D0301712

Polari – The Lost Language of Gay Men

Polari is a secret form of language used mainly by gay men and lesbians in London and other cities in the UK during the twentieth century. Derived in part from the slang lexicons of numerous stigmatised and itinerant groups, Polari was particularly popular among actors and gay men in the Merchant Navy. Initially used in order to maintain secrecy, Polari was also a means of socialising, acting out camp performances and reconstructing a shared gay identity and world-view among its speakers.

This book examines the ways in which Polari was used in order to construct such gay identities, linking its evolution to the changing status of gay men and lesbians in the UK over the past fifty years. Social explanations for Polari's decline are given, as well as an analysis of the ways in which it has been adopted and modified in the 1990s by newer groups of users. A Polari dictionary is included in the Appendix.

Essential reading for students of queer studies, this book will also be of great interest to scholars of sociolinguistics, anthropology, cultural studies and media studies.

Paul Baker is a Lecturer at the Department of Linguistics and Modern English Language, Lancaster University. His research interests include endangered and minority languages, language and sexualities, and corpus based approaches to language research. He has published papers in the *Journal of Computer Mediated Communication*, *Literary and Linguistic Computing* and *Computer Assisted Language Learning*. He is a committee member of the Foundation for Endangered Languages.

Routledge Studies in Linguistics

1. Polari – The Lost Language of Gay Men
Paul Baker

Polari – The Lost Language of Gay Men

Paul Baker

London and New York

First published 2002
by Routledge
2 Park Square, Milton Park, Abingdon, Oxon OX14 4RN

Simultaneously published in the USA and Canada
by Routledge
711 Third Avenue, New York, NY 10017

Routledge is an imprint of the Taylor & Francis Group

© 2002 Paul Baker

Typeset in Times New Roman by
Florence Production Ltd, Stoodleigh, Devon

British Library Cataloguing in Publication Data
A catalogue record for this book is available
from the British Library

Library of Congress Cataloging in Publication Data
A catalog record for this book has been requested

ISBN 0–415–26180–5

Contents

Illustrations

Figures

Tables

Acknowledgements

Special thanks to:

Barry Took and his representative for permission to reproduce excerpts from the radio programme *Round the Horne*.

Emma Hindley (director) and Juliet Margetts (producer) for permission to reproduce material from the television programme *A Storm in a Teacup* (broadcast 19th August 1993 as part of Channel 4's *Summer's Out* series). The London Co-ordinating Committee of the Campaign for Homosexual Equality for permission to use a cartoon in *Lunch* magazine, credited to 'NMY'.

David Hudson, editor of *Boyz* magazine, for permission to quote material from the Back-chat column and *Beginners Guide: Palare*, Issue 410. Jason Finch, managing director of OUTEVERYWHERE LTD for permission to quote the results of a poll on Polari which was published on the website www.OUTintheUK.com.

Additional thanks to Sally Johnson, Mark Sebba, Jane Sunderland, Andy Medhurst, Joan Swann, John Heywood, the Polari speakers who were interviewed for this book, the London Order of the Sisters of Perpetual Indulgence, David Raven and friends, Richard Maggs, Craig Hutchinson, Sue Blackwell, Lynne Murphy, Alan Sinfield, Bill Leap, Liz Morrish, Peter Burton, Kevan Mai, Ian Lucas and the members of the Out In Linguistics (Outil) Internet mailing list.

1   What is Polari?

Introduction

Well hello ducky, it's bona to vada your dolly old eek again. Order to your mother dear. Take the lattie on wheels did you? Fantabulosa! Oh vada that cod omee-palone in the naff goolie lally drags. Vada her gildy ogle fakes! Get dooey veras! I've nanti dinarly!

The above paragraph is written in Polari – put simply, a secret language mainly used by gay men and lesbians, in London and other UK cities with an established gay subculture, in the first 70 or so years of the twentieth century. That definition is a generalisation, but it serves well enough for the time being.

Polari was popularised during the late 1960s when the BBC comedy radio programme *Round the Horne* showcased a pair of camp, out-of-work actors called Julian and Sandy. These two unapologetic, in-your-face 'queens' used a version of the language which was just sophisticated enough to allow jokes that were high in gay content to get past the censors, and just simplistic enough so that the majority of listeners would be able to understand exactly what they meant.

After *Round the Horne*, Polari appears to have become unpopular, practically falling into disuse. At the time of writing, many gay men under the age of thirty have never heard of it, and of those who do know about it, a large number are only aware of a handful of words that were made famous by Julian and Sandy: *vada*: look; *bona*: good; *eek*: face; *lallies*: legs, for example.

My own association with Polari stemmed initially from listening to tapes of the Julian and Sandy sketches in the early 1990s. Shortly afterwards I tried to find out more about this intriguing use of language, but was disappointed by the lack of forthcoming information. However, the interest held, and was eventually developed into a doctoral thesis. It is the intention of this book to explain the history of Polari, looking back to its diverse origins, and charting the different ways in which it was used to help construct what can be referred to as 'gay identity' or, perhaps more accurately, 'gay identities'. My research has been concerned primarily with relating changes in how Polari was used (or rejected) to the ways that gay men have perceived themselves over time (or how they've been viewed or represented by others). Therefore, I am equally interested in the period after 1970, when Polari appears to have been in decline.

Is this book being written in order to revive Polari? While groups of people exist who have continued to use it, albeit in modified forms, and would perhaps like it to be revived, there are others who would prefer it to be forgotten (for reasons that are discussed in Chapters 6 and 7). By writing this book, it is inevitable that Polari will become demystified, spoiling whatever was left secret about it. But the book could also raise Polari's profile, to the annoyance of those who wish it to remain buried. My personal opinion is that the set of circumstances that led to gay men and lesbians taking up a secret language, initially for the sake of their own protection, should never be repeated again. However, if the current micro-revivals of Polari are anything to go by, it is likely that, if it is taken up once more, the motivations behind its use will differ from those of the past. The phenomenon of Polari is an important part of British gay social history, and for that reason alone it is worth documenting. When languages die out, a way of describing the collective experiences and world-view of a group is potentially lost for ever. Even if nobody intends to use that language again, it is worth being recorded and studied, adding to our existing knowledge of humanity and history.

All languages offer a potentially unique perspective of a particular society or subculture, and research into Polari is especially useful to those who are interested in linguistics, or the history of gay subcultures. This book therefore was not written with a single audience in mind: gay men, lesbians, bisexuals, linguists, queer/cultural theorists, historians, or people who enjoy camp or liked Julian and Sandy may have picked up this book for different reasons. I have therefore tried to write clearly, avoiding impenetrable academic prose whenever I can (this chapter is the most theory-heavy, incidentally).

What garnered my interest in Polari in the first place was the fact that the Julian and Sandy tapes made me laugh. Polari was, and still can be, a way of expressing humour – comedy that was often in the face of adversity. Polari is playful, quick and clever – a constantly evolving language of fast put-downs, ironic self-parody and theatrical exaggeration. The lexicographer, Eric Partridge, once referred to Polari as a 'Cinderella among languages', but I prefer to think of it as one of the Ugly Sisters: brash, funny and with all the best lines in the show.

As my research into Polari progressed, I uncovered a number of instances that contradicted the short definition that I began this chapter with. However, before re-examining that definition of Polari, it is useful to outline the research issues that I encountered, some that were relevant to the analysis of any 'dead' or 'secret' language and others that were more specific to Polari. The following section also covers the sources of information and types of texts that have been referenced in this research.

Researching Polari

When a linguist wants to research the way in which a particular group of people use language, one of the most obvious methods would be to take some sort of ethnographic approach, studying how people talk in natural settings – either by recording them, or by entering their community and joining in. Permission is usually obtained as it's ethically unsound to record people unawares. However, this can lead to the 'observer effect' – the fact that a group who know that they are being studied will behave less naturally to some degree. While the observer effect can be difficult to eliminate, generally people tend to giggle nervously into a tape recorder for ten minutes and then forget about its existence.

But in the case of a 'dead' language, it is often not possible to tape-record speakers, because they no longer exist. As Polari hasn't been used much since the 1970s it can safely be classed as 'endangered', if not 'dead'. And while it was possible to locate a number of people who remembered using it to varying degrees, if they were recorded now we wouldn't be able to replicate the original conditions that existed when Polari was used privately in the 1960s or earlier. The Polari they spoke into a microphone would be subject to the observer effect, and taken out of its original context by a gap of several decades. In some cases individual memories of Polari would have faded anyway, making such an exercise pointless.

In cases where linguists find ethnographic studies difficult to set up, they can refer to other sources: archives of texts in the form of letters, diaries, graffiti, old tape recordings etc., which may tell us how the language was used. It is easy to gain access to scripted forms of Polari, such as the Julian and Sandy sketches that were written to be spoken. However, scripted texts aren't spontaneous – they've been carefully constructed and edited. So they may reveal something interesting about, for example, how Polari was used to contribute towards stereotypical constructions of gay men as they were presented in the media, but they aren't the same as naturally occurring conversations. I wasn't able to locate any spontaneous recordings of Polari speakers from the 1950s and 1960s, incidentally.

Naturally occurring written Polari texts have proven almost as difficult to locate. This is hardly surprising: it was a form of language that was mainly spoken. Kenneth Williams (who played Sandy in the Julian and Sandy sketches – see Chapter 5) included the odd word of Polari here and there in his diaries, but an analysis of that wouldn't run to more than a few paragraphs. While it's the case that people have written novels that occasionally have people talking in Polari (e.g. Carson 1988), again, these are scripted.

So the fact that Polari was used secretly, at a time when people didn't have a great deal of access to audio recording equipment, and it was spoken rather than written, indicates that potential researchers are unlikely to have access to the kinds of naturally occurring texts that many linguists can take for granted.

But that's not to say that researching Polari is impossible. Other approaches can be considered, and subsequently the questions that are asked about Polari may have to be reframed. The Julian and Sandy sketches are perhaps the largest source of Polari data, and while they were the result of collaboration between script writers and actors, they were at least created by people who had worked in the theatre (one of the places where Polari originated) and who were therefore familiar with certain aspects of it. Julian and Sandy may have been humorous exaggerations of homosexuality, but they were at least grounded in reality. Additionally, other versions of scripted Polari, such as a scene in the film *Velvet Goldmine* (1998), or the three sketches set on the Piccadilly bus from the documentary programme *A Storm in a Teacup*, shown as part of Channel 4's 1993 *Summer's Out* series, can tell us something about how 'historic' Polari-speaking identities have more recently been recreated for public consumption, as part of an ongoing narrative of gay British history.

Access to another type of data that can tell us something interesting about Polari is via interviews. This can be referred to as attitude data – people are talking *about* a language rather than *in* a language (although they may slip into Polari occasionally to give examples of how it was used). Interviews are useful because they can relate Polari to real-life contexts – people can describe situations that happened. However, it should be noted that it is sometimes difficult to verify the authenticity of the accounts given by interviewees, as many of them may be asked to recall specific events from 30 or 40 years before. Even with the best intentions, groups of people may possess different memories of the same situation. Unintentional exaggerations or simplifications may also occur during interviews – for example, one person I interviewed told me confidently, 'nobody speaks Polari any more'. A week later, I received a telephone call from somebody who told me that he used Polari every day and, what's more, had taught all of his heterosexual friends at work how to use it.

Therefore, when reading quotes from people being interviewed about Polari, it's important to interpret them as opinions, not facts. While I feel confident to vouch that my interviewees were giving honest accounts about their own experiences of Polari, they were speaking for themselves, and not for every single person who spoke Polari.

A final type of 'text' that can be considered in relation to Polari is its lexicon. Taken out of context, a simple list of words (given with pronunciations, meanings, spellings and possible origins) doesn't tell us a great deal about how Polari was used. However, a closer look at the lexicon can begin to provide us with hypotheses about its use. The words in the Polari speaker's lexicon tell us which aspects of their lives they considered important enough to give names to – perhaps because there were no existing English words; or which parts they wanted to reconstruct or reclaim, because the existing words and meanings were somehow inappropriate. For example, words such as *gay* and *homosexual* already existed – but weren't really used by Polari speakers from the 1950s, who instead employed a whole catalogue of words to describe themselves and each other. There were also words relating to the mechanics of male–male sex, some of which, like *rimming*, weren't normally known to the average English speaker.

Also, the concept of over-lexicalisation is important to the research of any language. Over-lexicalisation in a language is one of the quickest routes to revealing the preoccupations of its users. For example, the claim that Eskimos have dozens of words for snow.[1] The phenomenon of having lots of words for a single concept in a secret language can be motivated by several factors. The fact that such words are discovered continually by outsiders (and often incorporated into mainstream slang as a result) may mean that new words have to be invented continuously. It can also be the case that a concept is so important that unrelated groups of users invent different words spontaneously for what they talk about most. Additionally, a single group may create lots of words for the same thing, in order to confuse others, or as a reflection of the thing's importance.

Another aspect of over-lexicalisation is that, if the words are examined closely enough, gradable distinctions can often be found between them. So in Polari there are lots of words for 'homosexual', but each word can then relate to other categories concerned with sexual availability, masculinity/effeminacy, attractiveness, age, particular sexual preferences etc. Additionally, sets of words based semantically around antonyms (binary pairs of opposites), may reveal something about the way that Polari speakers categorise their experiences as positive or negative. In this way, hierarchies can be created, and concepts and people can be positioned in opposing factions, with one word relating to something good (e.g. *TBH*: to be had), and another meaning something bad (*NTBH*: not to be had).

Finally, the Polari lexicon can be considered in terms of metaphor use. Many of the words in the lexicon existed first in English, and have therefore been borrowed and subverted by Polari speakers. The relationship between an original and new meaning of a word can be revealing. For example, Deignan (1997) carried out an analysis of the metaphors used in words that were related to sexual desire. She found that this concept is often constructed in terms of health or cleanliness metaphors; for example, 'a dirty weekend', which reveals the way that subjective judgements (e.g. sex being somehow related to (un)cleanliness) are encoded within words. It is possible that similar sorts of metaphors can be found within Polari words, and these relationships may uncover something about how Polari speakers constructed their own identities and those of others. Over-lexicalisation and metaphor are considered in more detail in Chapter 3.

Who spoke Polari?

Although researchers in the 1970s wrote about the subject of 'gay language' or 'homosexual language', it is no longer meaningful to make such generalisations. In the past it was often assumed that people could be placed into socially discrete categories,[2] and that each category would contain instances of language use that could be differentiated according to a number of verifiable features such as prosody, lexicon, grammar etc. So it was possible for researchers to make a priori assumptions about categories such as 'Black English' (Dillard 1972), 'Women's language' (Lakoff 1973) or 'Gay language' (Hayes 1976, Farrell 1972). Leaving aside the question of whether or not Polari *is* a language for the time being, I encountered a number of problems in identifying what is meant by 'gay' or 'homosexual' without resorting to unhelpful stereotypes.

For the purposes of this book, I define 'gay men' or 'homosexual men' as adult males who are self-identified as preferring other males as sexual and/or romantic partners. This is a limiting definition, but I defend it on the basis that the people who are willing to self-identify in this way are at least going to answer more honestly my questions concerning their sexual identity. Also, crucially, this places the issue of identity at the personal level – rather than imposing an identity on someone from afar. In any case, the issue of definition in relation to this book means that I should take into account Polari speakers, who, in the 1950s and 1960s, probably would not have defined themselves as *gay*, a word which gained widespread usage during the 1970s, by which point Polari was well in decline. *Gay* was a newer identity associated with openness, pride and liberation. Therefore, it could be argued that it is anachronistic to refer to these early Polari speakers as 'gay men', as this assumes that their sexual identities were the same as the post-Wolfenden gay men of today.[3] While there were some similarities, there were also significant differences – the idea of 'coming out of the closet' (as a choice), for example, was invalid, as were concepts such as 'gay pride' or 'gay liberation'. And for many Polari speakers, camp and effeminacy were ways of being – they wanted to have sex with a masculine man, but they were not masculine themselves; in fact, their use of Polari was one of the many ways in which they were marked as effeminate. Many constructions of gay identity since the 1970s have tended to be more focused towards the potential in all gay men to be masculine.

In the 1960s and earlier, Polari speakers who had sexual or romantic relationships with other men may have sometimes referred to themselves as *omee-palones* (literally men–women) or *queens*. Other people who had same-sex relationships may have used euphemisms to describe their sexual identity, or in many cases they may not have used *any* word. So, although the word *gay* is often used as a general term in this book, it is with the acknowledgement that, when it refers to people from before the 1970s, it may be anachronistic. However, *gay* is used for want of a better word to describe people who were same-sex oriented (either Polari-speaking or not) across the twentieth century. *Queer* was a pejorative term in the 1950s and 1960s, while *homosexual* is somewhat clinical, with medical and legal implications.

Perhaps the most important way that people define their sexuality is in accordance with the manner in which they relate to others. In this book I also use the term 'gay subculture', which could be interpreted as 'gay community' or, arguably, just 'gay culture' by those who would argue that, collectively, gay lifestyles have by now transcended the term 'subculture' in terms of size, influence and acceptance by mainstream society. However, much of the focus of this book is the early to mid-twentieth century, when 'subculture' was perhaps a more appropriate word to be used when referring to the UK. Again, the idea of a 'gay subculture' as an easily definable entity is subject to debate. Given that a society has permitted or constructed sexuality in such a way that those who are gay-identified are allowed to interact, the concept of a single gay subculture is quickly shattered. Just as there are many different types of gay men, there are also many different types of gay subcultures, which reflect race, background, social class, geographic location, sexual preferences, closet status, or combinations of some or all of these. In any given society there may be a dominant or hegemonic form of gay subculture, whereby certain types of identities are constructed as being more preferable to or more desirable than others, but that does not make it the only gay subculture or even the most accessible one (hegemonic subcultures can be aspirant – creating unobtainable ideals), only the most visible.

It can also be argued that possession of a gay identity is not necessary to be part of a gay subculture. For example, the concept of the *fag hag* – a heterosexual female friend of gay men – challenges the notion that the gay subculture consists entirely of gay males. So, when I write of a gay subculture, it is in the broadest sense, based around a collective notion of associated (but not necessarily shared) gay identity. While the idea of a gay subculture can most traditionally be considered in terms of actual physical location – for example, Old Compton Street in London or The Castro in San Francisco – it can also be the case that gay subcultures may exist in more virtual forms, such as in cyberspace or via subscription to specific magazines or newsletters. For many gay men, their relationship to the subculture is not defined as either belonging or not belonging, but as a fluctuating state, with different levels of attachment at different times.

Not all gay men spoke Polari. Those who did use it could be viewed as a subculture within the gay subculture – but again, Polari speakers shouldn't be thought of as a homogeneous set, all interacting with one another. Furthermore, while many Polari users were gay men, there were other people who used it but did not fit into this category. As Chapter 2 shows, Polari had roots in the theatre, and because of this there were numerous actors and actresses who knew of it, or used it, but would not normally have been identified as gay. Additionally, there are cases of *omee-palones* teaching words of Polari to heterosexual friends who had no or little direct association with gay subculture or the theatre. Finally, Polari was not just a gay *male* phenomenon. To a lesser extent, lesbians have been reported as using it. So, while *omee-palones* are the most well-documented users of Polari, they were by no means the only users.

One question that is difficult to answer is 'What constituted a Polari speaker?' It is difficult to define a set of criteria that would label someone as a Polari speaker and someone else as not. It should be pointed out that this is not because of any special features of Polari – defining who speaks any language is challenging, and the situation often appears especially complex when considering a language that is not someone's mother tongue.

The men I interviewed seemed happy to self-identify as Polari speakers, because they spoke Polari – circular reasoning. But questions such as 'How many words do you need to know before you can class yourself as a speaker of Polari?' impose a ridiculous level of quantification. The world cannot be divided neatly into two sets: Polari speakers and non-Polari speakers (it's easier to make statements like 'this person knows no Polari', but even that might not be strictly true, due to linguistic cross-over between Polari and English). And, clearly, a person's mere knowledge of Polari does not imply that they are a Polari speaker: the person may never use any of the words. One of my early contacts knew some Polari, but had to construct each phrase carefully in advance, often hesitating and self-correcting. He admitted that he never used it except in cases where he was asked to give examples of Polari. I would argue that he was not a Polari speaker.

Therefore, my definition of a Polari speaker is not overly concerned with how many words a given individual knows, or whether they use it as an add-on lexicon to supplement their English, or as something with a unique grammar. The context of its use became increasingly important in enabling me to decide whether someone was a Polari speaker. While I was careful not to extrapolate too much from any general statements about Polari from the men I interviewed, their reminiscences about how, where and why they used Polari as individuals (admittedly combined with a degree of familiarity with the language) gave me a much better picture of what constituted a Polari speaker, as opposed to someone who knew *about* Polari, or someone who knew the mechanics but was not a speaker.

Putting aside for the moment the inherent difficulty in defining a Polari speaker, another trick(y) question can be asked: 'How many people spoke Polari?' As researchers have found, trying to find the number of speakers of commonly known languages is an arduous task – 'language' questions have remained absent from the British National Census for exactly that reason. In the case of Polari we are not only dealing with an unofficial 'secret language', but also one that is endangered, or even 'dead'. We'll never know how many people spoke it. If forced to estimate, I would put the figure at tens of thousands at least, and this figure would not include people who would have heard Polari via the mass media phenomenon of Julian and Sandy, but instead focus on numbers who learnt it from within the gay subculture.

The concept of subcultures as problem-solving devices (Blachford 1981: 184) is particularly relevant to gay subcultures. Hall and Jefferson (1975) stress the connection between subculture and dominant culture; their framework suggests that subcultures intersect the dominant order (which generates problems) and other cultural forms (which mediate problems). Plummer (1975: 85–6) has suggested that homosexual subcultures may resolve problems resulting from the taboo placed upon homosexuality in mainstream society: secrecy, guilt, identity and access. Blachford (1981: 185) sums up the limitations of subcultures: they 'solve, but in an "imaginary way", problems . . . which at a more fundamental level remain unresolved'.

Barrett (1997: 186) argues that subcultural communities have no overall definition of what constitutes membership – notions of community and identity cannot be externally definable categories. Gay communities, for example, are not isolated pockets, having no contact with mainstream society. This echoes Pratt's view, which, instead of placing community at the centre of linguistic enquiry, instead puts the focus upon:

> the operation of language across lines of social differentiation, a linguistics . . . focused on modes and zones of contact between domi-nant and dominated groups, between persons of different and multiple identities, speakers of different languages, that focused on how speakers constitute each other relationally and in difference, how they enact difference in language.
>
> (Pratt 1987: 60)

Another related theory concerning subcultures is that of *communities of practice* first put forward by Lave and Wenger (1991: 29) in their exam-ination of situated learning: 'a person's intentions to learn are engaged and the meaning of learning is configured through the process of becoming a full participant in a sociocultural practice'. For Lave and Wenger (1991: 98), a community of practice is: 'a set of relations among persons, activity and world, over time and in relation with other tangential and overlap-ping communities of practice. A community of practice is an intrinsic condition for the existence of knowledge.' Language becomes an impor-tant facet of maintaining a community of practice, in that speakers will develop linguistic patterns as they engage in specific activities. These linguistic patterns or repertoires will change constantly through interac-tion between different members of one or more communities of practice. Also, communities of practice do not assume role homogeneity within a particular community – for example, there may be teachers and students within a community of practice, and the same person can take different roles in different communities. If the gay subculture can be seen as a 'community of practice', then Polari was one of the developing linguistic repertoires as different members interacted with each other.

So the study of the ways in which gay men use and structure their language provides insight into the construction and maintenance of gay identity across multiple contexts. Thus, *language* becomes a key factor in the construction of gay identities.

Redefining Polari

Language is perhaps an even more problematic term to identify than *gay* or *subculture*, being composed of numerous disciplines relating to its study: phonetics, morphology, grammar, semantics, pragmatics etc., each with its own methodologies and theories.

In the past, linguists who wanted to study what they had deemed 'gay language' began with an assumption of difference – that gay people used language in a way that was different from that of heterosexuals. There was also the assumption that there was something intrinsically similar in the way that, as a group, gay men or lesbians used language. Early research in this field focused initially on building lexicons (Legman 1941, Cory 1965, Rodgers 1972, Stanley 1970, Farrell 1972). Later researchers examined other features such as gaze and posture (Webbink 1981), code-switching (Lumby 1976), stress patterns (Moonwomon 1985) and intonation (Goodwin 1989, Moran 1991, Gaudio 1994).

It could be argued that a subculture will create its own social identity based upon recognisable stereotypes that can be imitated by its members (Le Page and Taboret-Keller 1985: 142). This theory would predict that, in order to 'index' a gay identity, speakers will use language (either consciously or unconsciously) in a way that reflects these stereotypical aspects of 'gay speech'. Because such aspects are stereotypical, it can be easy to categorise and mark these as 'differences', in comparison to 'non-stereotypical gay speech'. Thus, a taxonomy of features can be gathered together, representative as belonging to gay male speech. Such a taxonomy could include the list given by Barrett (1997: 192): lexical items specific to gay language, wide intonational pitch range, hyper-correction and hyper-extended vowels, and an H*L intonational contour. Barrett acknowledges that, although such indexes of gay identity might be recognised by other gay people as such, actual usages might only occur among a subset of gay men, and then only in certain contexts.

Attempting to find something 'universally homosexual' in language is as unproductive as trying to uncover something 'universally heterosexual'. Therefore, what I write about Polari is highly specific – it relates to individual uses from particular subcultures, over a finite time-period, and even then it is not the case that the Polari speakers I interviewed all used it in the same way, or even used the same words. In part, this diversity in use is due to synchronic and diachronic variation.

To describe synchronic variation, a researcher would look at a language variety or number of varieties that occurred at the same point in time – for example, by comparing how present-day speakers from London and Liverpool use glottal stops. Saussure (1966: 101) explains that synchronic, or static, linguistics examines the principles of a language-state, which in reality is not so much a point, but rather a finite span of time during which the number of modifications that have changed the language variety are minimal.

Diachronic variation involves looking at how a variety (or varieties) change over time; for example, how does the use of glottal stops by present-day speakers in London differ from the way they were used 20, 30 or 40 years ago? Synchronic variation, therefore, takes the form of comparing two or more linguistic 'snapshots' taken at the same time, whereas diachronic variation consists of snapshots of the same variety taken at different periods in time.

When I began interviewing Polari speakers, I sometimes found that they gave conflicting reports, particularly when assigning meanings to words. I originally interpreted this in terms of certain speakers being either right or wrong. I had assumed that Polari words would have specific meanings that would have been known to all speakers. It quickly became clear that this was not the case. It wasn't that people were giving wrong answers, just different ones. And that suggests that the idea of a single, standard version of Polari isn't viable. While Polari speakers may agree on certain well-known words, it's unlikely that two speakers would agree on everything, particularly if they came from different parts of the country or spoke Polari at different points in time. The fact that Polari is sometimes spelt *Palare* is testament to this. *Palare* appears to be an older spelling, while *Polari* has been used by the majority of academics who have written about it since the 1980s. But it should be pointed out that neither one is the 'correct' spelling – there are no definitive standards in Polari – only alternatives that were used by different sets of people at different times. It's almost certainly an exaggeration to speak of as many versions of Polari as the number of people who spoke it, but at the same time the idea of there only being one 'correct' way of speaking Polari is a simplification. The reality lies somewhere between these two standpoints.

To give another example of synchronic variation, I return to the definition of Polari that I offered at the beginning of this chapter – as a secret language. For many of the people who knew it, Polari wasn't a language but a lexicon – a set of words (mainly nouns, verbs and adjectives) that could be used in place of English words. However, in Chapter 3 I illustrate how some speakers used it in a way that began to suggest the beginnings of a grammatical system, which would make it more akin to being a language in its own right. Bearing this in mind, can we refer to Polari definitively as a lexicon or a language?

Perhaps it would be useful to think of Polari as a *language variety*. Hudson (1980: 24) speaks of varieties of language, which he defines as a 'set of linguistic items with similar social distribution'. Unfortunately, such a definition immediately raises further concept-definition problems, such as what is meant by a linguistic item? Chomsky (1965) would give examples such as lexicons, rules of pronunciation and meaning, and constraints on rules. However, Hudson (1980: 22) notes that definitions of linguistic items are dependent on the particular theory which a given linguist thinks best supports language structure. Determining exactly what is meant by, and therefore calculating, a 'similar social distribution' is also difficult. Another disadvantage of such a definition is that it is so broad that it includes phenomena such as 'languages', 'styles' and 'dialects'. Hudson (1980: 71) points out that there are considerable problems in distinguishing one language variety from another, and in determining one type from another: e.g. language from dialect. Therefore, the term 'language variety' can only be used informally, without intending it to be taken as a concrete theoretical construction.

Could we call Polari a dialect then? Hudson (1980: 36), in his analysis of language and dialects, concludes that 'there is no real distinction to be drawn between "language and dialect"', except for prestige. So is Polari a dialect of English, considered to be prestigious by its speakers, but non-prestigious by most non-speakers? Or is Polari a language in itself, with different dialects? However, either definition rests on locating Polari as something akin to a language and, for many of its speakers, it was not used this way.

The term *sociolect* is used by Wardhaugh (1986: 148) when classifying work carried out by Labov, Trudgill etc. in describing the speech characteristics of members of social groups, as opposed to *idiolects*, which represent the speech characteristics of individuals. Wardhaugh describes sociolects as 'statements about group norms arrived at through counting and averaging'. As with *language variety*, the term *sociolect* is general enough to be applied uncontroversially to Polari, but by concentrating on group norms we don't allow for the kinds of synchronic and diachronic variation that were especially characteristic of it.

Pidgins are languages with a reduced grammatical structure that can develop when one or more speakers of mutually unintelligible languages interact with each other, often around a specific social context such as trading. It could be argued that there are elements of *pidginisation* in Polari's development – for example, the combination of different subcultures (as discussed in Chapter 2), and the creation of a means of communication based around a specific number of purposes. However, in numerous ways, Polari fails to meet the criteria for being a pidgin language. It was spoken within a group (gay men), rather than as the only means of communication between two or more groups who couldn't understand each other, and all of its speakers already had a language (English) that they could use for communication if they wanted to. Perhaps then, Polari is a *creole* – a more complex form of language, which has developed from a pidgin and is generally used by the children or grandchildren of the original pidgin speakers. While Polari fulfils some of the criteria of a true creole, this definition doesn't take into account the fact that Polari was used secretively, in the place of an existing language.

The term *slang*, which is less broad than *language variety* is described by O'Grady *et al.* (1996: 555) as a 'label that is frequently used to denote certain informal or faddish usages of nearly anyone in the speech community'. However, slang, while subject to rapid change, is widespread and familiar to a large number of speakers, unlike Polari. The terms *jargon* and *argot* perhaps signify more what Polari stands for, as they are associated with group membership and are used to serve as affirmation or solidarity with other members. Both terms refer to 'obscure or secret language' or 'language of a particular occupational group' (O'Grady *et al.* 1996: 557). While jargon tends to refer to an occupational sociolect, or a vocabulary particular to a field, argot is more concerned with language varieties where speakers wish to conceal either themselves or aspects of their communication from non-members. Although argot is perhaps the most useful term considered so far in relation to Polari, there exists a more developed theory that concentrates on stigmatised groups, and could have been created with Polari specifically in mind: *anti-language*.

For Halliday (1978), anti-language was to anti-society what language was to society. An anti-society is a counter-culture, a society within a society, a conscious alternative to society, existing by resisting either pas-sively or by more hostile, destructive means. Anti-languages are generated by anti-societies and in their simplest forms are partially relexicalised languages, consisting of the same grammar but a different vocabulary (Halliday 1978: 165) in areas central to the activities of subcultures. Therefore a subculture based around illegal drug use would have words for drugs, the psychological effects of drugs, the police, money and so on. In anti-languages the social values of words and phrases tend to be more emphasised than in mainstream languages. This phenomenon is termed *sociolinguistic coding orientation* (Halliday 1978: 166).

Research in the past has looked at the reasons why people use anti-languages. Mallik (1972) found that 41 per cent of the criminals he interviewed gave 'the need for secrecy' as an important reason for using an anti-language, while 38 per cent listed 'verbal art'. However, Podgorecki (1973), in his account of the anti-language or *grypserka* of Polish prisoners, describes how, for the prisoners, their identity was threatened and the creation of an anti-society provided a means by which an alternative social structure (or reality) could be constructed, becoming the source of a second identity for the prisoners. The *grypserka*, therefore, was the means of creating and maintaining such a reality: 'An individual's subjective reality is created and maintained through interaction with others, who are "significant other" precisely because they fill this role: and such interaction is, critically, verbal – it takes the form of conversation' (Halliday 1978: 170). For Halliday, anti-languages are reconstructions of reality, which contain processes that enable individuals to establish identification with 'significant others'. Anti-languages have no mother tongue; they exist only in the context of resocialisation: 'Anti-language arises when the alternative reality is a *counter*-reality, set up *in opposition to* some established norm (Halliday 1978: 171).

Anti-language is therefore a good example of what Bourdieu calls symbolic power. Although he does not refer to anti-language, Bourdieu demonstrates the potential of language for changing one's perception of reality:

> Symbolic power – as a power of constituting the given through utterances, of making people see and believe, of confirming or *transforming* the vision of the world and, thereby, action on the world and thus the world itself, an almost magical power which enables one to obtain the equivalent of what is obtained through force ... is a power that can be exercised only if it is recognised, that is misrecognised as arbitrary [my italics].
>
> (Bourdieu 1991: 170)

It is the tension between the two alternative constructions of reality (society and anti-society) that creates the linguistic distance between language and anti-language. Again, both sets of concepts should be considered as notional extreme ends of a continuum based on a social system, with considerable overlap occupying the middle ground. Anti-languages are therefore concerned with the definition and maintenance of alternative (and often secret) identities, organised through ritual participation in alternative social hierarchies:

> What distinguishes an anti-language is that it is itself a metaphorical entity, and hence metaphorical modes of expression are the norm; we should expect metaphorical compounding, metatheses, rhyming alterations and the like to be among regular patterns of realization.
>
> (Halliday 1978: 177)

The theory of anti-language provides a useful framework when considering the speakers of Polari. Stigmatised by society, gay men had resorted to anti-language as a means of creating and maintaining an anti-society. Halliday (1978: 172) points out that anti-languages are necessarily secret because the anti-society is secret. In order to access the anti-society, the anti-language acts as the key. But, as well as allowing people of a shared identity to recognise and communicate with each other, anti-languages are the tools that create both that identity and the alternative society that houses them. Beier (1995: 64), in his study of Cant (a distant linguistic ancestor of Polari – see Chapter 2), suggests that Cant is more probably conceptualised as a jargon rather than an anti-language – the sixteenth- and seventeenth-century rogues were more likely to use it in order to disguise their speech and crimes, rather than to demarcate boundaries between themselves and other groups, or to construct reality in a partic- ular way. Similarly, it should not be thought that when people spoke Polari they were consciously thinking, 'we're doing this to construct ourselves as different from this group, in *these* ways . . .'. But, unlike Cant, which Beier (1995: 65) suggests has few words that attack social, religious or political systems, Polari is full of critical disdain. As I'll discuss in Chapter 6, the accusation that the world-view behind Polari was not always the most ideologically all-embracing was one of the factors associated with its eventual decline. And in Chapter 3 I show that, while *anyone* was fair game for Polari speakers (including other Polari speakers), special reserves of venom were used to create antagonistic words for opposing groups such as the police or heterosexuals. For this reason, Polari can more readily be classed as an anti-language than Cant.

Identity and performance

Positioning Polari as an anti-language allows us to expand upon its linguistic description to ask questions about, for example, how it was used in order to construct identity or, more accurately, identities. However, the term *identity* is perhaps more susceptible to multiple interpretations than any of the other slippery terms discussed in this chapter. In recent acad- emic writing it is common to find terms such as homosexual identity (Heywood 1997: 196); gay identity (D'Emilio 1993: 467); sexual iden- tity, bisexual identity, monosexual identity (Rust 1996: 64); political identity (Duncan 1996: 89); and gender identities (Cameron 1997: 60). Barnstein (1998: 5) says that identity is 'the parts of ourselves we show to others . . . an accurate reflection of who we feel we are. Some people . . . call it "The Real Me".'

Gleason (1983: 918) points out that the more general term *identity* is relatively new, emerging into social science literature in the 1950s and made popular by the psychoanalyst Erik Erikson.[4] For Gleason, most defi- nitions of identity tend to fall into one of two opposing conceptions, which reflect essentialist and constructionist standpoints. In the former sense, identity can be called 'intrapsychic', in that it comes from within, is fixed and stable, and is what people speak of when they talk about 'who we really are'. But in the latter sense, identity is seen as being 'acquired' in that it is a conscious or internalised adoption of socially imposed, or socially constructed, roles – therefore, someone can be said to identify, for example, as a goldfish fancier, a mother or a priest. Epstein (1998: 144) points out that Habermas's discussion of *ego identity* is a useful mediation point between the two definitions. For Habermas, ego identity is a socialised sense of individuality: 'a growing child first of all integrates itself into a specific social system by appropriating symbolic generalities; it is later secured and developed through individuation, that is, precisely through a growing independence in relation to social systems' (Habermas 1979: 74).

Identity can therefore be considered in terms of thoughts, feelings, beliefs and behaviours (e.g. language, dress, posture). Thus a person's *sexual identity* might involve their sexuality (whether they are oriented towards same-sex relations, opposite-sex, both or neither), the sorts of sexual activity that they prefer or dislike, their attitudes towards sex and sexuality, their preferences towards other people (e.g. age, race, body type), and the ways in which they present themselves to others as a sexual being. This multilinear conceptualisation suggests that we should really be thinking in terms of sexual identities, rather than a single sexual identity. Identities that refer to more specific traits are equally complex. For example, there are many different ways to be masculine, and there are many different perceptions of what masculinity is. Therefore, we should think in terms of masculine identities rather than a single masculine identity (Meinhof and Johnson 1997: 19–21).

Weeks (1985: 28) observes that, in modern society, marriage has been de-emphasised in favour of the concept of the couple as the constant in Western life. Even more central to people's concepts of their own identity is sex, which has become 'the cement that binds people together'. Therefore, during the twentieth century, sexual identities were considered with growing scrutiny. Becker (1963: 33–4) suggests: 'One will be identified as a deviant first, before other identifications are made.' While, for Goffman (1963: 14), it is not only outsiders who place a premium on stigmatised identities; those who are stigmatised must constantly 'manage' their identities along dichotomies such as excuse/confront and reveal/conceal. In some cases, identity management becomes the central tenet of a person's life. Epstein (1998: 145) echoes these points in his discussion of labelling theory, arguing that stigmatised or deviant identities are likely to subsume other aspects of identity – *all* behaviour of people with a stigmatised identity could therefore be seen by others as a product of the stigmatised identity.

I define identity as a constantly evolving state of being, composed of multiple, interacting, socially acquired and internally inherited characteristics. Primarily, for this book, I am concerned with the ways that Polari (as a language variety) has contributed towards changing constructions of gay identities over time. My research is therefore underpinned by Butler's (1990) conceptualisation of gender as performance, drawing on Austin's (1962) work on speech act theory. For Austin, certain statements such as

'I promise' were conceptualised as being 'performative', bringing a state of affairs into being, rather than describing something that already exists. Butler (1990: 33) related this idea to gendered identities, suggesting that their presentation is a never-ending process: 'Gender is the repeated stylization of the body, a set of repeated acts within a highly rigid regulatory frame that congeal over time to produce the appearance of substance of a natural sort of being.' This conceptualisation of gender extends earlier feminist theory (e.g. Simone de Beauvoir) that one is not born, but becomes, a woman. According to Butler (1990: 33), becoming a woman is 'a term in process, a beginning, a constructing that cannot rightfully be said to originate or to end'. Such a model is useful when thinking of gender in terms of speech. In the past, sociolinguists have thought that people talk in certain ways because of who they are. However, the postmodern perspective reverses this belief, so that people are who they are, because of the way that they talk (Cameron 1997: 48).

Performativity theory is useful in highlighting the ways that sex (man/woman) relates to gender (masculine/feminine). However, the idea that we continually construct or perform gender can be expanded to cover other forms of identity, such as sexuality. When Polari is spoken, one type of gay identity is 'performed'. Performances, however, do not normally occur as soliloquies. It is also important to consider the role of the audience (Leap 1996: 110). As speakers, we may use language as one means of performing identity, but the success of our performance is dependent on the comprehension of those with whom we interact.

Overview of the book

In this chapter I've attempted first to define and then to redefine the subject of this book – Polari. While Polari can be conceptualised as a secret subcultural lexicon used by some homosexual men, or even a 'gay language', I have tried to show how these definitions are over-simplifications by problematising concepts that are generally taken for granted: 'gay', 'subculture', 'language' and 'identity'. The theoretical underpinning for my research into Polari is based around the notion that language use contributes towards the construction or 'performance' of identities – in this case gay identities, and that Polari was specifically used as an 'antilanguage', not only to construct alternative identities, but also to set up an alternative reality for its speakers.

Keeping the idea of diachronic change in mind, I have based the remainder of the book around a loose historical narrative. Starting with the period before Polari properly came into existence, Chapter 2 examines its diverse historical origins, and should go some way in explaining its association with other stigmatised identities. Chapter 3 gives a description of Polari from a purely nuts-and-bolts linguistic perspective, while Chapter 4 examines how it was used in the pre-Wolfenden homosexual subcultures of the twentieth century before the 1960s. Chapter 5 takes up the story at this point, by focusing on the Julian and Sandy period of 1964–9, while Chapter 6 considers the decline of Polari over the 1970s and 1980s. Chapter 7 looks at the revival of interest in Polari during the 1990s.

Finally, for those who are interested, a Polari dictionary is included as an Appendix. It is by no means exhaustive, and it is likely that some people will read it and think 'that doesn't fit in with *my* knowledge of Polari', or 'that word isn't Polari, it's something else'. As the dictionary was compiled with reference to multiple, and sometimes conflicting, sources, it would be incredible if everyone who read it did agree about every word, spelling and definition. Many of these inconsistencies and boundary cross-overs are due to the rich source of linguistic diversity underlining Polari's history, which is discussed more fully in Chapter 2.

2   Historical origins

Introduction

Polari was not developed by *omee-palones* in an isolated bubble, separate from other influences. Rather, it emerged as the result of a number of converging subcultures over many decades. It is impossible to chart exactly how each linguistic item found its way from one subculture into another, and finally into Polari, but an examination of the lexicons of these historically related subcultures reveals similarities in terms of pronunciation and/or meaning (spelling is a moot issue, as these words were rarely, if ever, written down by the people who used them, and even when they were recorded on paper, it is unlikely that they became standardised, except by professional lexicographers who imposed their own spelling standards on them).

In this chapter I examine the origins of Polari, up to the point where it started to be recognised as something that was used primarily by gay men. The motivation behind this is to demonstrate, through tracing the evolution of various subgroups and lexical items associated with them, that Polari's influences are multiple and diverse. In order to explain the difficulty in pinning down the notion of a single version of Polari or a typical Polari speaker, we need to look to the past – to the relationships of an interrelated network of subcultures spanning social class, time and physical position, all contributing to each other, and to what was eventually to become Polari.

Also, the history of Polari is something that has never really been thoroughly examined – almost all researchers on the subject devote space to it, but, apart from perhaps Hancock (1984), who focuses on the Romance aspects of Polari, they do not examine in detail the links between subgroups. It is therefore my intention to examine the possible parent language varieties of Polari, in order to postulate exactly how much influence (if any) each had on its creation.

Methodological issues

Historical language research (especially of spoken language) is often problematic if the researcher wants to use naturally occurring texts to find out about the language. Examining the written data (manuscripts, carvings, parchments etc.) of dominant language(s) of any culture at a given time poses questions surrounding translation, origin, verifiability and so on, while the situation when dealing with subversive underground forms of language, such as slang, is even more difficult. Slang is less likely to be written down (with the exception of graffiti), and many subcultural forms of language were not written down at all, because those who spoke them were not part of a dominant mainstream culture and had no access or interest in publishing accounts of the uniqueness of their own language variety. Indeed, one of the driving forces behind anti-language is secrecy. Language variations are passed down via existing speakers, and in-group membership is required in order to gain access to that knowledge. Thus, subcultural language varieties are at once too important to the subculture to be revealed in print, and are often too unimportant, socially undesirable or subversive for members of an establishment to want to show enough interest in them.[1] Sources of data, when available, are scant and often unrealistic examples of the anti-language.

In order to find out about spoken language (whether standardised English, or Elizabethan slang) before the advent of tape recorders, we must therefore rely on written records or the memories of people who were around at that time, which at once presents a problem surrounding the validity of the data. Secondary sources can provide a window onto spoken language, but, because they are not themselves spoken language, they cannot give a full, true picture. For example, Graddol *et al.* (1996: 113), in their work on the sounds of Old English, flag their findings with the remark that they can never say for certain how Anglo-Saxons pronounced certain sounds, and that some of their work consists of educated guesses based on different types of evidence.

Similarly, in looking at the historical precursors of Polari, we must look to the work of earlier lexicographers and written texts. In some cases, the bulk of information we can obtain about a particular subculture is written from the (typically biased and negative) perspective of the mainstream culture via criminal records. Often, we can only make educated guesses about how these subcultures really used their languages when in private.

Cant and pelting speech

One of the earliest recorded language varieties that probably influenced what was later to become Polari was Cant, a secret code language used by criminals in the sixteenth to eighteenth centuries. Wilde (1889: 306) claimed that Cant could be traced back as far as the eleventh century when, under the Norman Conquest, many Saxons became outlaws and thieves – with their language becoming that of the conquered and continuing for generation after generation with little change. Cant, also known as pedlar's French or St Giles's Greek was most probably derived from the earlier Elizabethan pelting (paltry) slang (Harman 1567). Pelting speech was concerned with the business of crime and its over-lexicalisation of criminal terms attests to this. Halliday (1978: 165) notes that there were over 20 terms for the main classes of vagabonds (*prigger of prancers, jarkman, bawdy basket, doxy, dell* and *mort* being some of the more evocative-sounding ones). As well as the various criminal roles, there were also words to describe criminal strategies, which were collectively known as laws (e.g. *lifting law*: stealing packages). There were also names for tools (*wresters*: for picking locks), the spoils (*snappings*), and various penalties that would be incurred if caught (*trining on the chats*: being hanged). These words show that Cant was a technical language, which, like many other jargons, was concerned with a form of trade. There were also words for objects, parts of the body, animals, institutions and places.

One of the most prolific compilers of Cant was Captain Francis Grose (1731–91), who published *The Classical Dictionary of the Vulgar Tongue* in 1785. By the third edition in 1796, the dictionary had over 4,000 entries, although not all of these words were considered to be Cant – others were 'burlesque phrases, quaint allusions and nicknames for persons, things, and places, which, from uninterrupted usage, are made classical by prescription' (Grose, quoted in Lovric 1997: 4). A true ethnographer, Grose carried out his lexicography via midnight trips into some of the less salubrious parts of London at that time – mixing with the 'rough squads' who inhabited the Black Slums of St Giles's, Turnmill Street, St Kitts and Saltpetre-Bank.

Cant/pelting speech shows a number of derivational processes in its morphology, based around the most usual actions attributed to an object or person. Both Harmon and Grose give examples of words containing *cheat*, used as a general element for 'thing which' – for example, *crashing cheats*: teeth; *smelling cheat*: nose; *hearing cheats*: ears; *belly cheat*: apron; and *lullaby cheat*: infant. *Queer*, meaning something bad, and *cove*, meaning man, were also used in this way to form words: *queer rooster*: informer; *queer cuffin*: Justice of the Peace; *queer Ken*: prison house; *cross cove, flash cove, leary cove*. *Cull*, like *cove*, was a general word for man, and was used in a similar way to *queer, cheat* and *cove* in that other words were derived from it: *bob cull*: good man; *chaunter cull*: writer; *bleeding cully*: one who parts easily with his money. In Cant, *cully* was often used to refer to a thief's mate. However, *cull* could also mean testicles. Beier (1995: 79) points out that, when it came to naming body parts, those who spoke Cant had a particular interest in evacuation and genitalia.

The Mollies

> 'Where have you been you saucy queen?'
> (*Hell Upon Earth*, Anonymous 1729)

Although the concept of 'the homosexual' as a sexual identity, as opposed to 'the sodomite' as a sexual practice, has its roots in nineteenth-century medical terminology (Foucault 1976), it is generally accepted that same-sex intimacies have always existed. Trumbach (1991: 130–3) argues that, in the 1660s and 1670s, sodomy was committed by 'rakes' who were libertine in religion and republican in politics. Sexually, they took the active, penetrating role, their partners being younger adolescent males. However, rakes were also sexually interested in women, and were not considered effeminate. Effeminacy, on the other hand, was associated with 'fops', who did *not* have sex with men. By 1710, however, a new identity, the *Molly*, had emerged – one who was effeminate *and* engaged in sex with other males. The word was possibly derived from the Latin, *mollis*, meaning 'soft'. The Mollies existed within a subculture based around what were known as Molly Houses.[2] These were clubs and taverns where working- and middle-class men would meet, for the purposes of socialisation and to make sexual contacts. Although the Mollies sometimes dressed as women, Norton (1992: 104) suggests that they were more 'vulgar than aesthetic, and evinced more vitality than effeteness' – their dressing up was more a means of 'letting off steam' than any real desire to be female.

However the Mollies are viewed, it is known that they subverted traditional heterosexual customs and rituals. For example, sometimes Molly 'marryings' would occur, meaning that two men would pair off and have sex in another room, known as 'The Chapel' (Norton 1992: 55, 100). There is also a description of an event known as 'lying-in' whereby one man, mimicking a woman, would pretend to give birth to a wooden baby, which would then be christened (Norton 1992: 98–9). Perhaps this humorous mocking of 'normality' was a response to mainstream society's attitude to the Mollies. 'Sodomy' was illegal and punishable by imprisonment. Blackmail of homosexuals was relatively common, and public opinion of homosexuality was largely negative. The Mollies were effectively criminalised, partly because of the growth of the Societies for the Reformation of Manners, and many of them were driven underground, mixing with criminals or being forced into their company in prison. Overlap between Cant and words that the Mollies knew is, therefore, hardly surprising.

It should not be implied that it's possible to draw an unbroken line of subcultural inheritance between the Molly subculture and the current gay culture in the UK. Also, it's unlikely that the Mollies would be viewed as being 'gay' in the way that most people nowadays would understand that word, but there were a number of elements about their identities that can be related to the later Polari speakers: the fact that they had sex with men, and their use of language to describe sexual acts.

While the Mollies had plenty of euphemistic phrases for male–male sex (*riding a rump, the pleasant deed, do the story, swive, indorse, caudle making*) and cruising (*strolling and caterwauling, bit a blow, put the bite, make a bargain*), there were also words in their lexicon (as demonstrated by Norton) that are less sexually oriented and more likely to be from Cant: *flash ken*: house of thieves; *nubbing cheat*: the gallows; *mish*: shirt; *shap*: hat; *stampers*: shoes; *poll*: wig; *queer ken*: prison; *queer booze*: bad drink; and *queer cull*: fop/fool. Although *queer* is used in some of the phrases that the Mollies used, there is no evidence to suggest that it was used as a word to describe homosexuals. However, it is possible that its use as a pejorative term may have originated here. A couple of Molly words have survived into present-day gay vernacular, via Polari – *trade* was (and still is to some gay men) a sexual partner, while to be *picked up* was to find a partner. The Molly lexicon at least tells us that cruising for gay sex is an age-old pastime.

Parlyaree and its variants

At this point it's useful to introduce a language variety that probably acted as a bridge between Cant and Polari. Until the end of the eighteenth century, actors were a despised group, and for self-protection they used a form of language known as Parlyaree. One of the most prolific lexicographers of the twentieth century, Eric Partridge, has perhaps written most widely on Parlyaree, noting its similarities to Cant (Partridge 1970: 223). He also links Parlyaree to circus people (1950: 117), who used a number of words taken from backslang, rhyming slang and gypsies. The more solitary strolling players (who were later succeeded professionally by troupers) and cheapjacks (pedlars) who mingled with showmen in fairgrounds also contributed to and used Parlyaree. In addition to these groups, some early-twentieth-century prison slang came from Parlyaree.

While Partridge compiled extensive dictionaries of slang (1950, 1961, 1964, 1970, 1974), his descriptions sometimes make for confusing reading.[3] He describes language varieties that have similar spellings, sometimes claiming that they're separate entities, sometimes saying that they're variants of one another, and sometimes asserting that they're the same thing. At times it is difficult to tell whether he's saying that the name of a language variety has two possible spellings, or whether he's actually talking about two completely different language varieties. The following three examples, each from different editions of his dictionaries, should make clear exactly how unclear he was:

> parlaree or -ry; parlyaree; or with capitals. The language of circus men, showmen and itinerant and/or low actors; based on Italian and to some extent on 'Lingua Franca' ... It often merges with the language of tramps.
>
> (Partridge 1964: 497)

Parlyaree

The 'Lingua Franca' – but actually as to 90% of its words Italianate – vocabulary of C. 18–20 actors and mid-C. 19–20 costermongers and showmen . . . Cf palarie . . . In line 8 pargliare is a misprint for parlare, which accounts for the Parlaree (-ry) form; the Parlyaree form has been influenced either by palarie or by e.g., parliamo, 'let us speak'. Parylaree is both less general and less serviceable than Parlary or parlary. In late C. 19– early 20, palarey or palary was very common espc. among music-hall artists; after ca. 1945, palary is demotic, parlary hieratic.

(Partridge 1970: 1391)

parlary. Slang: prostitutes': since ca. 1930.

(Partridge 1974: 1318)

Attempting to pick this apart becomes difficult. We have *parlaree, parlyaree* (with or without capitalisation, although it's debatable as to whether there's a difference). Then there's *pargliare* (which we can fortunately discount as a misprint in an earlier edition of one of Partridge's books), *parlare, palarie* and *Parlary* (in upper case). In addition are *palary* and *parlary* (now in lower case). A number of groups are mentioned: circus men, showmen, itinerant and/or low actors, tramps, costermongers, music-hall artists and prostitutes.

The question of whether it is worth treating all of these varieties as separate lexicons can be answered easily. The slight difference in the spellings of the words is the best indicator of how similar they were, or whether, apart from a few profession-related idiosyncracies, there were any differences at all. Being a minority spoken language variety, used by a number of (generally poorly educated) groups, and thus rarely written down, it is not surprising that there were few standardised spellings, and that Partridge encountered such difficulty when he attempted to tease them apart from one another. It is also unsurprising that he refers to certain words as being Parlyaree, others as Parlary, and still others as both. Back in 1950, in an essay entitled *Parlyaree*, Partridge uses his first sentence to say that it is also occasionally known as Parlaree, Parlarey, Parlary or Palarie. He probably should have left it at that.

So what sort of words were found in this language variety? Citing an out-of-print publication by Sydney Lester (1937) called *Vardi the Palary*, Partridge notes that there are references to money (*saltee*: penny; *bianc*: shilling; *funt*: pound) and numerals (*una, dewey, tray, quattro, chinqua, say, setter, otter, nobber, daiture, lepta, kenza*: 1–12). Lester gives the following example of a Parlary conversation:

'What's the bottle, cull?'
'Dewey funt, tray bionk, daiture soldi medza, so the divvi is otta bionk nobba peroon and tray medzas back in the aris.'

Translated, this would read:

> 'How much have we taken, pal?'
> 'Two pounds, three shillings and tenpence ha'penny, so we get eight shillings and ninepence each and put three ha'pence back in the bottle.'

There are a number of interesting features in this example: the 'bottle' refers to the day's takings. Without knowing the context of the excerpt, it is impossible to tell whether the speakers are prostitutes, entertainers or thieves, or if the bottle refers to a real bottle or not. It is later described as an *aris* – which appears to be Cockney rhyming slang: *aris* being a truncation of *Aristotle*, rhyming with bottle. The word *aris(totle)* also occurs as a possible Polari word in the later Julian and Sandy sketches (see Chapter 5), most likely meaning 'arse'.

The word *cull* which was used previously by the Mollies (who took it from Cant) and circus people, suggests that Parlyaree has origins that date back to at least the 1800s. Here *cull* is used to mean 'mate'. *Divvi* is perhaps a truncation of 'division', and still survives as a verb in certain regions of England today, meaning 'to share'. Although it is used in its noun sense in the example above, it appears to have retained its original meaning. *Peroon* possibly means 'per man' or 'per one'.

The link between beggars and showmen can be demonstrated by the following busker's song, which was sent to Partridge in a letter by Herbert Seaman, and is quoted in *Slang, Today and Yesterday* (Partridge 1970: 1391):

> Nantee dinarlee: The omee of the carsey
> Says due bionc peroney, manjaree on the cross
> We'll all have to scarper the jetty in the morning,
> Before the bonee omee of the carsey shakes his doss.

Translated, the song means:

> We've got no money: the landlord
> Says two shillings per person, we've got our food by cheating
> We'll have to leave in the morning,
> Before the good landlord wakes up.

Despite all of his confusing definitions, Partridge at least took pains to find the label (or labels) to this complex form of language, which he found running across several subcultures over a long period of time. Other lexicographers merely labelled language according to the group they were studying. So Frost (1876: 305–11) describes 'circus slang', which has many similarities to Parlyaree. Although, like many of the other language varieties discussed in this chapter, this slang contains a number of the terms that are related directly to the circus (*slang*: a gymnast's performance; *jeff*: rope; *ponging*: tumbling), some are more general (*bono*: good; *dona*: lady). Other words are indicative of the itinerant life of the circus people; namely, *letty*: lodgings, and *John Scaparey*: to abscond (usually without paying). There is some cross-over between this lexicon and the Cant lexicon. For example, the word *cully* has similar meanings in both lexicons, although each one has been given a more specific meaning within the subculture (circus man's mate; thief's mate). Incidentally, one of the verses of the circus song *The Man On The Flying Trapeze*, written by George Laybourne in 1868, contains the line 'This young man by name was Signor Bona Slang'. Note the similarity between *bona* and Frost's *bono* – both having the same meaning.

Allingham, in the novel *Cheapjack* (often referenced by Partridge), tells of the author's 'adventures as a fortune-teller, grafter, knocker-worker and mounted pitcher on the market-places and fairgrounds of a modern but still romantic England'. The author refers to something called 'Grafter's Slang', which again has a lot in common with Parlyaree:

> Grafters speak a language comprised of every possible type of slang. Some of the words they use come from the Romany, others are Italian, and quite a number of words are Yiddish. These include 'gezumph', which means to cheat or to overcharge: 'snodders', for people who don't spend: and 'yocks', for chumps. Although it is all very childish, I suppose, I have known times when it has been very useful to be able to speak a language which is universally known by the grafters and seldom comprehensible to anyone else. There are times when earwigs, that is to say people who listen to one's conversations, can be very dangerous.
>
> (Allingham 1934: 189)

Although Allingham makes no reference to Parlyaree, many of the grafter's words are described by Partridge as Parlyaree, e.g.: *bevvy*: drink; *charver*: despoil; *chavvy*: child; *denar*: shilling; *donah*: women; *homey*: man; *letty*: lodgings; *munjary*: food; *nanty*: beware; *scarper*: run; *tober*: fairground; *tober'omey*: toll collector; and *tosheroon*: half a crown. A number of other words refer explicitly to the trade of the grafter: *crocus*: a doctor; *dookering*: to tell fortunes; *flash*: grafter's display; *gear*: stock; *lark*: line of business; *tober*: fairground; and *vardo*: caravan, while others refer to monetary units: *coal*: penny; *denar*: shilling; *phunt*: pound; *smash/suzie/spraser*: sixpence; *thrummer*: threepence. There is also another set of words which refer to crime, police and imprisonment: *brass*: prostitute; *gezumph*: swindle; *moon*: a month's imprisonment; and *splits*: the police.

There are words in Allingham's slang which can also be found in Cant, circus slang or the variants of Parlyaree. For example, compare Allingham's *phunt* with Lester's *funt* (both meaning 'pound'), or Allingham's *munjary* with Partridge's *manjaree*. For Allingham, *nanti* meant 'beware', while for Partridge it could mean 'be quiet', 'no', 'none', 'nothing' or 'don't'. Similarly, Allingham's *charver* meant to despoil, while a *charvering donna*, according to Partridge was a prostitute. Another example from *Cheapjack* shows *charver* in context:

> 'E'll keep you gassing all the blinking night if you let 'im,' he said to me. 'What about slippin' up the apple and pears and getting in feather? I'm just about charvered.' . . . 'Charvered' is not a very nice expression, and no doubt Charlie would not have used it had he realised that Madam Eve was present.
>
> (Allingham 1934: 189)

Writing around the same time as *Cheapjack*, George Orwell, in *Down and Out in Paris and London* (1933), although not mentioning Parlyaree, includes a chapter on the slang of beggars and tramps that contains a number of words also used by Allingham: *deaner/dener*: shilling; *clod*: money; *kip*: lodgings; *tosheroon*: half a crown; *sprowsie/sprasy*: sixpence; *gee*: accomplice; *Smoke*: London; and *mug-faker*: photographer. Orwell's novel is semi-autobiographical and is interesting in that it makes a couple of links between the tramp subculture and homosexual men. In one part of the book he describes how a tramp makes sexual advances towards him when they are locked up together for the night. The tramp later explains that their low status made interaction with women impossible, so most had sex with men by default. Orwell (1933: 161) also describes a doss-house, which was frequented by 'ambiguous-looking youths in smartish blue suits' and wealthier men who were prepared to slum it, perhaps because they were after sex with the younger youths.

It is clear that many of the Parlyaree words have Italian origins, and Hancock (1984) has perhaps best explored the relationship between Polari and Italian to date, although his essay only touches on Polari's relationship to the homosexual subculture of the twentieth century. Indeed, the Polari lexicon that Hancock presents at the end of his essay contains many Parlyaree words, and only a few that have a specific relevance to gay men.

It is almost certain that the word *parlarie* (or whichever way one chooses to spell it) is derived from the Italian *parlare*: to speak. Hancock (1984: 395) acknowledges two possible ways that Italian may have influenced Polari (or Parlyaree). First, Britain saw an influx of Italian Punch and Judy men, organ grinders and pedlars during the 1840s. These individuals would have worked with existing show-people and other travellers. The second association of Italian with Polari is concerned with the importation of a 'great number of Italian children' (Ribton-Turner 1887: 303–4) to England during the nineteenth century who were subsequently sent out to busk or perform for the financial benefit of persons known as 'padroni'. These children rarely would have had any substantial knowledge of English, and their most likely contacts would have been other street performers. Therefore, it is possible that more Italian entered into the lexicon of show-people in this way.

Hancock includes a 109-item lexicon at the end of his essay, of which about two-thirds appears to be derived from Italian. A few words relating to sex or prostitution are apparent, such as *aspro* (perhaps derived from the phrase 'ass pro(stitute)', *bagaga*, *kerterver cartzo* (a venereal disease – literally 'bad penis'), *pont* (which in other lexicons meant 'pound'), *charver*, *punk* and *carsey* (now having the extra meaning of 'brothel'). As well as this there are a number of performance-related words such as *wallop*: dance; *mazarine*: platform below stage; *fake the fatcha*: shave the face; and *muck*: stage makeup, while the word *barkey*, which referred to a sailor, suggests connections with seafaring Lingua Franca, or at least the docklands. As well as including Partridge's number terms, there are additional numbers: *say oney*: seven (literally 'six and one'), and *say dooe*: eight (six and two). *Long dedger* is used for eleven, rather than Lester's *lepta*.

Lingua Franca

The phrase 'Lingua Franca' has been used several times so far, without explanation. Linguists sometimes use the term *lingua franca* in reference to cases where two (or more) people possess different first languages (e.g. one is French and one is English) and neither is able to understand the other, so they communicate in Spanish. In this case, Spanish is viewed as a lingua franca. However, there is another meaning of Lingua Franca, which refers to a language variety spoken in ports along the Mediterranean coast and originating from the time of the Crusades (Hancock 1984: 391). Lingua Franca had a number of grammatical rules, making it more akin to a pidgin – a simplified form of language derived from two (or more) different languages. Some Lingua Franca words that appear to be at least related to Parlyaree are: *barca*: boat; *mangia*: food; *bona vardia*: all's well; *capello*: hood; and *parlamento*: conversation (Kahane *et al.* 1958).

Lingua Franca was almost certainly known to English sailors, who most probably brought it back to England with them (Coelho 1880). In the eighteenth and nineteenth centuries, many wounded seamen, upon returning to England, were subsequently put ashore miles away from the place where they were to be paid. As a result they were obliged to take to the roads against their will, becoming rogues and beggars as they made their way across the country (Hancock 1984: 393). Other retired sailors would have joined the travelling classes of showmen, players and pedlars in order to make a living (Ribton-Turner 1887, Salgado 1977: 138). The distinction between sailors and beggars is blurred somewhat when it is considered that an Act of 1713 made wandering illegal, except for sailors. As a result, many beggars pretended to be sailors until the law was repealed in 1792.

Therefore, in numerous ways, the Lingua Franca words learnt by sailors would have entered the various versions of Parlyaree used by beggars, pedlars, strolling players and other travelling people. Alan Corré notes that the Lingua Franca words used within Polari have been influenced by Occitan, a Romance language intermediate between French and Spanish, usually regarded as a French dialect.[4]

The traditional sexual fascination of sailors for some gay men has been noted by a number of writers: Green (1987: 128): 'The automatic union of ... sailors ("rum, sodomy and the lash") and the gay world is clichéd, politically no doubt far from correct, but unavoidable.' Donaldson (1990: 1174) describes the 'erotic mystique' of sailors, who, in their figure-hugging uniforms could be seen as sexually casual, easily plied with alcohol, and willing to do almost anything for money. The hypersexual sailor has been constructed in fantasies by Jean Genet, Tom of Finland, Bob Mizer's Athletic Guild and countless other purveyors of gay pornography. Rodgers (1972: 22) continues the theme:

> the Navy ... is fantasised [by gay men] as full of young doll-like boys who have signed up at seventeen; when out to sea, boredom is relieved by boring a bud and playing drop the soap ... Sailors in general are known as seafood.

Spencer (1995: 335–40) describes how, in 1919, an American YMCA at Newport, Rhode Island was the subject of scandal as dozens of sailors were found to be involved in homosexual parties. An investigation carried out by the Navy backfired when it transpired that decoys who were used to find information about the gang were also having male–male sex, but did not consider themselves to be gay. The lines between who was homosexual and who was not became so confused that, by 1920, an Inquiry condemned the original investigation, and the Navy offered clemency to some of the men who had been imprisoned.

While it is unlikely that the majority of sailors would be able to live up to such high sexual expectations, or whether they would be willing to admit to having a man in every port, even if this was the case, an argument can be made for the link between homosexual men and the Navy. Some gay men would have joined up simply because of the all-male environment. Despite the fact that homosexuality was illegal in the Navy, a significant proportion of gay men joined the Merchant Navy or passenger cruise ships, many working as stewards or waiters. Other gay men, while not sailors, would have hung around dockland areas, hoping to make new friends. Chesney (1972: 328–9) suggests that 'it was probably in the great ports that the most genuinely professional male prostitutes were found'. It is almost certainly the case that, in England, sailors were linked to the development of Polari in the East End of London (see Chapter 3). These *sea queens* or *boat-queens* also coined several terms that were related to their lives at sea. For example, a ship was known as a *lattie on water*, a berth full of queens was a *fruit locker*, and a curtain hung across a bunk to enable privacy during male–male sex was known as a *trade curtain*. The sea queens are discussed in more detail in Chapter 4.

Rhyming slang and backslang

A book describing Polari would not be complete without mentioning (Cockney) rhyming slang, which at once ties it to the geographic region of London, and gives a robust format for deriving words. The first Cockney rhyming slang lexicon was published in 1821 as *The Flash Dictionary*, and was reprinted as appendices to *Poverty, Mendacity and Crime* (1839) and *Sinks of London Laid Open* (1848), both without acknowledged authors. Although it has been suggested that the rhyming slang and backslang used by costermongers derives from a secret language of the criminal underworld, Franklyn (1960: 7) notes that there were differences between Thieves Cant, which was complex and 'grim', and rhyming slang, which was amusing and intelligible even to the uninitiated. He suggests that rhyming slang was developed by Cockney navvies in the early nineteenth century, as a means of mystifying the Irishmen who worked alongside them on the docks, canals and railway embankments. It is likely that unemployment led the navvies into contact with the criminal underworld, where they passed on rhyming slang to professional thieves.

The majority of rhyming slang consists of two- and three-word phrases, such as *field of wheat* or *half inch*, with the latter part of the slang phrase rhyming with the original English word. In the cases above, the former means 'street', while the latter means 'pinch' (steal). The phrase can also be abbreviated, so that only the first part of it is used. Therefore *stairs* becomes *apples and pears*, or just *apples*. Generally, the phrases translate into nouns or verbs, although there are exceptions, e.g. *ruddy* is rhyming slang for 'bloody', and *raughty* means 'naughty'. Some rhyming slang words that appear to have been used in Polari are shown in Table 2.1.

Table 2.1 Rhyming slang words used in Polari

Rhyming word	Derived from	Meaning
barnet	Barnet Fair	hair
hampsteads	Hampstead Heath	teeth
irish	Irish jig	wig
minces	mince pies	eyes
plates	plates of meat	feet
scotches	Scotch peg	legs
two and eight	two and eight	state
steamer	steam tug	mug (prostitute's client)

Backslang is formed simply by saying the word as if it was spelt backwards, so *face* would be *ecaf*, *hair* would be *riah*, and *nose* would be *esong* or *eson*. These first two examples are well-known Polari words (with the third being less well-known, but still classed as Polari). As with rhyming slang, not all backslang words found their way into Polari's lexicon – *doog gels*: good legs; *foop*: poof; and *larro*: oral sex being three that don't appear to have made the cross-over (Green and Williams 1999).

Romani

Romani (also Romany) is a member of the Indo-European family of languages (Katzner 1986: 107). The gypsies, or 'Egyptians' as they were first known, moved westward at some period, no later than the ninth century AD, and spread over western Asia, Europe and eventually to America. By the early sixteenth century they had reached Britain, the first recorded account of them in Britain being from 1505.

By the twentieth century, Romani had lost its distinctive syntax, phonology and morphology (in that order) and was simply a lexicon consisting mainly of verbs, adjectives and nouns. Kenrick (1979) suggests that Romani English originated as a pidgin (and later became a creole) between Romanies and the English people who joined their bands in the sixteenth century, or that it gradually changed through contact with the host language.

Burton (1979: 120) links Polari to a number of groups, including the gypsies: 'It owed allegiance to and was curiously linked with the curious argots developed by the "underworld groups" – the Gypsies, the blacks, the drug sub-culture, the criminal, the racing fraternity.' However, Hancock (1984: 395) disagrees:

> Burton's labelling of Gypsies and Blacks as 'underworld' peoples speaking 'curious argots' is scarcely justifiable ... there is nothing clearly Gypsy or Black in Polari, and Sephardic immigrants would more likely have contributed Romance words to the dialect than would have Ashkenazim from Russia and Poland.

An examination of Borrow's Romani English lexicon (1874) (Borrow 1982) reveals only a handful of words which appear to be related to Polari or Parlyaree. For example, *boona*: good; *chavi/chavali*: girl/daughter; *chavo/chauvo*: boy/son; *dui*: two; *warda*: guard or take care; and *pani/pawnee*: water. The Romani English word *fake* (work illegally or steal) is also found in Frost's list of circus words, with a similar meaning. Finally, there is a word for the number seven which is interesting. Many Romani English speakers used the phrase *dui trins ta yeck*, which translates in Romani English as *two threes and one*. Hancock (1984: 400) gives the phrase *say oney*, translating to *six and one* for the number seven.

So, while these terms are different, there is at least a parallel in the additional format of some of the larger numbers in both Romani English and Polari.

The lexical similarities between Polari and Romani English, however, are slight at best, and there is no guarantee that any cognate words are a result of any genuine cross-over between the two varieties of language. It could be the case that words such as *bona/boona* and *fake/fakement* found their way into both languages from a third source, such as circus language. However, the gypsies were another itinerant group of people, and most certainly would have encountered other travelling groups such as tramps, circus people and costermongers, ensuring some degree of linguistic cross-over. And although they are separate languages, the circumstances under which Romani is used are similar to those of Polari. Unlike, say, Lingua Franca, which was used so that different groups of people could understand one another, both Polari and Romani were used as secret languages to exclude outsiders.

Theatre speak

> I was living with a dancer ... and they all talked it, regardless of sex, it was nothing to do with sex – it was just a kind of professional slang.
>
> (Sandy Wilson, BBC Radio 4 1998)

It is difficult to cite a date (or even a decade) when Polari became something separate from Parlyaree, although Partridge (1970: 249) points to some time in the nineteenth century, writing that Parlyaree had become 'moribund'. By this point, the strolling players and performers had been succeeded by those who worked primarily in music halls. While many actors and dancers continued to work around the country and abroad, it was London, with its numerous entertainment venues, that became the base for Polari. As well as its theatres and music halls, London, like many big cities, became home to gay men, who moved there for numerous reasons: anonymity, greater tolerance, a more cosmopolitan lifestyle, work opportunities, access to other men etc. By the late 1930s, gay subcultures had become established in the UK's large cities, especially London. Dancers, known as *wallopers*, and singers, known as *voches* (voices) delighted in the language derived from Parlyaree, which they claimed for themselves. While many of these performers were gay, there were plenty who weren't, and for them Polari, or *Palare* as it was more commonly known in the first half of the twentieth century, was simply the language of the theatre, with words associated with the stage, many taken from the older Parlyaree. However, Polari was quickly picked up by chorus boys, particularly those who were gay, and they adopted the language as their own.

In 1969, Peter Gordeno published a brief description and 19-item lexicon of something he called the 'dancer's language', which in reality was Polari. Asserting that many of these terms came from the circus, he went on to say that they were known by thousands of dancers the world over. While this language variety wasn't linked explicitly to gay men in the article (after all, he was writing for the family-oriented *TV Times* magazine), the list included words like *camp*: outrageous, eccentric or twee; *omme-polone*: homosexual; and *frock*: female attire.

Polari's links with the theatre continued with the Julian and Sandy sketches of the late 1960s (see Chapter 5). These radio comedy characters were cast as out-of-work actors, and could be viewed as stereotypical Polari speakers, being good representatives of the link between the gay subculture and the theatre. This form of theatre-speak could also be classed as 'West End' Polari (see Chapter 4), which has been described as a more simplistic version than that influenced by Lingua Franca and the multi-ethnic East End communities in London.

Prostitution

Polari's association with prostitution has a long history – Partridge referred to *parlary* as being a prostitute's slang since the 1930s, and the links between male prostitution and sailors has already been noted. Quentin Crisp (1968: 30–1) describes how he and his young effeminate friends who hung around the Black Cat café in Old Compton Street may have had jobs during the day, but were 'prostitutes by vocation'. In an era of guilt and oppression, for Crisp, accepting money for sex absolved him 'from the charge of enjoying sex for its own sake'. Piccadilly Circus (or *The Dilly* as it was renamed in Polari) was a popular haunt for male prostitutes, as the song *Piccadilly Palare* by Morrissey ascertains:

> The Piccadilly palare
> Was just silly slang
> Between me and the boys in my gang
> 'So Bona to Vada. OH YOU
> Your lovely eek and
> Your lovely riah'.
> We plied an ancient trade.

However, it was not just male prostitutes who would have introduced their *steamers* (clients) to Polari. A relationship between gay men and female prostitutes is suggested below:

> The reason why gay men linked with prostitutes and the other criminals was we gave each other protection in a roundabout way. If girls were caught with condoms they would be charged with prostitution.

If a gay guy was caught with a tin of vaseline he would also be charged with prostitution. So the girls would carry the vaseline and the boys would carry the condoms. It made for a rather strange relationship.

(Jim, *It's Not Unusual*, BBC2 1997)

Jewish influences

In London, there was a strong Jewish community (particularly in the East End) which also contributed a number of linguistic items to Polari. There were 100,000 Jewish people living in London between 1870 and 1914, and many times that number stayed in the East End before going on to New York (Mazower 1987: 9). At the start of the Second World War there were 11 million speakers of Yiddish, representing between 65 and 70 per cent of the world Jewish population (Goldsmith 1997: 15). Yiddish dates back to at least the fifteenth century, when it was introduced to Poland from Germanic lands. Emerging in the Rhinelands, Yiddish was a composite of Rabbinic Hebrew, Loez or Laaz (Jewish dialects of Old French and Old Italian), dialects of medieval German, and forms of Slavic. Like Polari, Yiddish borrowed and adapted words from many different sources.

Terms such as *kosher homie*: Jewish man; *schinwhars*:[5] Chinese man; *schonk*: to hit; *schvartz homie* or *schvartzer homie*: black man; *vonka*: nose, *sheitel/shyckle*: wig; *schlumph*: to drink; *schwarly*: man; *schnozzle*: nose; and *nosh*: oral sex, are likely to be influenced by Yiddish words. It is likely that such terms entered the Polari lexicon as a result of people belonging to both the gay and Jewish subcultures in London, just as rhyming slang and backslang entered Polari via the influence of the London Cockney dialect. Yiddish theatre was extremely popular in the East End of London around the beginning of the twentieth century, and it's therefore possible that the Parlyaree-based theatre slang would have been influenced by the Yiddish spoken by Jewish performers.

American Airforce slang

'Got any gum, chum?'
(Common catchphrase called out to American servicemen in the UK, 1940s)

In times of war, sexual taboos tend to be relaxed – many people, facing the threat of occupation or death are less likely to worry about upholding rigid moral codes based around sexual behaviour. The periods of extended separation and ensuing loneliness experienced by those in wartime are ideal conditions for otherwise unlikely sexual pairings. Sex becomes a much more opportunistic and matter-of-fact affair. In the Second World War, while many gay men joined the Army – experiencing sexual freedom for the first time – some, like Quentin Crisp, remained at home, excluded on the grounds of 'suffering from sexual perversion'.

The Blackout effectively made public sex a much more frequent affair than before – doorways, parks and underground stations all became viable locations for a chance encounter. And then, as Crisp (1968: 157–60) discovered to his delight, the Americans arrived:

> As they sat in the cafés or stood in the pubs, their bodies bulged through every straining khaki fibre towards our feverish hands . . . Above all it was the liberality of their natures that was so marvellous . . . Never in the history of sex was so much offered by so many to so few.

The US troops, called GIs after the words 'Government Issue' which appeared on their equipment, formed the majority of the 1,421,000 allied troops who were accommodated in the UK by the late spring of 1944 (Calder 1969: 308). With their nylons, gum, Hershey bars, soap, razor blades and Lucky Strike cigarettes, the young, lonely GIs had plenty to offer in exchange for companionship. While women were happy to help ease their loneliness, according to Crisp, a good proportion of these Americans didn't seem to be overly fussy about the sex of their British bed-fellows. London in particular played host to the American Airforce, and, unsurprisingly, it was about this time that American slang terms started to creep into Polari. When the war ended, the Americans returned home, but they had left behind a legacy of words such as *butch*: masculine; *cruise*: look for sex; *blow-job*: oral sex; and *naff*: bad.

1960s drug culture

In the 1960s, recreational and experimental drug use soared, transcending class and ethnic boundaries, but based primarily around teenagers and young adults. Bohemian youth was influenced heavily by the 1950s' beatnik style, pioneered and mythologised in America by Allen Ginsberg, Jack Kerouac, Neal Cassady and William Burroughs. While people who used drugs were criminalised and the popular press was quick to sensationalise and stigmatise those who were caught, unlike many earlier generations of drug-users, this subculture did not consider itself in terms of being criminal or hopelessly addicted. Peter Burton's 1979 article on Polari in *Gay News* asserts that, during this time, a few words and phrases referring to drug use entered some Polari lexicons:

> Many of the words used in Polari also belong to the slang of . . . other groups . . . dubes, meaning pills, had – and may well still have – exactly the same meaning in drug-users slang. And of course, at that point in time, a lot of us seemed to live on 'uppers' and 'downers.'
> (Burton 1979: 23)

Uppers, such as cocaine and speed, have stimulating effects, whereas *downers* – heroin, alcohol, sleeping medication and tranquillizers – create a calming, mellow 'high'. Mods had popularised the use of drugs such as Drynamil, which were prescribed for anxiety but also had an amphetamine-like effect when two or more were taken together. These drugs were called *purple hearts*, because they were shaped like a rounded triangle and had a reddish-blue colour. In the 1960s they would have been taken by gay men who wanted energy for a 24-hour, dance-till-you-drop lifestyle. To get high on pills was to be *blocked*, while an intense desire for sex after the effects of drugs had worn off was known as a *randy comedown*. As well as referring to pills, *doobs* (also *dubes* or *doobies*) was slang for marijuana cigarettes.

Conclusion

Partridge (1970: 1391) notes that, by about 1970, 'gay slang has come to be known, in raffish, homosexual circles, as *polari*'. However, other writers (e.g. David 1997: 199) claim that, by the late 1960s, Polari had become 'almost extinct'. It is certainly the case that, by the 1970s, Polari had begun its decline (as discussed in Chapter 6).

One aspect of Polari that I have not covered in this chapter is the fact that gay men invented their own words, independently of the other subcultures under discussion. *Cottage*, *rimming*, *auntie*, *active/passive*, *bedroom*, *dress up*, *trade*, *bitch* and *jennifer justice* – these words appear to be more related to the experiences of gay men than words such as *lallies*, *bona*, *dooey*, *palone* and which could have come from any slang lexicon, or words like *purple hearts*, *walloper* and *barkey*, which clearly have been imported from specific groups. Some of the people I interviewed were reluctant to class these 'gay' words as being Polari at all – one man referred to them as 'nelly words', while others have referred to them as 'nonce words', 'gay slang' or Gayspeak.

Is it the case that Polari developed separately, alongside something that could be considered as 'gay slang'? Or perhaps the 'nelly words' began as Polari, but were quickly dropped by Polari speakers when a wider audience were exposed to them? I think these explanations are unlikely. It is more credible that these words were so well-known by both Polari speakers and the gay men who didn't speak Polari, that they weren't considered to be secrets and therefore not Polari in the proper sense. Tellingly, many of these 'nelly words' survived Polari's decline and are still known by gay men, if not always used. In any case, it is ironic that the very words considered to be most relevant to gay men are the ones that are also most likely to be dissociated from Polari – supposedly a 'gay' language.

How can we explain the ways that words and phrases from different subcultures at different times in history coalesced to become Polari in the twentieth century? Perhaps we can view each group in terms of 'speech communities'? Lyons (1970: 326) refers to speech communities as all the people who use a language, whereas Hockett (1958: 8) gives a definition which delimits sets of people who communicate with each other via a common language, emphasising the importance of social contact. Bloomfield (1933: 42) and Gumperz (1972: 54–5) give descriptions that allow for members of speech communities to communicate multilingually, whereas Labov (1972: 120) emphasises shared attitudes to language. Finally, there is an approach that refers to groups in society which have distinct speech characteristics and other social traits. This is the view put forward by Le Page (1968: 189–212) and Bolinger (1975: 333).

Theories have come under criticism for their inherent implications that speech communities exist as discrete groups in societies (Hudson 1980: 30), and that binary distinctions of membership or non-membership can be made. It is clear that identities such as 'grafter', 'tramp', 'circus person' etc. were not absolute, but rather could be considered as loosely overlapping and transient roles, changing over time. A person may initially have taken work as a sailor, but later become a beggar, or worked as a grafter in a market or a performer in a circus. A gay man may have worked in the theatre, but also as a prostitute. Speech communities are therefore best considered as prototypical concepts.

It is clear that many of the linguistic items I have described were known to more than one group, sometimes with alternative spellings (which is more probably the result of differing transcription practices of multiple authors), and sometimes with semantic differences (e.g. *nobber* can mean 'nine' or 'one who collects money for a beggar'). Such homonyms are significant and can be accounted for in a number of ways. For example, one group may have borrowed a linguistic item from another but incorrectly understood the meaning, or they may have adapted it for their own needs. In some cases, the meaning of a shared word or phrase would change over time for one group but not the other.

Both Lave and Wenger's (1991) theory of *communities of practice* and Pratt's (1987) theory of *linguistics of contact* work well in this context. Communities of practice theory places a focus on groups of people coming together to carry out activities, and using a form of language based around those activities – whether the activity is performing in a circus, begging, or looking for sex with other men. Linguistics of contact theory recognises that there is overlap between members of communities and between the communities themselves. This places emphasis on the changing identity of the individual rather than on separate and homogeneous group identities, each with its own jargon or anti-language. By observing crossover features (e.g. occurrence of the same linguistic items in different groups) both diachronically and synchronically, it becomes necessary to view each group not so much as different links in a chain, but as overlapping states of being that an individual can inhabit serially or multiply at different times.

However, to view all Polari speakers as possessing multiple identities is to over-complicate the story somewhat. There would be cases where Polari speakers would not possess other identities, but simply come into contact with other stigmatised subcultures for reasons such as incarceration, sexual attraction, prostitution, migration to cities, employment trends or shared activities (e.g. drug use). Many of the linguistic items described in the earlier sections of this chapter would not be recognised by Polari speakers from the 1960s onwards. It is clear, however, that Polari has evolved from these earlier varieties that were known as Parlyaree or Parlary, and the most direct link between twentieth-century Polari speakers and nineteenth-century Parlyaree speakers would have been via London's music halls and theatres.

Having traced Polari's roots from Cant up to the twentieth century, the next chapter is concerned with providing a linguistic description – in particular the different classes of words that were used (vocabulary), the ways that new words could be formed (morphology), and the ways that words could be strung together to make meaningful sentences (grammar).

3   Polari as a language system

Introduction

It is worth bearing in mind an important distinction when considering Polari (or any language variety). It can be viewed as an abstract language system, defined by its *linguistic items* (Hudson 1980: 24; Wardhaugh 1986: 22), but it can also be thought of in terms of language use, or rather, the social contexts, mores and motivations for using language. This is perhaps similar to Saussure's (1966: 9, 13) concepts of *langue* and *parole*, where *langue* refers to the 'language habits of all speakers of a language' and *parole* refers to 'the individual uses and variations we observe' (Wardhaugh 1993: 19).

It is the intention of this chapter to examine Polari, not from a social or historical perspective, but from a more expressively linguistic or *langue* point of view. Therefore, this chapter attempts to break Polari down into its working parts by examining its vocabulary, grammar and accent. While the Appendix works as a glossary, listing Polari words in alphabetical order, with a pronunciation guide, and possible spellings and meanings, this chapter deals with Polari as a language system on a more abstract level, revealing the processes that go into the creation of Polari words and utterances.

Vocabulary

> *Interviewer*:   How close did [Polari] come to being a language in those days? Is it just a vocabulary?
> *Peter Burton*:   It's just a vocabulary.
> *(Word of Mouth, BBC Radio 4 1995)*

It is undoubtedly the case that the most distinctive feature of Polari is its lexicon, and for many speakers the lexicon was sufficient. However, later in this chapter I will show that, for some speakers, Polari appeared to go beyond the status of a vocabulary, with the beginnings of a grammar that did not simply mirror that of English. But for the moment we must accept that Polari was in essence spoken in English, with a number of key words replaced with Polari equivalents. Adept speakers would use a high number of Polari words, often modifying existing linguistic items or combining them in novel ways (see the section on morphology in this chapter). Therefore, the extent to which Polari resembled a 'language' is dependent, among other things, on the Polari:English ratio employed.

This ratio is obviously related to the number of Polari words the speaker knew. Studies of slang (e.g. Stanley 1970) have found that many subcultural lexicons include *core* and *fringe* vocabularies. Core vocabularies contain a few words or phrases that are known to many people, including those who are not part of the social group who use the slang. Fringe vocabularies are much larger, but each word in the fringe vocabulary will only be known to a few speakers. This phenomenon can be applied to Polari. For example, most speakers, and a significant proportion of non-Polari speakers, will be aware of a core Polari lexicon. This includes words such as *bona*, *vada*, *eek*, *lallies* and *riah*. Seven of the Polari speakers I interviewed agreed to be 'tested' on their knowledge. I asked them to identify a list of 200 Polari words, and to add any words they knew that were not on the list. Each speaker was able to identify between 35 and 78 words, of which only 20 (the core) were known to every interviewee.[1] The other words, consisting of the fringe vocabulary, tended to be understood by only one or two speakers. So, while Polari may appear to have a large lexicon (consisting of over 400 terms), it is extremely unlikely that the average Polari speaker would have known all of these words, and hence the Polari:English ratio any one speaker could achieve had limitations.

These limitations grow when we consider that Polari over-lexicalises. As discussed in Chapter 1, over-lexicalisation refers to a phenomenon where lots of words exist for the same concept in a particular language. It is particularly well-documented for concepts that have taboo or criminal associations: consider the number of slang terms for marijuana: *hash*, *brown*, *pot*, *Mary-Jane*, *weed*, *dope*, *grass* etc. In other cases, over-lexicalisation can refer to extremely subtle distinctions within a concept. Given that the core Polari lexicon was relatively small, and that items in it were products of over-lexicalisation, the opportunity to substitute a Polari word for an English word is further limited. With this stated, it is useful now to consider how Polari words are distributed according to parts of speech.

Nouns

The majority of Polari lexical items (70 per cent) are nouns, with verbs and adjectives contributing to a significant proportion of the remaining 30 per cent.[2] The nouns tend to be concerned with the following broad semantic fields:

- types of people (for example, occupation)
- body parts (including genitalia)

- clothing
- terms of endearment/address towards people.

Before looking at these types of nouns in more detail, first a word or two about proper nouns.

Proper nouns

There are hardly any proper nouns in Polari, exceptions being *The Dilly* (Piccadilly) and a number of terms used to describe, and notably feminise, the police: *betty bracelets*, *lily law*, *hilda handcuffs* etc. One practice (discussed in Chapter 4) among some Polari speakers was to give themselves and each other female names (also known as 'camp names'), a practice some gay men continue to use today. There would usually be a link, perhaps near homophony between the male name and the female name – so *Martin* becomes *Martina*, and *Harold* is *Harriet*. Otherwise, the name could reflect a personality trait that would perhaps 'suit' a particular person, as a sailor who was interviewed notes:

> When I came to sea the older ones had names like Lana Turner, and you know, Ginger Rogers, after the Hollywood stars. And you maybe had one called Dockside Doris, or the rougher ones: there was one called Gilda Gash. There was another one called Three Way Mavis, cos obviously the things she got up to.
>
> (Mark)

Classifying people

Many of the words used to classify different types of people (a category comprising 30 per cent of all nouns) appear to work in terms of their relationship to *binary constructions*. For example, a Polari noun will refer to someone's sexuality as homosexual or heterosexual, to their sex (male or female), gender[3] (e.g. butch or camp), age (young or old) or attractiveness (beautiful or ugly). In many cases, Polari words that labelled types of people would be used in order to refer to several of these binaries at once. For example, the term *antique h.p.* refers to an ageing gay male, referencing three sets of binaries (age, sexuality and sex). Certain combinations of binaries are more common than others. So there are lots of words that describe feminine men, or gay men, or feminine gay men, but fewer words are used to refer to masculine men, lesbians or masculine gay men.

The four most common types of occupation that were referenced in Polari words were prostitution, show business, the police and hairdressing. The existence of words for these professions can easily be explained. Some Polari speakers had possibly worked as prostitutes at some time in their lives, and prostitutes would almost certainly be a feature of a large underground gay scene, especially in cities. As well as terms for prostitution, there were also words that referred to clients of prostitutes.

Moving on to consider why many of the words describe occupations connected with the theatre, this is likely to have been because the theatre was one of the places were Polari first originated, and many actors (both gay and straight) continued to use Polari. With respect to hairdressers, this was a stereotypically 'gay' occupation. The inclusion of the police in the lexicon has quite a different genesis, however. While words for prostitution, the theatre and hairdressing reflected the (stereotyped) lifestyle and occupations of gay men speaking Polari, the police loom large in the lexicon as they were a principal threat to that lifestyle, as discussed in Chapter 4. So, the prominence of occupations in the Polari lexicon defines in part the gay world (hairdressers, entertainers and prostitutes being part of the Polari-speaker's world and those most likely to be gay or use Polari) in contrast to the principal agents of the 'straight' world that a Polari speaker had reason to come into contact with and fear (the police were 'the enemy').

The police are not alone in being identified as outsiders in the Polari lexicon. *Flatties* and *gillies* were words derived from the older Parlyaree lexicon (see Chapter 2), referring respectively to males and females in a theatre's audience, while the word *naff*, although mainly used as an adjective, could also be employed as a noun. A *naff* was the personification of the adjectival form of the same word (a feature I look at more closely in the section on adjectives below). A *naff* was therefore a heterosexual person who was unattractive/unavailable to Polari speakers precisely because of their heterosexuality.

The use of the words *omee* (man) and *palone* (woman) reveal an interesting formula in deriving categories. While an *omee* refers to any man, and *palone* to any woman, the word *omee-palone* (man–woman) refers specifically to a homosexual man. The combination of the two words cannot be taken as a literal translation (the closest thing to a 'man–woman' would be a hermaphrodite). However, the ordering of the words appears to be important, as the example *palone-omee* (lesbian) testifies. It appears that the first word of the pair refers to sex, while the second to sexuality or gender, or a combination of both. Clearly, 'otherness' in terms of sexuality/gender is being marked here – as heterosexual men and women are simply the default *omee* and *palone*, not *omee-omee* and *palone-palone*. Perhaps when *omee-palone* was coined, it was based on the folk belief that 'homosexual men were women trapped in men's bodies'.

Some words could have unfixed meanings, so the same word could be used to refer to different types of people, for example, *butch, queen, trade, sea queen* and *steamer* (all discussed below). The semantic categorisation of a word in different ways could be attributed to Polari's status as a secret, unwritten language – with no standards, meanings are more likely to shift.[4] Or it could be due to processes of explicitly highlighting either the similarities between supposed binary pairs, or the shift which comes from unfixed gay identities. The process appears to be a form of under- rather than over-lexicalisation, where the same word has many meanings, rather than there being lots of meanings for a single word.

For example, the word *queen* could be used by Polari speakers to refer to any gay man, but it could also just refer to a subcategory of men who were effeminate, or who took the passive role in intercourse. When premod- ified by another noun, *queen* could simply denote someone who is 'into' a particular fetish: for example, *drag queen* (a gay man who wears femi- nine clothing, not a transsexual), or *sea queen* (one who pursues sailors). However, a *sea queen* can also be a gay sailor. In the same way, a *rice-queen* could be a gay Asian man or someone who pursues sexual relationships with Asian men. Therefore, the construct *x-queen* can refer to both what is pursued, and who is pursuing, existing simultaneously on either side of a binary divide.

Butch, which refers to masculinity, can be used in different ways to refer to males or females, whereas *trade*, which denotes a casual sexual partner, can apply to someone who is ostensibly heterosexual (possibly a male prostitute), but can also mean someone who is gay and available for sex. A gay aphorism 'today's trade is tomorrow's competition' (Gardiner 1997: 123) implies that the sexual identity of 'trade' is unfixed. A *steamer* could be a client of a prostitute or a gay man who seeks passive partners, the two not necessarily being the same thing.

There also appears to be a link between some of the surface meanings of the Polari lexical items for people, and their 'real meanings'. While not all of the words have been borrowed from English, many of them were. For example, the use of the word *seafood* (commonly used to refer to an attractive sailor) employs a food metaphor. The use of metaphor therefore becomes an interesting factor in the derivation of Polari words. Table 3.1 shows some examples.

Sexual attraction is often marked in terms of food metaphors in Polari (apart from the derogatory word *fish* which refers to females). Many of the metaphors used in slang depend on the five senses, and taste is often used as a metaphor for sexual terms:

Table 3.1 Common metaphors associated with Polari nouns

Metaphor	Examples
food	chicken, dish, fish, fruit, seafood
royalty	queen, duchess, lady
animal	bull, bitch
money	trade, rent, renter
femininity	betty bracelets, bitch, dolly, fairy, lily law, manly alice, mary, minnie, mollie, nelly, zelda, fag hag
family	auntie, sister, orderly daughters, husband

Many words with primary standard meanings of food have sexual slang meanings. The body, parts of the body, and descriptions of each, often call food items into use ... This primary relation between sex and food depends on the fact that they are [our] two major sensuous experiences ... Sex and food seem to be related in our subconscious.

(Flexner and Wentworth 1960: xxvii)

The popularity of food items in Polari supports Flexner and Wentworth's remarks about slang per se. However, in Polari, I would suggest that the 'subconscious' relating of sex to food is rather more explicit than they suppose.

A strong feminising metaphor runs through many Polari nouns. Although the words are gender-marked as female (either because they are a female name: *betty bracelets*; or because they imply a female relationship: *auntie*; or female status: *queen*), they are often used to refer to males. Most commonly the words are applied to gay males (*queen, lady, sister*), but there are cases where nominally heterosexual males are also feminised; for example, words for the police (*betty bracelets, lily law, orderly daughters*). Like Julian and Sandy, many Polari speakers were camp (or at least they were when they spoke Polari). The female words referred to this, and perhaps also positioned gay men as being similar to heterosexual women in that they both had men as sexual partners.

Not all of the feminising words are used to refer to men who are camp. For example, the phrase *manly alice* refers to a masculine gay man. Nor are feminising words just used to describe men. A *zelda* is an unattractive woman, while a *fag hag* is a woman who usually consorts with gay men. Therefore the feminising metaphor is not linked exclusively to sexuality, gender, or even sex. What the Polari lexicon potentially appears to be able to do is to construct *everyone* in terms of femininity, whether they are feminine/female or not.

This process was interpreted as sexist by some opponents of Polari (see Chapter 6). However, it is interesting to view it in terms of the binary male/female distinction, especially in relation to power. Often when dealing with binaries in the social world, there are inequalities in the way that power is divided between each side of the binary (Derrida 1972). For example, traditionally, men are viewed as possessing more power than women, while the same theory can generally be applied to white/non-white and heterosexual/homosexual distinctions. Therefore, to refer to gay men as female could have the effect of highlighting their status as 'other' or disempowered. To use a feminising word on a heterosexual man would be a way of insulting him by referring to him as somehow being 'less than a man',[5] while the same word used on a gay man is only half-mocking; there is also a sense of reclamation and identification, of the term and of the person it is used upon. It is unsurprising that some of these words are concerned with relationships (e.g. *sister, auntie*) and would have been used to refer to friendships between gay men. The use of feminising terminology is therefore multi-fold: it addresses the difference between heterosexual and homosexual, and can be used as a weapon against outsiders, or as a means of consolidation within the gay subculture. However, it can also be employed ironically or aggressively within the subculture where needed.

Body parts and clothing

Following words that describe types of people, the next most common type of noun refers to body parts (about 20 per cent of all Polari nouns). Again, words to do with body parts allowed Polari speakers to describe each other. About a third of the words for body parts in Polari refer to facial features (eyes, nose, ears, mouth etc.), and another third refer to sexually taboo parts (genitals, breasts, anus etc.). There are about equal numbers of words for male and female body parts.

After body parts, the next biggest noun category was clothing (15 per cent of all nouns). There were about equal numbers of words that referred to men's and women's clothing, with many clothing words referring to accessories (jewellery, glasses etc.), hats, wigs or shoes. Metaphor use in words for clothing and body nouns is less marked than for nouns that refer to types of people, but it is still present. Again, similar categories are found, for example, the feminising metaphor: *aunt nells* (ears), *lills* (hands), *maria* (sperm) and *slingbacks* (shoes). A food metaphor is also found with reference to body parts: *beef curtains* (vagina), *brandy* (backside), *dish* (backside), *meat and two veg* (male genitalia), *minces* (eyes), *pots in the cupboard* (teeth), *plates* (feet) and *winkle* (small penis). Body parts (especially sexual body parts) are seen as tasty meals, to be devoured.

Terms of endearment

Several words exist in Polari that are used as general terms of address: *dear*, *ducky*, *heartface*, *girl* and *treash* (an abbreviation of 'treasure'). Although it can also be disputed that some of these words might have simply been features of English spoken language in the 1950s and 1960s, the use of certain terms of endearment was (and still is) also a notable aspect of language use by some gay men. One interviewee respondent explains why he uses such words:

> I myself use *sweetie* a lot because it is very convenient if you don't remember the other person's name, a very frequent occurrence on the gay scene. Older people use *dear* for that reason, as well as its camp value.
>
> (Lucas)

I would suggest that the use of words such as *dear* and *ducky* has a similar function to the working-class heterosexual male's use of the word *mate*[6] in contemporary spoken English, or even *cull* in the eighteenth century. However, a couple of the men I interviewed noted that these gay equivalents could often be used sarcastically or ironically. *Heartface*, for example, can be used towards an old or unattractive man. To address someone as *dear* can be patronising if the hearer is *not* a close friend or lover. *Dear* can be a dismissive label suggesting femininity or frailty – the term 'silly old dear' implies a forgetful, elderly lady. To use the same address to everyone, as the interviewee describes above, makes all acquaintances the same: undistinguishable, and unimportant. Therefore, the Polari terms of address are ambiguous, containing subtle shades of meaning depending on the context in which they are used.

Verbs

After nouns, the next largest grammatical category of lexical items found in Polari contains verbs (comprising about 13 per cent of the lexicon). Table 3.2 shows some of the most frequent types.

Words for anal sex in Polari are relatively few in number (*charver, arva*) and both can be used to refer to heterosexual intercourse, hence they may have the broader meaning of penetrative sex. A larger proportion of Polari words for sexual acts therefore involve forms of oral sex, although there is also a significant percentage of words that are used for the act of looking for sexual partners. Two of these words, *solicit* and *importune*, are taken from legal terms, being criminal charges used against homosexuals.

As with the nouns, the other categories of verbs are concerned with socialisation, relationships and identity construction. Verbs concerning

Table 3.2 Common classes of verbs in Polari

Type of verb	Examples
sex	arva, go on the batter, blag, blow, charver, clean the kitchen, cottage, cruise, gam, importune, jarry, nosh, plate, reef, rim, solicit, tip, tip the ivy, tip the velvet, tip the brandy, troll
go/walk	cruise, mince, minnie, orderly, scarper, troll, vaggerie, zhoosh
eat/drink	bevvie, jarry, mungaree, schumph, zhoosh
talk	bitch, dish the dirt, nellyarda, polari, send up
perform	chant, jogar, slang, wallop
dress up	drag up, facha, zhoosh
fight	battery, battyfang, schonk
look	charper, vada, ogle, cruise, cold calling
other types	do the rights, fake, lau, parker, parker the measures, savvy, screeve, shush, turn my oyster up

performance (in the show business sense) are almost certainly a result of the overlap between gay identities and theatre/carnival identities. The 'dress up' words are also possibly associated with the same overlap: gay men may *drag up*, or *zhoosh their riah* because they are going on stage, or it may be part of their gay identity to appear attractive. Both explanations are conjecture to a certain extent, but with persuasive evidence, such as the theatrical connections of Polari, to support them.

Words for movement (or walking around) are common in Polari. *Mince*, meaning to walk with short steps in an affected manner, dates back to the sixteenth century, and was originally used to describe the movement of females.[7] By the end of the eighteenth century, the verb could be used with reference to males.[8]

While *mince* refers to an effeminate way of walking, *troll* and *cruise* have more sexual meanings, as both refer to walking with intent to find sexual partners. *Troll*, which has several meanings, is probably derived from an earlier definition: 'to move, walk about to and fro, ramble, saunter, stroll or roll', which dates back at least to the fourteenth century.[9] Other definitions of *troll* are also concerned with movement: it can be a bowling term, or mean 'to spin', 'to wag the tongue', 'to turn over in one's mind', 'to sing something in a round', or 'to draw on a moving bait' (*Oxford English Dictionary* 1994). Another meaning of *troll* is concerned with witchcraft; trolls were mythical creatures, formerly, in Scandinavian mythology, conceived as giants, and now as dwarfs or imps. The word *trolla* in Swedish means 'to charm or bewitch'. It is possible that the gay use of *troll* has taken both of these other sets of meanings into consideration: to walk around, seeking to charm a man into the act of copulation. As a Polari word, *troll* can mean 'to walk effeminately', or 'to walk, seeking sex'.

Cruise originated in the seventeenth century and was first used in connection with the movement of ships, corresponding to the Dutch word *kruisen* (to cross).[10] By the end of the seventeenth century, its meaning had been generalised to other types of movement, including that of people. However, the gay meaning of *cruise* most probably comes from twentieth-century America, where it was used to mean walking or driving the streets, either aimlessly, or to look for casual sexual (especially gay male) partners. Laud Humphreys, in a book describing the sexual behaviours of gay men in public lavatories, *Tearoom Trade* (1970), describes how cruising had become a popular activity for gay men, as a result of the popularity of the car and the installation of a comprehensive water system across American towns, which preceded the creation of a number of public conveniences in secluded areas in parks. *Cruise* is therefore a relative latecomer to Polari, possibly via the American Army during the Second World War. Finally, the term *cold calling* is used euphemistically to refer to the act of walking into a pub or bar, on the off-chance that there might be someone attractive there. Interestingly, this word was used by lesbians.[11]

Connected to words associated with movement are a number of lexical items that involve the act of looking at people. *Cruise*, as a Polari word, can simply refer to the acting of looking, e.g. in constructions such as '*he cruised me*'. *Ogle* also refers to looking at someone in a sexual manner. *Vada* is a more general term, often used in imperative constructions: '*vada that palone*', being a verb that draws attention to someone or something, but not necessarily because the object of attention is desirable. It is therefore the effeminate queen, the stereotypical Polari speaker, who is in the position of observing other men as possible sexual conquests. To *vada* is not only to look at someone, it is also to make an implicit evaluation about their worth, which leads to the next grammatical category in the Polari lexicon – adjectives.

Adjectives

Many of the Polari adjectives tend to be evaluative rather than neutral, depicting the speaker's emotional attitude, either positive or negative, towards a subject. So words such as *bona, cod, dolly, naff* and *tat* are not only describing someone or something, they do it in terms of whether or not the speaker approves or disapproves.

Four adjectives can be used as superlatives, in that they were used to label something as either *very* good or *very* bad: *gutless, large, mental, too much*. The meaning of the word would be dependent on the context. For example, 'she's too much', used on a friend, could mean that the friend was behaving in an embarrassing way. Or it could mean that the friend was being funny. Therefore, the key to interpreting these words isn't in the direction of the evaluation (good or bad), which would either be obvious, or perhaps left deliberately ambiguous. The communicative force of the word is to highlight extremities of behaviour.

About half of the Polari adjectives I collected are used to describe sexuality or gender (*butch, bitch(y), camp, dizzy, queeny, screaming, swishing* etc.). As with the nouns, the majority of the words refer to homo- rather than hetero- sexuality, and effeminacy rather than masculinity. Several adjectives combine an evaluation component with a sexuality component, in order to create words that describe someone's potential availability and/or attractiveness. For example *TBH* is always a word with a positive evaluation. If someone is *TBH* (to be had), then one meaning of the word is that the person in question is viewed as being attractive, and, as it were, worth having. However, *TBH* may simply be used to enquire of a person's sexuality. If someone is *TBH* then they must also be gay (or willing to experiment). It is not so much that they are to be had, but that they *can* be had. The adjective used in this way makes the assumption that, potentially, anyone who is gay is *TBH*, but it is likely that the word was used most often on people who were attractive, and it was hoped were also gay, or at least willing to participate in gay sex. The acronym *NTBH* (not to be had) implies the opposite: that the person was unattractive, or attractive but not willing to participate in gay sex (either because they weren't gay, or perhaps because they weren't interested). *TBH* and *NTBH* are both ambiguous terms that work in terms of availability, with sexuality and attractiveness being interlocking components.

In a similar way, the adjective *naff* implies someone who is heterosexual, and by implication unattractive or unimportant as a consequence. The word's association with negativity eventually became more important than its association with sexuality, so it could be used at first to deride objects that could have been seen by Polari users as being bad (i.e. heterosexual taste), e.g. 'look at those naff gnomes', but later it was used by heterosexuals to refer to *anything* that was simply in bad taste.

The sexuality adjectives and nouns can be seen as existing as a continuum (see Figure 3.1), sometimes with the same word occupying different places on it. At one end are 'homosexual' words (*gay, camp, dizzy*), while at the other are 'heterosexual' words (*naff, NTBH*). After the 'homosexual' category is 'bisexual' (*bibi, acdc*) and then a category that identifies as heterosexual but is 'willing to have gay sex' (*TBH, trade*).

The link between adjective and noun words in Polari was mentioned briefly earlier, with the fact that the adjective *naff* could be personified. The same is true of other Polari adjectives: *gay, butch, trade, queen, camp* and *nelly*, which can function as either noun or adjective. This conversion accentuates the importance of the adjective, in that it is used here as the description of a person's identity – they become the adjective personified.

Prepositions

There is only one well-known Polari preposition: *ajax*, which is most probably a shortened form of *adjacent to*, but which is usually taken to mean 'over there'. The fact that this preposition exists is testament to the fact that Polari was frequently used to talk about people who were in view of the speakers, and perhaps close enough to overhear (e.g. '*vada the omee-palone ajax*'). As prepositions are closed class items and generally

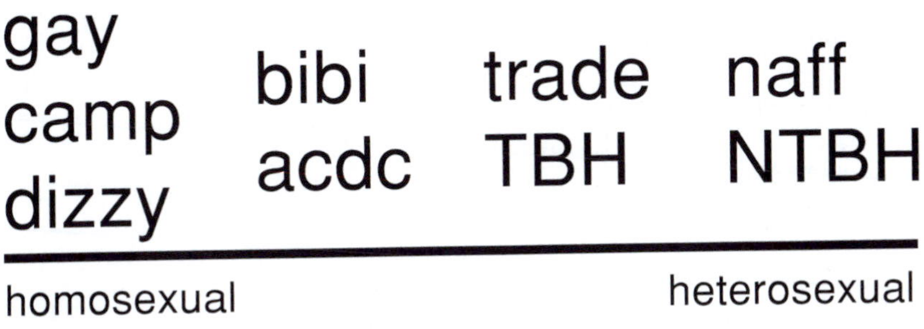

gay camp dizzy	bibi acdc	trade TBH	naff NTBH
homosexual			heterosexual

Figure 3.1 Continuum of sexuality labels in Polari

not prone to lexical innovation, the lack of unique Polari prepositions (and articles, conjunctions and pronouns for that matter) is not surprising.

Adverbs

None of the men I interviewed were able to tell me of any Polari adverbs, although, as with English words, adverbs can possibly be derived from adjectives, for example by adding the suffix *-ly* to them, or by the position of the word in the sentence. The section on grammar below describes this type of transformation in more detail.

Pronouns

Like the nouns, Polari pronouns are feminising. Female third-person pronouns (*she*, *her*) can be used to refer to males or females in the third person, with similar intent to that discussed in the section on nouns above.[12]

An interesting replacement of the first person pronoun occurs when the word *I* or *me* is replaced by a noun phrase which functions as a pronoun. For example, consider the phrase '*your mother's a stretcher case*'.[13] The noun phrase *your mother* is used in place of the word 'I', while the noun phrase *a stretcher case* is used as an adjective to mean tired – the person is ready to be carried away on a stretcher. The speaker isn't implying that his or her mother is tired, but is saying '*I* am tired!'

Other than being a distinctive way of making Polari more difficult for outsiders to understand, I believe that this process also has two other values. First, it marks a distance between the speaker's everyday identity – the *I* – and the speaker's 'Polari identity' – *your mother*. If a male Polari speaker uses 'your mother', then he both reveals his Polari identity (e.g. gay and/or feminised), and at the same time disowns it, because he appears to be talking about somebody else. Second, the possessive construct of *your mother* places emphasis on the relationship between the speaker and hearer, from the *hearer's* perspective. In Polari, someone's mother is likely to be an older, more experienced gay man.

Another interesting aspect of pronoun use in Polari relates to the gender-neutral pronoun *it*. This can be used to refer to a short-term sexual partner. The following example from Kenneth Williams' diary is illustrative:

> Wednesday 28 August [1968]
> I met Harry who said Tom picked up a boy in the Piano and Harry said 'It's got a huge cock so Tom is silly, with that pile and all . . .' so I thought hallo! It certainly gets around in Tangier.
>
> (Davies (ed.) 1993: 331)

In the past, such a practice has been said to minimise the importance of a person or objectify them, in the same way that *it* is used on babies

(White 1980: 244). While *she* feminises and familiarises, *it* sexualises and makes anonymous. For Polari speakers, a binary distinction is not only made between *he/she*, but also between *she/it*.

Articles

The articles *the*, *a* and *an* are sometimes inserted in unexpected ways in the Julian and Sandy sketches, as this example from *Bona Pets* shows:

> *Sandy*:   You wanna make him big. And butch!
> *Julian*:   Butch!
> *Sandy*:   And be butch you see. With the bulging biceps.

In this example most people would be likely to simply say 'With bulging biceps' rather than 'With the bulging biceps'. However, this unusual use of the definite article may be a result of the speaker's London dialect rather than any linguistic feature that is attributable to Polari's structure.

The can also be used as a possessive pronoun. In the following example, *the* (in bold typeface) appears to be used in place of the possessive pronoun *her* (which itself is used in place of the possessive pronoun *his*).

> Well, she schlumphed her Vera down **the** screech at a rate of knots, zhooshed up **the** riah, checked **the** slap in the mirror behind the bar, straightened up one ogle fake riah that had come adrift, and bold as brass orderlied over as fast as she could manage in those bats and, in her best lisp, asked if she could parker the omi a bevvy.
>
> (Gardiner 1997: 123)

Negators

Several negators exist in Polari (*nish*, *nishta*, *nanti*, *nix*, *nantoise*), all of which can generally be used to mean *nothing*, *no* or *don't*. From interviews with Polari speakers, *nanti* appears to be the most generally well-known negator, appearing in the core Polari lexicon. Nanti usually precedes another Polari word: for example, *nanti hambag*: no money.

Fixed expressions

Polari contains a number of fixed expressions, which could be referred to as idioms or discoursal expressions. Although these expressions can contain several words, I have treated them as linguistic items in their own right, and included them in the Appendix. Other expressions only contain one word, but are used in a way that refers to a longer English phrase.

Many of the phrases in this category can simply be used as nouns (*meat and two veg*: male genitalia), or to give more complete descriptions of nouns. While the Polari word *pots* means 'teeth', the phrase *nanti pots in the cupboard* translates as 'no teeth'. While it is possible that this phrase translates word-for-word to 'no teeth in the mouth', I was unable to find any cases of the word *cupboard* being used as Polari for 'mouth' in any other phrase, or occurring on its own. Table 3.3 gives a list of some commonly heard phrases with translations.

Grammar

Polari is not often considered to be a 'language', but is more generally viewed as a collection of words. However, there is evidence that those who knew it well made use of a form of grammar which was sometimes different from that of English. In its simplest form a typical Polari phrase such as '*vada the lallies on the omee-palone*' could be translated directly into English as long as the hearer was familiar with the lexical mapping. Even by making an educated guess, an uninitiated hearer might be able to decipher some meaning from the utterance. Each Polari word maps on to an English word, the word order does not differ, and function or closed-class words tend to be English.

However, some adept speakers combined Polari words together in ways that meant they could not be translated so easily. For example, consider the phrase *nanti Polari*. The standard Polari interpretation would be 'don't say anything', but many people I spoke to who are reasonably familiar with the core Polari lexicon translated this utterance differently, for

Table 3.3 Fixed expressions in Polari

Polari phrase	Translation
on the team/in the life	gay
on your tod	alone
don't be strange	don't hold back
I've got your number	I know you're gay
	I know what you're up to
bona nochy	good night
that's your actual French	I've just spoken French (subtext: aren't I sophisticated!)
aunt nell	listen!
nanti polari	don't say anything
alamo!	he's attractive! Derived from an acronym of the phrase 'Lick Me Out' (LMO).
mais oui	yes
the colour of his eyes	penis size
sharda!	what a pity!

example as 'someone who has no Polari'. Obviously, the context of such a phrase would be important in its interpretation, and it could also be the case that the second solution *could* be a valid one. The problem with the phrase *nanti Polari* is that the words can be mapped to English in several different ways. *Nanti* can mean no, nothing, or don't, while *Polari* can mean to talk, or can refer reflexively to the secret gay language itself. So only when *nanti* is mapped to *don't*, and *Polari* is mapped to *speak* will the English syntax be matched. Also, *nanti* when mapped to *don't* is a case of mapping one word to two (*don't* being a contraction of *do not*).

To take a number of longer examples, Terry Gardner (in Jivani 1997: 15) gives the following example of a Polari sentence: *Palone vadas omi-palone very cod*, which he takes to mean 'that woman is giving me dirty looks'. A direct word-to-word mapping of Polari to English would result in 'woman looks gay-man very bad', which is an ambiguous interpretation. Anyone who has tried to learn a second language will be familiar with the fact that word-for-word translations are not always effective, as languages tend to have different grammatical structures and word order.

So if we were to translate this sentence into word-for-word English, the following issues are raised:

1 'Me' is marked simply as *omee-palone* or 'gay man' – the speaker refers to himself in the third person, which is something that most English speakers tend not to do. As noted above, this type of construction also occurs with the Polari phrase *your mother*;
2 No articles are used – 'that woman' or 'the woman' is simply *palone*;
3 *Vadas* seems to function as a verb in the sentence, but the translation converts it into a noun – 'dirty looks';
4 The word *cod* is separate from the verb/noun *vadas*. It appears to be functioning as an adverb ('that woman is looking at me very nastily') but is not marked as such. In English, an adjective is often converted to an adverb by the addition of the morpheme *-ly*. So *cod* could be expected to be *codly* or *coddily* here.

As discussed above, there are other terms in Polari that consist of fixed expressions and can be translated euphemistically. Two such terms are concerned with penis size: *nada to vada in the larder* (small penis) and *the colour of his eyes* (penis size). Such idiomatic phrases contain semantic and pragmatic elements that cannot be translated directly word for word with a lexicon.

Female impersonator Lily Savage gives a number of Polari phrases (Savage 1998: 103), some of which can be translated word for word:

Varda the naff hommie with nante pots in the cupboard
Look at this unsightly wretch with the appalling dentistry

Varda the groyne on the antique h.'s martini
Look at the size of that ring on the elderly homosexual's hand

Get that bona jarrie down the screech
Eat this wonderful food

Varda the cartes on the hommie
Look at the size of the bulge in that man's trousers.

Other phrases are not translated so directly into English:

Nantois trade
I didn't encounter a sexual liaison tonight

Naff feeley hommie
I'm very jealous of that young man

Palare the antique h. for the bevois
If you engage our elderly friend in conversation he might stand a round of drinks

I had bona arva off the hommie back at the lattie
My masculine gentleman friend shagged me senseless in my house.

Like English (and other European languages) Polari tends to follow subject–verb–object word ordering. However, unlike English, it is clear that Polari has a 'telegraphic' quality to it. A short phrase can be expanded pragmatically, taking into account the social situation – for example, *naff feeley hommie* translates directly into *unattractive young man*. However, in the context of the gay subculture, a young man may arouse jealousy from older men, hence a negative evaluation might not indicate that the young man was unattractive; rather, he is envied. In the above example, *palare the antique h. for the bevois*, there is no indication of the conditional verb 'might'; this must also be inferred from the social context of the situation. A direct translation would simply read 'talk the old gay man for the drink'.

Other non-standard grammatical formations are most probably a result of the East London dialect where many Polari speakers were based. So pronouns are often altered, as in the following example where *theirselves* is used instead of *themselves*:

Sandy: We will be happy to oblige on the fifteenth. We are your great all-round entertainers. Sand and Jule. A show in theirselves.
                                         (Bona Performers, BBC Radio Collection 1992)

Below, *hisself* replaces *himself*:

Sandy: Don't run yourself down. You should see his bread poultice.
Now, no really, no he's always denigrating hisself Mr Horne.
(Le Casserole de Bona Gourmet, BBC Radio Collection 1992)

Similarly, tenses are used creatively, for example: *done* in place of *did* (the past participle in place of the past form), and *wasn't* in place of *weren't*:

Sandy: Oh we're just filling in ain't we. Filling in between commercials. We just done one commercial where Jule was playing this big film director wasn't you.
(Bona Pets, BBC Radio Collection 1992)

In Bona Books, below, *come* is used instead of *came* or *had come* (present tense in place of past tense):

Julian: You gotta personalise him. Give him a name like Rock or Tab or Dorian. Gotta dramatise it you see. Who was this watervole? Nobody knew where he come from but nothing was ever the same after he'd been there.
(Bona Books, BBC Radio Collection 1992)

Below, the singular verb *is* replaces the plural *are*:

Julian: No. In a close-up my knees is dead naff. I mean they're all wrinkled.
(Bona Promotions, BBC Radio Collection 1992)

In the following example, *what* is used as a conjunction, where *which* or *that* would usually have been the appropriate word:

Julian: Well we've got some new strains what we've bred ourselves.
(Bona Pets, BBC Radio Collection 1992)

In the past, linguists have associated non-standard forms of grammar with the speech of working-class males (Labov 1972), and it is possible that Polari speakers would use such forms, even when not speaking Polari. This relationship of Polari to social class is discussed in Chapter 4.

Looking at many of the Polari words, it's not always easy to associate them with homosexuality, although some words might be said to be 'homosexual' in tone, such as those to do with male–male sex acts, male sexual body parts, looking for sex etc. However, others such as terms for clothing or body parts could just as easily apply to any subculture where the object of sexual desire was considered to be unacceptable in some way by the standards of the dominant society. Another set of Polari words, such as those appropriated from earlier Parlyaree, Lingua Franca and Cockney rhyming slang lexicons (see Chapter 2), for example, are even more sexually neutral in tone.

Therefore, it seems that what identifies Polari as a gay language variety is not its words (although they are important), but the way the words are used – in context and in connection with one another, and finally, in what they are used to do (as discussed in Chapter 4). Polari is much more than the sum of its lexicon; the words themselves are merely a means to an end. So, returning to the question of whether Polari was a language or a lexicon, it appears to exist on the cusp of both, having the (often unrealised) potential to transcend its status as a simple list of words. The fact that its lexicon is relatively small, being based around nouns (and, to a lesser extent, verbs), means that more context-based guesswork is needed when creating and understanding Polari utterances. English words that don't exist in Polari (many of the closed-class words, for example) are simply absent from such utterances, giving Polari the *appearance* of a reduced grammar which is somewhat different from that of English. The problem is compounded by the fact that different people used Polari to varying degrees of complexity.

One test in determining whether or not Polari can be viewed as a language different from English is in terms of whether the two are mutually intelligible (Akmarjian *et al.* 1997: 262) – to what degree would English speakers be able to understand a piece of overheard Polari if they had never heard it before? It's likely that an utterance that contains a high number of Polari words would be difficult to understand by the uninitiated (and such was its original purpose). However, another test in deciding Polari's status regarding language would be to ask 'could it be used to communicate *anything?*' And here is where Polari falls down. It may be ideal for gossiping about potential sexual conquests on the gay scene, but outside this genre its usefulness becomes less viable – English words would need to be relied on to a much greater extent and, as a result, mutual intelligibility would increase. Thus, it is not Polari's grammar (or lack of it) that causes it to fail as a language, but its lexicon.

Pronunciation

Most Polari speakers had English as their first language. However, as many of its speakers came from London, its pronunciation would have been influenced by Cockney with numerous lexical items in Polari being derived from backslang or rhyming slang. The Julian and Sandy characters have exaggerated Cockney accents and use dialectal forms of speaking that are different from standard 'received pronunciation' English, although not all the variations in their language can be attributed to the Cockney or London dialect.

In the absence of naturally occurring data, it is difficult to make statements about prosodic features of Polari such as pitch, tone, speed or rhythm. From an analysis of short bursts of fluent Polari such as Julian saying '*order lau your luppers on the strillers bona*' in a couple of the *Round the Horne* sketches, and various Polari sentences spoken by David McKenna in the documentary *A Storm in a Teacup*,[14] it appears that it was spoken quickly and rhythmically, making use of a wide intonational range. It was *not* to be spoken gruffly.

Julian and Sandy also have what could be described as 'camp voices', indexing many features that are commonly thought to be stereotypical of a 'gay' accent: dragged out vowel sounds, a high to low pitch, frequent exclamations and a tendency to affect an upper-class way of speaking (which often clashes with the Cockney accent).

Idiomatic French

As well as using the Polari lexicon (with a good number of its linguistic items derived from Italian via Parlyaree) the Polari speaker can also rely on other non-English forms, code-switching between English, Polari and French. For example, the characters in the Julian and Sandy sketches borrow a large number of stock French idioms, such as *artiste*, *très passé*, *intimé*, *pas de deux*, *entrepreneur* and *nouvelle vague* (*sic*). The Polari words *bijou* and *maquiage* are also from French.

The following example shows how French is combined with Polari:

> *A:* Vada well: zhooshed riah, the shyckle mauve, full slap, rouge for days, fake ogle-riahs, fortuni cocktail frock and mother's fabest slingbacks.
>
> *B:* Freeman, Hardy and Willis.
>
> *A:* **Mais oui** ducky. Then **la tout ensemble**. Gert with a macintosh.
>
> (*A Storm in a Teacup*, Channel 4 1993)

Lily Savage (1998: 103) notes that some Polari words have '-ois' added to them as in French: *nanteois*, *bevois*. Why incorporate French phrases into Polari? One explanation would be in order to make the language yet more difficult to understand. As many Polari speakers were associated with itinerant professions (for example, the theatre or the Navy), they would have been likely to come into contact with speakers of languages other than English, so perhaps French (or other languages) would have been added to the existing lexicon.

However, it could also be the case that these French phrases would help to glamorise the speaker, suggesting that he or she was well-travelled or multilingual (other than knowing Polari and English). French, therefore, would enable Polari speakers either to claim a 'sophisticated' identity, or to mock those people who thought they were sophisticated, by imitating them. Julian and Sandy's use of French is almost certainly ironic.

Morphology

Because of its playful, secretive nature, the invention of new words is an essential part of Polari. Affixation, which is one of the most common morphological processes for creating new words in Polari, is often applied to words using English rules (see Table 3.4).

Other types of morphological processes are also employed to create new words.

Clipping

Martini (ring) is shortened to *marts* (hands), while *manjaree* (a word used in Parlyaree for food) becomes *jarry* in Polari. The new word can still mean food, but can also mean 'to eat', and is used in a sexual sense, so to *jarry the cartes* would be to perform fellatio. One of the few proper nouns, Piccadilly Circus, a place well-known to gay men in London as a hang-out for male prostitutes, is shortened to *The Dilly*, while *charva* (sexual intercourse) can be shortened to *arva*, retaining the same meaning. The backslang term *ecaf* (face) was shortened phonetically to *eek*.

Acronyms

Two of the most well-known Polari words derived from acronyms are *TBH* and *naff*. *TBH* literally means 'to be had', and was used as an adjective or label for someone who is sexually available, but not always for someone self-identified as homosexual: e.g. 'Is he TBH?'. It could also be used to indicate that someone was attractive/sexually desirable: e.g. 'He's very TBH'.

Table 3.4   Creating new words via affixation in Polari

Original word	Meaning	Affix	New word	Meaning	Change
wallop	dance	-er	walloper	dancer	verb → noun
vogue	cigarette	-s	vogues	cigarettes	sing. noun → plural noun
zhoosh	(to) style	-ed	zhooshed	styled/titivated	present tense verb (non-third person singular form) → past tense verb
fabe	great	-est	fabest	greatest	adjective → superlative form
varder	(to) look	-ing	vardering	looking	verb/noun → adjective/-ing form of lexical verb

Naff (or *naph*) was originally used as a Polari word to mean 'not available for fucking', although it has a rather varied set of origins which are discussed in greater detail in the Polari dictionary in the Appendix. Other Polari acronyms include *BMQ* (Black Market Queen), *vaf* (vada, absolutely fantabulosa!) and *alamo* (Lick Me Out!). One possible origin of the word *camp* is from the acronym meaning 'Known As Male Prostitute'.

Blends

Two known blends are used in Polari, both of which have been popularised by the Julian and Sandy sketches: *fabulosa* and *fantabulosa*; both are extensions of *fab* or *fabe*, which themselves are most probably truncations of *fabulous*. *Fantabulosa* is also likely to have been derived from *fantabulous*, itself a blend of *fabulous* and *fantastic*, which the *Oxford English Dictionary* cites as occurring in the late 1950s.

Compounds

A number of new words are derived from morphological compounds, with word stems such as *fake*, *covers*, *queen*, *curtains/drapes*, *Polari* or *riah* providing base forms for several linguistic items. *Fake*, which originally meant 'to make, or do' in Parlyaree, has since seen a return to its English meaning of 'artificial', and signifies words to do with accessories: *ogle* (eye) plus *fake* gives *ogle fake* which can mean glass eye, or spectacles.[15] Taking this rule further, *ogle fake riahs* are false eyelashes, whereas *aunt nelly* (ear) plus *fake* gives *aunt nelly fakes* (earrings). Table 3.5 sets out these and other Polari compound formations.

One way of creating Polari words, which is most probably based on Cant (see Chapter 2), is by relating the word literally to some aspect of its essential nature. In Cant this was facilitated by the suffix *cheat* which literally meant 'thing which'. So a *hearing cheat* is an ear, and a *smelling cheat* is a nose.

While *cheat* is not employed much within Polari, the practice of naming words via some descriptive aspect of their nature (which is also common to many of the compound constructions described here) has continued. Some additional examples being: magazines: *glossies*; perfumes: *smellies*; a watch: *timepiece*; and a sex change: *remould*.

Suffixation

Julian and Sandy regularly make use of the suffix *-ette* at the end of a number of nouns, in order to indicate when something is small:

Julian: Right now drinkettes.
Sandy: Oh, drinkettes. Yes, drinkettes.
                              (Bona Caterers, BBC Radio Collection 1992)

Table 3.5 Common compounding structures in Polari

Base	Meaning	Compound	Meaning
fake	accessory/false	ogle fakes	glass eyes, glasses
		aunt nelly fakes	earrings
		ear fakes	earrings
ogle	eye	ogle shades	spectacles
		ogle riahs	eyelashes
		ogle fake riahs	false eyelashes
riah	hair	riah shusher	hairdresser
omi, palone	man, woman	omee-palone	gay man
		palone-omee	lesbian
		filiome	young man
		kosher homie	Jewish man
		schwartzer homie	black man
covers	coverings	stimp covers	stockings
		mart covers	gloves
tip	lick/kiss/taste	tip the velvet	oral/anal sex
		tip the ivy	oral/anal sex
queen	gay man	size queen	gay man who likes large penises
drapes/curtains	skin	town hall drapes	uncircumcised penis
		coliseum curtains	foreskin
		beef curtains	vagina
matlocks	teeth	matlock mender	dentist
polari	talk/hear	polari pipes	telephone
		polari lobes	ears
fashioned	false	fashioned riah	wig
lattie	house	lattie on wheels	car, taxi
		lattie on water	ship
the full	totally	the full drag	women's clothing
		the full eke	wearing makeup
		the full harva	to be fucked anally

While -*ette* is an English suffix, and has been used in the derivation of words such as *cigarette*, *flannelette*, *launderette* and *statuette*, it is used in Polari to modify words that are generally not modified by -*ette* in English. For example, the suffix is encountered in the following words in the Julian and Sandy sketches: *masterpiecettes*, *tourettes*, *restaurantette*, *glassette*, *futurette*, *telegramette*, *treashette*, *publisherettes*, *trippettes*, *studioette* and *bootettes*. Three of these form part of the title of the company Julian and Sandy have set up in a particular sketch (Bona Publisherettes, Bona Trippettes, Bona Tourettes), suggesting that the suffix -*ette* is a high-profile linguistic device, which is used to 'Polarify' an existing English word. By downplaying quantity, a concept is perhaps trivialised. A glassette of wine is less substantial than a glass of wine. However, the word could be used ironically, to refer to a *huge* glass of wine. As well as appearing to make things smaller, -*ette* can also be used to feminise, e.g. *usherette*, *majorette*, which fits with other feminising aspects of Polari, such as pronoun usage.

Conclusion

This analysis of Polari vocabulary suggests it is a language variety that places a high value on words concerning social and sexual identity (as in Chapter 4). More than two-thirds of the nouns in Polari are concerned with people: their identities, what they are wearing, and the various parts of their bodies. Other types of noun categories are also concerned with people or social structures: names for money, terms of address, terms for relationships between people, and names for places and food. Many of the non-abstract nouns are terms for everyday items used by people: *dog and bone* (telephone); *glossies* (magazines); *polari pipe* (telephone); *rattling cove* (taxi); and *vogue* (cigarette), whereas many of the abstract nouns are concerned with language: *billingsgate* (bad language); *cackle* (talk); *lav* (word); *lingo* (language); *polari* (gay language); or sex/sexuality: *catever cartzo* (venereal disease); *cherry* (virginity); *colour of his eyes* (penis size); *lamor* (kiss); *randy comedown* (desire for sex after taking drugs); *remould* (sex-change); and *wedding night* (first time two men have sex).

The proliferation of words to do with people, body parts and clothing testifies to the importance of people and their appearance in the Polari-speaker's world. At a first glance, binary constructs such as masculine/feminine, gay/straight, young/old and attractive/unattractive seem to be a dominant classificatory feature in Polari. However, the existence of words such as *TBH* or *trade* shows that the binary distinctions themselves are ideals, open to subversion. Terms such as *sea queen* can be used to refer to both who is pursued sexually, and who is doing the pursuing. Also certain adjectives (*gutless*, *large*, *mental*, *too much*) can function as superlatives, in either a negative or a positive sense. As always, context appears to be extremely important in deriving meaning from certain words.

One of the most important roles of the Polari lexicon is in providing the Polari speaker with numerous *person nouns*, e.g. *trade*, *queen*, *butch*, *naff* etc., many of which categorise according to gender, sexuality or sex. Taken with verbs, which are concerned mainly with sexual acts or processes involving finding sex (by actively walking around or by looking at people passing by), the lexicon's common denominator is *sexual availability*. Adjectives describe whether someone is good or bad (worth having sex with), and their sexual identities. Again, the lexicon allows for the identity construction of others in terms of their sexual potential: the 'nouning' of adjectives (*camp*, *butch*, *queen* etc.) shows how important such a classification scheme based on gender and sexuality is to Polari speakers.

This chapter functions to a greater or lesser degree as a stand-alone Polari grammar. However, it describes Polari in a decontextualised way, not explaining in any detail why it was used or what it was used to achieve. The following chapter examines Polari from a sociological perspective, placing it within the context of the UK homosexual subculture in the 1950s or thereabouts, by relating the experiences of Polari speakers to the social conditions for homosexual men who lived through that period.

4 Uses and abuses

While the previous chapter examined Polari as a language system, it is the intention of this chapter to look at *situational* uses of Polari in order to determine why it became known as a 'gay language' and what it was used to achieve. It is worth bearing in mind that, just as there were numerous versions of Polari in existence, the number of ways that it could be employed was also diverse. Not only did Polari change depending on who was speaking it, but location, audience or time period could also affect the reasons for its use. As this chapter concentrates particularly upon the varieties of Polari that were spoken in the 1950s, it is worthwhile beginning with a brief description of the conditions surrounding the legal and social situation for homosexual men and lesbians who lived in the UK at that time.

Gay oppression

Male homosexuality was illegal in Britain until 1967, when it was legalised under certain restricted circumstances. However, this simple fact does not indicate the extent to which homosexual men and lesbians were oppressed by the authorities and the British public until (and beyond) decriminalisation.[1] According to Halsey (1972: 533), the yearly number of reported indictable homosexual offences rose almost exponentially in the first two-thirds of the twentieth century. In 1921, there were 178 convictions, but by 1963 this figure had risen to 2,437, more than twice the number of indictments for heterosexual offences in that year.

While, for most of the twentieth century, the law criminalised homosexual acts in any form, this did not stop homosexual men from meeting each other, conducting relationships and making sexual contacts. Clearly, such activities created a need for secrecy – they were criminal acts. Many homosexual men and lesbians moved to large cities, where their numbers were higher, anonymity was easier and attitudes tended to be more progressive, and it was in cities that the gay subculture was shaped. Such circumstances allowed clandestine pubs and bars to develop, generally requiring membership and discretion on the part of their members. Behind closed, and sometimes locked, doors, men could slow-dance cheek-to-cheek, cruise one another, and express their sexualities in relative privacy. Away from established drinking and dancing quarters, men found partners in cruising grounds: deserted parks, picnic areas and beauty spots, public toilets (or *cottages*), darkened cinemas, and bath-houses.

In the first half of the twentieth century, one period does stand out, in which by all accounts a degree of tolerance of homosexuality was shown that was not to be seen again until after 1967. As discussed in Chapter 2, during the Second World War, a number of factors had led to a relaxation of sexual mores in the UK (Humphries 1988: 71), especially in cities that were subjected regularly to air raids. As people huddled together in shelters, the thought 'this could be the last night of my life' prompted more than a few to seek affection from unlikely sources. In the armed forces, homosexuality was one way for men who didn't normally identify as gay to release sexual tension and to have access to affection from another human being at a time when they were away from family and friends. As already discussed, the Blackout meant that there were many more places to engage in discreet outdoors sex at night.

However, after the war ended, the moral climate shifted. Many people wanted to forget about the hardships they had endured and return to 'normality'. Soldiers came home and the family unit was seen as more important than ever (Ferris 1993: 148). A survey of sexuality carried out in 1949 claimed that most British people were horrified and disgusted by homosexuality (England 1950: 153) and, according to Ron Storme, who was interviewed in 1993 for the Channel 4 television programme *A Storm in a Teacup*, around the time of the Coronation of Queen Elizabeth II (2 June 1953), London was 'cleaned up', drag shows were banned and the police became less tolerant of homosexuality:

> If you went out in a frock, if the police ... saw you in a car, they would stop you and ask you to get out of the car, which you didn't do because as soon as you got out of the car then they would pinch you for soliciting.
>
> (Ron Storme, *A Storm in a Teacup*, Channel 4 1993)

During the 1950s the police became increasingly zealous when it came to prosecuting homosexuality: once they had uncovered its existence they looked for more (Ferris 1993: 156). Homosexuals had generally been viewed as easy targets by bullies on both sides of the law. They tended not to fight back or complain, and were relatively easy to attack or arrest in cruising areas. Those with high-status jobs or families were particularly at risk from blackmail, which often proved to be a lucrative scam for criminals. One team of blackmailers were reported as making at least £100 a night, netting £15,000 within seven months, and obtaining £26,000 from one of their victims (Jivani 1997: 114–15). The owners of the gay bars, pubs and private clubs had to tread a thin line between making a living and not allowing too many 'obvious queens' into their establishments:

> The pub was raided. They took your names and addresses. It was a form of harassment in those days. The pub would go quiet for a week or a month, and then people would start drifting back again ... If you had a height of powder too much on one cheek, you might have missed it as you got ready to go out. The barman would say 'Sorry dear, out'. And you'd have to leave.
> (Daniel, *A Storm in a Teacup*, Channel 4 1993)

Quentin Crisp (author of *The Naked Civil Servant*, 1968), describes how he was barred from a private drinking club:

> Everyone protested and they rushed up to the proprietor and said, 'How can you do this'. And the proprietor said 'I don't give a damn what he does or what he is. The police come to this pub and they say "You run a funny sort of place"'. And when the owner said 'What funny? How?' they say 'That funny' ... You see, your mere manner would get you into jail. Nobody had to prove anything. They said they saw you walking up and down the street between the hours of this and that and the magistrate would say 'Have you anything to say for yourself?' and the moment the victim said [*uses effeminate voice*] 'Well it was like this, your honour'. 'Six months'.
> (Quentin Crisp, *A Storm in a Teacup*, Channel 4 1993)

John Alcock talked about the panic of the 1950s:

> I thought that every policeman coming up to me on the street was going to arrest me. I always looked over my shoulder when I was bringing a gentleman home to entertain, usually a labourer ... The temperature of the time was quite unpleasant. We thought we were all going to be arrested and there was going to be a big swoop.
> (Hall-Carpenter Archives 1989: 52)

No gay man or woman was immune to the threat of 1950s British homophobia. Alan Turing, who was instrumental in cracking the Germans' Enigma machine codes in the Second World War committed suicide in 1954, three years after he was arraigned for an 'act of gross indecency'. Richard Davenport-Hines described a 'pogrom' at Taunton in 1954–5 where frightened younger men gave evidence against older men, while Lord Montagu of Beaulieu, Michael Pitt-Rivers and Peter Wildeblood were sent to prison in 1954 for participating in homosexual acts. In the latter case, it was believed that this was a show-trial, using the titled status of one of the defendants in order to make an example and ensure publicity (Ferris 1993: 157).

Needless to say, the police, in using Montagu as an example, had a willing ally in the form of the British press. Newspapers contributed to much of the hostile climate experienced by gay men in the post-war years. The *Sunday Pictorial* published a series of articles in 1952 on homosexuality entitled 'Evil Men', describing its aim as a 'sincere attempt to get to the root of a spreading fungus' (Weeks 1981: 241). In 1963, Soviet spy, John Vassall, was discovered to be gay. The tabloid newspaper, the *Sunday Mirror*, published an article about him encouraging the public to hunt out homosexuals. Entitled 'How to Spot a Possible Homo', it was designed to whip viewers up into a paranoid frenzy by accessing negative folk stereotypes about homosexuality (including the association of homosexuality with paedophilia) in order to induce and justify further witch-hunts:

> It is high time we had a short course on how to pick a pervert . . . Basically homos fall into two groups – the obvious and the concealed . . . THEY are everywhere, and they can be anybody . . . I wouldn't tell them *my* secrets. 1 The Middle-aged man, unmarried . . . 2 The man who has a consuming interest in youths . . . 3 The Crawler . . . 4 The Fussy Dresser . . . 5 The Over-clean man.
>
> (*Sunday Mirror* 1963)

Members of the medical profession often viewed homosexuality as a disease, and attempts to 'cure' gay men involved electric shock treatment, the administration of drugs intended to induce nausea (David 1997: 181–4), or even female hormones (which caused Alan Turing to grow breasts) (Jivani 1997: 123).

Given that gay men were victimised by blackmailers, the establishment and the press, it is fair to say that to appear openly homosexual in the 1950s in the UK was to court danger. The police, who in other cases would be expected to protect citizens from assault, would at best be unsympathetic when faced with a cry for help from a gay man under attack, and at worst, as Alan Turing found, be liable to add to the victim's problems by prosecuting them. In public, most gay men were careful not to broadcast their sexuality, for their own safety. Even in the home they had to be careful: snooping neighbours[2] and police raids could breach the intimacy of that space. So, both within and beyond the home, the way one walked, dressed, wore one's hair and spoke had to be subject to constant self-evaluation and adjustment. Quentin Crisp's effeminate voice, sandals and makeup, being intrinsically linked to homosexuality in the consciousness of the British public, were always going to mark him and other 'gender outlaws' as potential victims:

it was the always-obvious queens that the general population saw and goggled at, and because such queens were undeniably recognizable men visible in the public sphere, they came to stand for male homosexuality itself.

(Medhurst 1997: 277)

Secrecy and exposure

You would say, 'Vada the cartes on the omee' because nine out of ten times [heterosexuals] wouldn't understand what the hell you were talking about and you would use it specifically as a hidden language in that case.

(Jim E)

Considering that homosexual identities were stigmatised and criminalised in the UK in the 1950s and 1960s, it is unsurprising that many homosexual men were fearful of exposure. The term *in the closet* (possibly derived from the American-sounding idiom *skeleton in the closet* to refer to a secret) was first used to refer to the maintenance of secret homosexual identities, but its meaning currently can be used in reference to any secret activity, e.g. *closet Star Trek fan*. It is unlikely that Polari speakers in the 1950s and early 1960s would have perceived their sexual status in terms of being 'in' or 'out' of the closet. However, by post-1970s standards we can say that one of the most obvious ways that Polari use contributed to the construction of homosexual identity was in the maintenance of the closet, even though the concept of the 'closet' in relationship to sexual identities was yet to come into popular use:

My friends and I picked up this language. It was marvellous because we could sit on a tube-train or a bus and talk about the person opposite using this Polari which no one could understand except theatrical people.

(Jo Purvis, *A Storm in a Teacup*, Channel 4 1993)[3]

In Jo's case, Polari could be used to conceal one's sexuality and allow her friends the means to carry on conversations about other people while they were present. Thus, conversations that contained references to homosexuality could occur in public places, without the speaker having to compromise or reveal his/her sexuality to multiple listeners.

Polari's relationship to the concept of the gay 'safe space' is interesting to analyse here. As this is a relatively recent term, there were no places during the 1950s and 1960s that were labelled explicitly as 'safe spaces' for homosexuals. The term is currently used to refer to places (usually physical, although not always so – websites can call themselves 'safe spaces') which are created so that gay identities can be disclosed or acted out in a non-judgemental, non-threatening atmosphere. For example, some universities have designated rooms as safe spaces in order to 'promote a more positive atmosphere for gay, lesbian, bisexual and transgender people'.[4]

Because Polari enabled such expressions of gay identity to occur in public contexts, the concept of a 'safe space' was widened. It became not so much a physical place (e.g. a private club or home) where people could be themselves away from prying eyes, or in sympathetic surroundings, but theoretically *any* place where Polari was spoken. Polari became a symbolic, linguistic, safe space. However, as I discuss below, whether or not it succeeded in creating a space safe, was dependent on other aspects of sexual performance.

The uninitiated listener who overheard a Polari conversation may have suspected that the Polari speaker was 'foreign', or at least purposefully using some sort of secret code. However, if audiences were not sized up correctly, humiliation could ensue, as the account below reveals:

> Two of my friends were on holiday in Italy and they were in a crowded shoe shop. One of them noticed an attractive man and brought this to the attention of his friend, by talking in Polari. However, the Polari he used was so similar to Italian that the man said 'Thank you!' Everyone in the shop had understood the Polari and started laughing. My friend was so embarrassed that he ran out of the shop.
>
> (Keith)

While Polari was used to conceal gay identity from outsiders, it could also be used as a tentative means of coming out of the closet. As one interviewee noted, 'it was used as a non-give-away that you were gay'.

> [The Polari words] were secret passwords. You could identify with other gay people if you thought they might be – you could drop a word in like 'camping about', or 'I'm going camping, but I'm taking my tent'.
>
> (Dudley Cave, *A Storm in a Teacup*, Channel 4 1993)

For Dudley, dropping an occasional 'gay' word into a conversation was a hedged means of dual identification. In essence, the speaker was relying on the hearer either recognising Polari, and therefore understanding that the speaker was gay, or not recognising Polari, and thus revealing themselves not to be gay. The use of Polari was therefore a complex interplay between speaker, hearer and social context. To simply characterise it as a 'secret language' is missing this important point. Polari clearly had an important role to play in both 'outing' oneself and revealing the sexual identity of the listener:

We were 'so'. Have you heard that word? We were so. Is he so? Oh yes. Oh he's so so, and TBH (to be had) was a very famous expression. The sentence would go simply like this, well he's not really 'so' but he's TBH. And you would know exactly.

(Unnamed interviewee in Porter and Weeks 1991: 75–6)

Using words like *so* in order to put out tentative feelers about someone else's sexuality is linked to the notion of Gay English as co-operative discourse (Leap 1996: 12–48), where two (or more) holders of a secret (e.g. gay) identity are able to negotiate the disclosure of such identities without having to be explicit. So Polari could allow a range of strategies, both for concealing an identity, and for communicating it to fellow speakers. However, the use of Polari for maintaining secrecy is dependent on whether such secrecy is initially tenable. In some cases, it was not, and then the flip side of Polari, as a tool of confrontation, comes into use:

We flaunted our sexuality. We were pleased to be different. We were proud and secretly longed to broadcast our difference to the world: *when we were in a crowd.*

(Burton 1979: 23)

Although Peter Burton describes Polari initially as a secret language, with hindsight he states that it must have been obvious to anyone what he and his friends were talking about. Although Polari could be used to 'confound and confuse' *naffs* (heterosexuals), *roughs* (aggressive men) and *orderly daughters* (police), it probably brought attention to the fact that the speakers were gay, rather than enabling them to stay in the closet. Polari might have concealed a specific message but it did not conceal homosexuality – how could it, if the speaker was also wearing makeup, feminine clothing and had deeply hennaed hair? In such cases, Polari was more likely to be used as a means of contributing towards a defiant 'out' identity. The hearers would know that something was being said about them, possibly derogatory, but would not be able to understand exactly what.

Of course, in other cases, as Dudley Cave points out, Polari *could* be employed to identify other people who were not obviously homosexual by their appearance. It is unlikely that the effeminate 'obvious' queens would have used it solely for this purpose, as others would have more immediate visual cues in identifying them. So Polari also varied in use depending upon whether the speaker was out or closeted. While the Polari of the closet was a means of conducting secret conversations and discreetly identifying fellow homosexuals, it could also be a means of constructing a highly visible gay identity when coupled with a 'mincing' gait, a loud, 'screaming' voice, outlandish and colourful clothes, makeup and a camp attitude. These were the visible and audible badges by which some gay men wore their identity.

So did Polari enable gay men to hide their sexual identities, or did it reveal them? The answer is dependent on the individual user, and the audience. There was an essential dichotomy in the uses of Polari, which depended upon occasion and speaker. At one extreme, the married man with the office job and the pinstripe suit would be able to make contacts without putting his closeted status at too much risk, simply by dropping a Polari word into a conversation with someone he suspected might be gay. If he happened to be wrong about his assumption, then little harm would have been done. At the other extreme, for the queens who minced, wore makeup and dyed their hair, the concept of the closet would have been redundant. Talking in Polari was another way of revealing (and revelling in) their difference, and even if the hearer did not understand the actual details of what they were saying, some sort of message about the speakers' variance would be conveyed. However, as noted, both of the above cases are extremes at opposite ends of a continuum. It is also likely that there would be homosexual men (and women) who could 'pass' for straight, but were able to use Polari in order to communicate secretly in public with one another. For them, the relationship between Polari and the closet was equivocal. It could help them to conceal their sexual identity, or to reveal it, in front of complete strangers. Polari, like many of the terms in its lexicon, had an ambiguous nature, and it was not only the meaning behind the utterance, but also the way in which it was conveyed – whether camped up to the hilt, with the word *girl*, *dear*, *ducky* or *heartface* tagged on to the end of every sentence, or spoken fleetingly and with a searching tone, which would have provided clues to outsiders about the speaker's sexuality.

East End and West End identities

It also appears to have been the case that social class was an important variable affecting the use of Polari. Personal reflections by Polari speakers reveal a perception that there were two dominant forms of Polari in London: one associated with show business and the West End, and the other with the more insular and stable East End community:

> The West End and the East End. There's a community difference. The East End queens were much more based in their community so it was their territory, whereas the West End queens were just like gypsies, moving from place to place.
> (Michael James, *A Storm in a Teacup*, Channel 4 1993)

There was rivalry between the two groups, as David McKenna, a gay man from the East End, intimates:

> I always used to feel very sorry for the West End queens, simply because they weren't allowed to really be themselves. They worked

in their various offices ... with their collars and ties on, and they
were George by day, and Fishy Frances by night.
(David McKenna, *A Storm in a Teacup*, Channel 4 1993)

From descriptions of the differences of 'West End' and 'East End' Polari
by Michael and David, it appears that, of the two, the West End Polari
was less complex, derived mainly from existing gay or theatrical words,
while the East End Polari speakers were influenced by a number of other
communities, and were more proficient at using it to confuse:

I think the difference between the East End Polari and the West End
Polari was the West End was fundamentally based on theatre – the
theatre-speak. And the East was based on the boats, the boat queens,
Yiddish, all sorts of communities there, and all their words and slang
got used in it in the gay Polari as well, which didn't happen in the
West End.
(Michael James, *A Storm in a Teacup*, Channel 4 1993)

The sea queen would accentuate or elaborate a lot more on the Polari.
If you were going to say 'Look at that guy standing next to me', the
shore-side Polari part would be 'Vada the omee standing next to me.'
A sea queen would say 'Vada the schwawarly on me jaxys way out.'
They just elaborated on it, because it was meant to sway people, so
they didn't understand what you were talking about. Even with the
sea queen not wanting a shore-side West End queen to understand
what she's saying. You'd be standing there and you'd say 'Oh vada
that naff queen. What a coddy kaffall dear. Oh vada the schnozzle on
it dear.' And you'd be doing all this Polari, they'd understand the
basics. They understood bona and camp and cod and riah and things
like that, but the sea queens would really go to town.
(David McKenna, *A Storm in a Teacup*, Channel 4 1993)

David's usage of East End (sea queen) Polari *is* potentially confusing
when heard, as it contains a number of terms which are from related
subcultures, for example *schwawarly* and *schnozzle* both have Yiddish
sch- stems. Additionally, some Polari words have undergone considerable
mutation. *Kaffall* is likely to be an elaboration of *ecaf*. *Coddy* is an elaboration of *cod*, whilst *jaxys* is an elaboration of *ajax*. These linguistic
sleights of hand, if one is unprepared for them, introduce another level of
complexity into the Polari lexicon, which even those who were familiar
with the basic items would have difficulty translating, especially if it was
spoken at high speed.
The two types of Polari speaker described by David and Michael are
interesting to analyse. While neither 'claims' an East End or West End
identity overtly, the East End identity is constructed as being the superior

ne. East End Polari is seen as being more sophisticated, and therefore
etter, while the West End 'queens' are pitied because they can't be 'true'
) their identities. By day they 'work in offices' and wear the clothing of
mainstream society (collars and ties), and by night they are 'Fishy Frances'.
For the West Enders, their gay identity is submerged in secrecy, and can
only be realised on a part-time basis. However, another construction of
the West End identity connects them with the theatre, and describes them
as being 'like gypsies', moving from place to place. While the East Enders
or sea queens have a home, a 'territory', the West Enders have nowhere
to call their home. So two forms of identity are described for the West
End queens – a theatrical itinerant identity, and a closeted, office-working
identity. The fact that these constructions come from different speakers is
interesting, as both appear to have different conceptions of what constituted a 'West End queen'.

However, a crucial difference between the working-class East End of
London and the business/entertainment-focused West End of London is
that the two forms of Polari were used by speakers of different social
classes. Ron notes the relationship between Polari and class when he claims
that, as he did not use it, he was viewed as being 'posh':

> I understand Polari. I know what they're talking about . . . I do use
> it on occasions. People think they can get one over on me by talking
> Polari but I know exactly what they're saying and talking about. I've
> never had a cause to use it. They've always referred to me as a posh
> queen but I'm just a working-class girl.
>
> (Ron, *A Storm in a Teacup*, Channel 4 1993)

Ron's account of Polari appears inconsistent. On the one hand he says 'I
do use it on occasions' while on the other he says 'I've never had a cause
to use it'. Polari is referred to as a thing that people use in order to 'get
one over on' him: a covert prestige form. Ron describes (unnamed) Polari
speakers as constructing an (unwanted) 'posh queen' identity for him,
which he rejects in favour of 'working-class girl'. The relationship of
social class to Polari is also mentioned by another speaker:

> I learned 'palari' when I was in the theatre, but it was a common
> language . . . It was common only among a certain class in the gay
> world. It was usually people like myself who were in the chorus, the
> common end of the structure, who used it.
>
> (John in Porter and Weeks 1991: 138)

John's use of 'common' (three times in this short excerpt) is worth noting.
Polari is seen as 'common' both in the sense of the frequency of its use,
and in the sense of it being a signifier of social status. Like Ron, John
labels Polari as a language that was used by working-class people.

Consequently, social class seems to have been a factor in determining whether Polari was used. The use of Polari, especially the elaborate East End variety, would have identified a speaker as working class or 'common', whether they were or not. Similarly, a reluctance to use Polari, or the use of the West End version, marked a speaker as 'posh', whether or not they identified themselves as actually being working class.

Cruising and bitching

As well as being an exclusive form of communication, some of the interviewees suggested that Polari could be used in an aggressive way – one of its main uses was for making evaluations about the physical characteristics of other people *while they were present*. Here the target may, or may not, be gay. Polari, with its lexicon of body parts, clothing and people types, could be used to point out potential sexual partners to friends, and could act as a way of exchanging information about various qualities and preferences of others:

> It became quite common chatting to each other . . . when you were talking about a person who was present at the time.
>
> (Jim L)

With its often telegraphic nature, Polari could also be used by pairs or groups of men as the means of a rapid sexual information exchange:

> It's useful gay shorthand when you're cruising.
>
> (Jim C)

> It was used . . . to draw attention to someone. Like, as we were saying, 'vada the homie' instead of saying 'look at that gorgeous person over there'.
>
> (David A)

As an adjunct to cruising, such evaluations, whether positive: *vada the cartes on the omee ajax* (look at the genitals on the man nearby), or negative: *vada that naff riah on the omee-palone with the cod lally-drags* (look at the terrible hair on the homosexual man wearing those awful trousers) can still be construed as offensive. In the former case, the subject of discussion is reduced to sexual object status, while in the latter the subject's taste is ridiculed.

Peter Burton describes how Polari could be used to wound:

> Polari has about it a particularly brittle, knife-edged feel. Nothing – in my chicken days – was more daunting than an encounter with some acid-tongued *bitch* whose tongue was so sharp that it was likely she

would cut my throat with it. Those queans,[5] with the savage wit of the self-protective, could be truly alarming to those of us of a slower cast of mind.

(1979: 23)

Verbal aggression was not, therefore, necessarily directed towards outsiders. As well as helping to establish a shared identity among gay men, to protect them from harassment and arrest, and to afford a face-saving means of recognition, Polari could be used as a means of expressing conflict within the gay subculture. Unlike male heterosexual subcultures, where conflict could involve a fist fight, the stereotypical Polari speaker would eschew physical violence, relying on insults as a means of aggression. Harris (1997: 15) notes: 'Straight men express aggression through fist fights and sports; gay men through quick-witted repartee and caustic remarks. Straight men punch; gay men quip. Straight men are barroom brawlers; gay men, bitches.' Another Polari interviewee described how he developed his critical wit as a young queen in the Merchant Navy:

> The older ones were so quick and so cutting, you had to think of a retort that was funnier and cleverer than theirs and say it back at them straight away. Of course, eventually this just became a second nature.
> (Barry)

However, it is important not to over-generalise. Physically aggressive gay men did, and do, exist, as do exchanges of verbal insults among heterosexual men (such incidents can also act as a precursor to physical attacks in either case). Many gay men would have been subjected to bouts of name-calling, possibly from a time before they even realised what homosexuality was. The over-lexicalisation of pejorative terms for 'gay man' which exist (for example: *faggot, pansy, puff, shirt-lifter, brown-hatter, fairy, batty-boy, queer* etc.) is further testament to their status as 'target'. Faced with verbal abuse from an early age, it is likely that some gay men would have responded by developing both a thick skin and a superior ability to remark upon the weak spots or oddities of others. This critical technique would be helped by the fact that gay subcultures are grounded in sexuality and desire, with the discussion of positive and negative physical attributes being one of the foremost ways of evaluating oneself and others. Even those who did not engage in such 'dishing' would possibly be used to the concept of verbal abuse as a mode of interaction.

While a surface analysis may conclude that gay men use Polari to be bitchy, predatory or bitter, I wish to examine their behaviour from the perspective of politeness theory (Brown and Levinson 1978: 107, 110). A distinction can be drawn between negative politeness and positive politeness. In the former, the speaker tries to satisfy the hearer's basic requirements of territory and self-determination. Negative politeness is therefore a deferential affair. Phrases such as 'Please, you go first' and 'Welcome to my humble abode' would characterise the ingratiating, genuflecting nature of negative politeness. However, in the case of positive politeness, the speaker takes care to maintain the positive self-image or 'face' of the hearer, treating the hearer as a friend, someone who is the same as the speaker, with the same in-group rights and privileges. Therefore, a strategy of positive politeness can be the employment of in-group markers such as *mate, buddy* or *pal*. Polari has several such in-group markers: *ducky, dear, heartface, treash* and *girl*. Another positive politeness strategy involves the implementation of an in-group language or dialect which can be easily applied to Polari use. Other positive strategies involve gossip and joking. Within gay communities (as with many communities), insults can serve dual purposes. On the surface, and to outsiders, they may appear simply to be aggressive, critical utterances. However, considering Polari as a tool of positive politeness, an insult takes on a different aspect. Where there is a sense of shared identity and similarity, insults are sanctioned, either because they are understood to be jokes, and/or because they act as positive politeness – the speaker can make the insult because the closeness between speaker and hearer means that no offence will be taken.

Acting camp

Considering that Polari insults could be playful, joking or remain ambiguous, it is worthwhile focusing on the main way that Polari was used humorously – as camp.

> *Interviewer*: Did you ever use it when there were just gay people together?
> *Respondent*: Yes, just only in a camping around sort of way.
>
> (Sidney)

Camp is notoriously difficult to define, partly because it is a broad concept, connected to taste, sensibility, comedy, parody, class, homosexuality and effeminacy, and because attitudes towards it have changed considerably over time. As Ross (1989: 146) notes, 'universal definitions of camp are rarely useful'.

Sontag (1966: 279) viewed camp as 'a certain form of aestheticism', evaluating objects 'not in terms of Beauty, but in terms of degree of artifice or stylization'. For Sontag, camp was playful, detached and apolitical. However, according to Ross (1993: 74), camp can be seen as a cultural economy. 'It challenged . . . legitimate definitions of taste and sexuality. But we must also remember to what extent this cultural economy was tied to the capitalist logic of development that governed the mass culture industries.'

Long (1993: 78) argued that camp is a 'moral activity'. For gay men who have been ridiculed because of their sexuality, their tragedy becomes trivial. Camp allows them to respond by taking the trivial seriously, 'parodying the forces of oppression' (Long 1993: 79).

Meyer (1994: 1) redefines camp again – as 'political and critical'. Putting aside the notion that camp is merely a 'sensibility', Meyer casts camp as a 'solely queer discourse' (1994: 1) and 'the total body of performative practices and strategies used to enact a queer identity, with enactment defined as the production of social visibility' (1994: 5). Medhurst (1997: 281) disagrees: 'Meyer's excessive claims for camp as always-and-only-radical cannot convince anyone who has spent time among camp queens, whose turns of phrase and ideological outlook can be frighteningly reactionary.'

Although Polari, with its reliance on playfulness, ambivalence, irony, gender subversion and parody can certainly be classed as a form of camp, the extent to which the *omee-palones* who used Polari in the 1950s and 1960s thought of what they were doing in terms of 'aestheticism', a 'cultural economy', a 'moral activity' or a 'queer discourse' will never be known. While this does not mean that Sontag, Long, Meyer and other theorists of camp should be derided, it appears that camp, like many things, can be as uncomplicated or as intricate as the people who choose to define it. My own definition is that Polari speakers used camp as a mindset or framework for making sense of the world, based on ironic, mocking and self-mocking humour, which was in turn based on their stigmatised status. If camp is the theory that allowed gay men to reconstruct reality, then Polari, as an anti-language, is one of its practices.

So far in this chapter Polari has been positioned as a language variety that either enabled protection or aggression. However, Polari also helped to construct a social gay identity, serving as a code that helped to affirm membership of a community, and to strengthen the collective identity of the subculture. From a language that was initially used as a form of protection (or aggression), either to 'confound and confuse' (Burton 1979: 23) outsiders, or to display one-upmanship over other homosexual men, Polari would also have been simply used for entertainment value:

> It was used to be camp ... you can have a camp laugh.
>
> (Darren)

> My boyfriend used to use it quite a lot to try and make me girlishly giggle. I only use it now when I want a cheap and easy laugh with my friends, usually after quaffing large amounts of eggnog.
>
> (Kevin)

Polari's link to comedy is crucial – but ultimately one that limits its potential as a true language. It could be used as a way to mitigate appalling circumstances faced by homosexual men: arrests, entrapments, blackmail and hostility etc., by rendering them comic. As a coping mechanism in the face of potential tragedy, Polari supplies an ironic distance from the real world, turning power structures upside down and viewing everything through the filter of a Hollywood movie (see Chapter 7). However, in making a joke out of everything, it becomes difficult to express emotions such as real sorrow or anger in Polari.

As Burton (1979: 23) points out, the people who used Polari tended to be those who were camp or effeminate (hence the over-lexicalisation of words connected to 'camp' in the lexicon). In the 1950s and 1960s, gay men used Polari to categorise various sexual identities according to gender performance and sexual roles. For example, one interviewee, who had worked in the Merchant Navy for 40 years, describes how the sailors he knew were classified as *omees* (heterosexual men), *omee-palones* (effeminate homosexuals, who were also known as *queens*), and *trade-omees*, who appeared to be heterosexual, but were willing to have sex with *omee-palones*. There were also *BMQs* (Black Market Queens) or *phantoms* (homosexual men who were closeted). These sexual categories were expected to be strictly adhered to – each having different standards of behaviour, both in and out of bed. *Omee-palones*, for example, were generally passive or receptive sexually, while *trade-omees* were active or inserters. *Omees* did not have sex with other *omees*, while the *BMQs* or *phantoms* would administer oral sex to snoring or groggy crew-mates, long after 'lights out'. The *omee-palones* would call each other by girl's names and refer to each other as 'girl' or 'she':

> Big May was . . . a sea queen. She'd been on the boats for years and years. They'd have a *husband* for the voyage . . . *Seafood* is the Polari word. They were all very married, they were in couples. There was the *butch* and the *bitch*, it was very aping the heterosexual thing. We called ourselves *girls*. It's to do with clinging to our youth, desperately and pathetically.
>
> (Betty Bourne, BBC Radio 4 1998)

It was not uncommon for an *omee-palone* to take a 'husband', perhaps one of the *trade-omees* who had become particularly attached to his partner. The husband might already be married to a woman, but for the duration of the voyage (and in many cases for years afterwards) the relationship would continue, sometimes with exchanges of rings.

> I was in London down the East End, with my boyfriend, and these three young fellows, they'd be called louts nowadays shouted 'Hey you bag' and all that. And my fella walked up to them and said 'Hey listen, that's my missus you're talking to. Piss off if you don't want filled in', cos he was quite big, in more ways than one.
>
> (Mark)

The queens would sleep in their husband's cabin at night, while their cabin would be converted into a living room. Mark, who worked as a chef, describes how he would make sandwiches for his husband while he was on the late watch. He describes his role as being like an 'unpaid housewife'. Polari use, or lack of it, was a further distinction that marked the queens and their husbands as having different status:

> Say me and Frances [his *omee-palone* friend] are sitting and talking, my husband's there. I'd say 'What are you doing tonight?' She'd say, 'What I'm going to do girl,' she'd say, 'I'm going to go round and dohbie the riah'. Dohbie is wash. And she'll say, 'I'll dohbie the riah dear, I'm going to do the brows, and then I'm going to get the eke on.' Well my husband will understand that she's going to go round the cabin and get ready. He knows she's putting on makeup, because that's 'putting eke on', you see. But *he* wouldn't use it.
>
> (Mark)

As noted earlier, Polari appears to have been deployed most often by working-class homosexual men. However, a further point should be made here. It was not *all* working-class homosexual men who used it. Before Gay Liberation in the 1970s, a much more traditional masculine–feminine role dichotomisation existed for working-class homosexuals, with masculine working-class men often not considering themselves to be homosexual:

> You might walk on a ship and say 'I always go with the chippie', which was the carpenter, and he might come round later and knock on your door. I mean he might be married, he might be straight, but it wasn't gay, you're classed as a queen. It wasn't this 'gay' business, no disrespect.
>
> (Mark)

As Mark explains, while the '*butch numbers*' would have understood Polari, it was generally just the stereotypically effeminate '*queens*' who incorporated it into their speech as a signifier of camp.

Bearing this in mind, it is not surprising that many female impersonators and drag queens took to Polari enthusiastically over the twentieth century. Described by Newton (1993: 43), female impersonators are 'a society within a society within a society'. Surrounding their society are the 'ordinary' homosexuals, and surrounding them is mainstream heterosexual society. Indeed, such was the frequency of usage of Polari by drag queens, that some people readily identified the language as belonging solely to them:

> Drag queens had their own language, which was called Polari, and if you were well-in they would explain some of the words to you, but you had to really get to know them before they would chat away in

this language which was a bit like backslang, and they would say, 'Nanti polari in front of the homi' which means don't speak in front of the straight person, and, 'Vada the ecaf' which is look at the face. It was like a total other planet, with its own language, its own life, its own little world – which just continued without anyone else knowing about it.

(Jose Pickering, *It's Not Unusual*, BBC2 1997)

In addition to such anecdotal evidence as this, many of the men I interviewed mentioned names of performers such as Lee Sutton and Mrs Shufflewick.[6] For drag queens, Polari became part of their act, as the following transcript of a song (a Polari version of 'Baby Face') used in a drag cabaret act by Lee Sutton reveals (the words in brackets are spoken directly to the audience, who attempted to sing along):

(We're going to do a little number now. Er, this may be a bit of a mystery to some of you because it is written in a foreign language. But in the second half we do explain it. What it's all about. We do our best.)

Bona eke
You've got the campest little bona eke
And when you vada me it leaves me weak
Bona eke
My heart starts a racket every time I see your packet

Bona eke
Your bon polari almost makes me spring a leak
I'd grant your every wish
I'd even grease my dish
Just to see your bona eke

You've got a tatty gaff
And all your drag is naff
But I love your bona eke

What's more your riah's cod
And all your pots are odd
But I love your bona eke

Your lallies look like darts
And you've got nanti cartes
But I love your bona eke

Explanation time . . .

Bona eke
(nice f . . . wait for me)
You've got the campest little bona eke
(you've got a nice face for a woman, even though you are a fella)
And when you look at me it leaves me weak
(when you look at me I feel as though I've done seven days inside)
Bona eke
(nice face)
My heart starts a racket every time I see your packet
(I get so excited when I look at your wages)

Bona eke
(nice face)
Your bon polari almost makes me spring a leak
(whenever you speak your mind I almost lose control of myself)
I'd grant your every wish
I'd even grease my dish
(I'd even cook for you)
Just to see your bona eke
(nice face)

You've got a tatty gaff
((*Irish accent*) your flat is full of potatoes)
and all your drag is naff
(your wardrobe's worse than mine)
But I love your bona eke
(nice face)

What more your riah's odd
(patriotic hair – red and white with a navy-blue parting)
and all your pots are cod
(there's something fishy about your teeth – take 'em out – have a
whale of a time)
But I love your bona eke
(nice face)

Your lallies look like darts
(your legs are so thin if they were bowed you could take up archery)
and you've got nanti cartes
(your old grey mare has nothing to pull)
But I love your bona eke!

The transcript shows how Polari is used as a form of positive politeness (discussed above). The song makes use of some of the more commonly
known words: *bona, eke, campest, vada, packet, polari, dish, drag, naff,*

riah, cod, pots, lallies, nanti and *cartes*. Over the course of the song, the singer dissects the physical attributes of a man, both in terms of body (*eke, packet, riah, pots, lallies, cartes*) and clothing/taste (*gaff, drag*). The song combines lusty appreciation in the first two verses ('I'd grant your every wish/I'd even grease your dish') with criticism in the final three verses ('Your lallies look like darts and you've got nanti cartes'). Therefore, the message that the object of desire is physically attractive is subverted towards the latter half of the song. The song's mix of compliments and insults, combined with its focus on appearance, is illustrative of the ambivalent nature of the aggressive Polari speaker.[7]

That is not to say that Polari used aggressively will always have a benign undercurrent. Individual personalities, existing relationships and rivalries will all have important parts to play in deciphering the true intent of a Polari utterance. Realistically, it is more likely that aggressive Polari, used within homosexual subcultures, probably contains measures of true aggression and positive politeness.

So, Polari was not always just used to show that someone was homosexual, it could also be used in order to be brutally, outrageously camp. However, the camp identity can also allow certain opinions to be expressed in a 'safe' way. To give an anecdotal example, one gay man I know uses Polari infrequently; usually when he sees an attractive man and wants to point him out. His Polari is characterised by phrases such as, 'ooh, vada the lallies on him!', uttered in a voice which echoes camp British 1960s comedians such as Kenneth Williams and Charles Hawtrey. However, this 'Polari identity' is very different from the way he conducts himself at other times (respectable, middle-class, non-camp).

In cases like these, the concept of 'language crossing' is useful. Rampton (1998: 291) defines language crossing as 'the use of a language which isn't generally thought to "belong" to the speaker . . . a sense of movement across quite sharply felt social or ethnic boundaries'. Language crossing can often occur at 'liminal' points in interactions, e.g. ritual abuse, transgressions, self-talk, boundaries of interactions (greetings, farewells), games and performance art (Rampton 1998: 298). This formulation of languages as 'belonging' or having owners is interesting when considered in relation to Polari. Gay men (especially *'queens'* or *drag queens*) may be considered to be the 'owners' of Polari, in that they were the people who used it most. However, as I have indicated in this chapter, not all gay men used Polari (even if they claimed to understand it) and it could be used within the gay subculture in order to exclude and confuse (e.g. the East End and West End varieties). With the passage of time and the decline of Polari since the 1960s, is it possible for anyone, other than the original users, to 'own' this language variety? It may be reclaimed, as I discuss in Chapter 7, but its more recent uses are different from the way its original 'owners' would have used it.

The gay man who uses a Polari 'voice' in order to point out an attractive man is using a form of double voicing or metaphorical code-switching:

'inserting a new semantic intention into a discourse which already has
. . . an intention of its own. Such a discourse . . . must be seen as belonging
to someone else. In one discourse, two semantic intentions appear, two
voices' (Bakhtin 1984: 189). Double voicing can be uni-directional or
vari-directional. In the case of uni-directional double voicing, the speaker
uses someone else's discourse 'in the direction of its own particular intentions' (Bahktin 1984: 193). In other words, they're saying something that
they mostly agree with, but putting on a different voice in order to maintain a bit of distance from the statement. In the case of vari-directional
double voicing, the speaker makes a remark that would be in opposition
to his or her own beliefs. For example, if I wanted to mock racist views
I might say something racist while putting on an 'Alf Garnett'[8] voice.

The use of Polari described above could be viewed as a case of uni-
directional double voicing; the speaker goes along with the momentum
of the second voice, but an element of otherness is retained which makes
the utterance conditional and hedged. It's not always the case, though,
that double voicing can easily be classed as uni-directional or vari-
directional. At times, the speaker described above, who sometimes 'puts
on a Polari voice', openly disapproves of predatory gay practices, which
makes his uptake of the predatory Polari voice even more ambiguous. Is
he mocking this identity, reclaiming it or using the voice as a convenient
filter to reveal a part of his personality he is otherwise at odds with?
Bahktin (1984: 199) notes that at times the boundary between speaker and
the 'voice' they are adopting can diminish so that there is a 'fusion of
voices' and the discourse ceases to be double voiced, becoming 'direct
unmediated discourse'.

In adopting, for a short time, an alternate identity, this Polari speaker is
able to voice a sexually predatory opinion, while discreetly distancing his
'everyday self' from it. By speaking in the voice and language of a stereotypically effeminate, predatory gay man he is simultaneously mocking the
stereotype (and thereby acknowledging that such opinions aren't necessarily 'acceptable'), but also recognising the usefulness of the stereotype in
allowing the release of the opinion. Polari, then, can act as an outlet that
allows some people to say what would normally be unsayable.

Initiation rites

While many gay men and lesbians had access to subcultural pubs, bars,
cafés and clubs in large cities, others (because of factors such as age,
geographic location, lack of knowledge about the gay subculture, or
guilt/shame about their sexuality) were excluded. However, when circumstances arose whereby such a person came into contact with the subculture,
one of the first obvious signs seems to have been hearing Polari. A good
example of Polari being part of the process of initiation into homosexual
life is given in the semi-autobiographical novel by Michael Carson, *Sucking*

Sherbert Lemons (set in 1963). Benson, the 15-year-old hero, is followed by a man who has seen him looking at a book containing photos of African tribes in the library and has deduced he is gay:

> 'How did you know?'
> 'Takes one to know one dear.'
> 'How do you mean?' asked Benson for whom the cliché was as novel as a mango.
> The man shrugged. 'I mean that I knew as soon as I saw you. When I saw you having a vada in the dinge section, I said to myself, Andrea – my name's Andy in real life actually, dear – Andrea, I said to myself, there's a gay one if ever I saw one.'
> 'A gay one?' asked Benson.
> 'A homo, a pouff, a queer, a gay boy. You really were born yesterday weren't you dear?'
>
> (Carson 1988: 203)

Another example comes from 'John', interviewed in the 1970s magazine *Lunch*, who said of his first sexual experiences:

> I used to have sex in the cottage . . . It wasn't until I was about sixteen and a half that I met this person and he was a taxi driver by the name of Ronnie and he proceeded to tell me what a golden little chicken I was and all the rest of it. Not in those precise words because I didn't know the parlare then. She wasn't an experienced queen.
>
> (John, interview in *Lunch* by Seligman 1973: 11)

Not only did Polari identify someone as belonging to a particular and different group (even if the hearer was not sure what that group was), the fact that an underground language existed would indicate that there were others like them. For gay men and lesbians who were yet to discover the 'scene', Polari was a connection between themselves and that subculture, whether heard via Julian and Sandy on the radio, or via a few words uttered by a stranger. It was crucially in these 'first contact' situations that Polari was encountered. As such, this makes its place at the heart of homosexual identity prior to 1967 all the more understandable.

This view of Polari – as a rite of passage into the gay subculture – was articulated clearly by Robin, another merchant seaman:

> Palarie was very commonplace on board ship when I was at sea. I joined my first ship at 16 and there were a lot of unfamiliar [Palarie] words to learn . . . There were many, spoken by everyone, officers and ratings. I was a steward, like the airlines today, many were H.P.'s [*homee-palones*]. The older queens looked after me though and I was soon christened my camp name, Rose. A lot of the older queens spoke

only Palarie. I'm not sure why it was so popular, maybe it goes back to national service. The 'Merch' was a good way out for the more feminine men at the time, when the Liners were in their heyday.

(Robin)

Learning the words for Polari was seen as part of the initiation rite into gay culture for new sailors, while the 'renaming' of a sailor with a 'camp name' was a way of sealing this new identity: a mark of social acceptance. Robin describes how he was looked after by the older *queens* on the ships, who passed down Polari words to him. The language also served as a focus of shared interest, by which older, established members of the gay community could impart knowledge to new members:

> When I was in Ipswich up until the age of 18, I was sort of out from the age of about 16 and Ipswich at that time had a very limited gay thing going on and there was a bunch of geriatric old queens sitting around in a living-room-sized pub, and they actually gave lessons. So that was my sort of initiation into it. It was quite extensive.
>
> (Sidney)

In this sense, Polari helps to construct a *social* gay identity, serving as a code which helps to affirm membership of a community, and to strengthen the collective identity of the subculture.

Conclusion

It is unlikely that every person interviewed would have used Polari in the same way. Rather, the interviewees each tended to give one or two examples of how they understood Polari was used. With interview data, caution must be applied in reading 'truths' into statements, even when (and as is the case with the interview data in this chapter) descriptions of usage tend to be verified by unrelated sources. However, even if we choose to disbelieve everything that the Polari speakers said, their descriptions still give us insights into how *they* construct their own versions of Polari-speaking identities.

From the interviews with Polari speakers it transpires that Polari could be employed in the construction of numerous gay identities, often all at the same time. As a means of enabling the maintenance of secrecy in certain contexts, Polari could also be used to construct either a cautiously 'out' identity, or a flamboyantly, aggressive 'out' identity, depending on how it was used. Within the gay subculture, Polari enabled the expression of effeminate identities, even to those who didn't always want to own up to them. It acted as a social lubricant, and also as a means of conveying gossip, expressing verbal aggression, cruising, being humorous, and playing the game of one-upmanship. In the case of aggression and one-upmanship especially, its use could confuse and hurt.

Finally, and perhaps most importantly, Polari was used as a way of tearing down 'heterosexual' reality, and remoulding it as a world seen through gay eyes, with gay standards. While many of the words in Polari appeared to have English 'equivalents', it is important to note that meanings weren't exact translations. '*Bona*' didn't just mean 'good' – it meant good *by the standards of the gay subculture*. For gay men and lesbians in the 1960s and earlier, Polari not only allowed them to recreate themselves, it also allowed them to recreate their whole world.

The next chapter examines the most high-profile speakers of Polari to date: Julian and Sandy. Occurring on the cusp of the Gay Liberation movement in the UK, the popularity of this camp pair of jobbing actors represents Polari's swansong before a long, slow decline into obscurity. While this chapter has focused on 'real-life' uses of Polari, which were restricted to the private spaces of the homosexual subculture, the phenomenon of Julian and Sandy saw this secret language launched on to unsuspecting, unprepared, mainstream family audiences across the UK. Polari was about to go public.

5   Julian and Sandy

Background to the sketches

The largest and most widely-known source of Polari could be found propping up a revue show broadcast on Sunday afternoons to homes up and down the UK. Julian and Sandy were two fictional characters, created by Barry Took and Marty Feldman, and voiced by Hugh Paddick and Kenneth Williams on the British BBC radio series *Round the Horne*. The show, which ran from 1964 until 1969, was immensely popular, attracting nine million listeners each week and winning the Writers' Guild of Great Britain Award for the best comedy script in 1967. *Round the Horne* consisted of a series of comedy sketches, linked together by 'straight man' Kenneth Horne (hence the show's title). Each episode tended to adhere to the same format, containing a film spoof, a musical number, a parody of a cooking or fashion programme, a folk song from the fictional character Rambling Syd Rumpo (also voiced by Kenneth Williams), and usually ending with a Julian and Sandy sketch. The fact that this sketch was almost always last suggests that it was the most popular part of the show – the part 'worth waiting for'. Barry Took agrees with this statement:

> They were the most popular part of the show. Marty Feldman got tired of them and wanted to leave them out, but I didn't want to. So we did a sketch where we did leave them out one week, and then had them come in and complain that it was a disgrace and make all sorts of suggestions as to what we could have had them doing.
>
> (Barry Took, personal correspondence 1997)

Julian and Sandy were the two 'friends' in each sketch, and although their sexual orientation or relationship to one another was never made explicit, it was implied in many other ways. They were both stereotypical effeminate homosexuals, although, of the two, it was Sandy who was the more experienced, aggressive and sharp, while Julian tended to be softer, although supposedly more talented and more physically attractive.

Small numbers of actors and comedians who performed camp, effeminate or implicitly gay roles existed both before and after Julian and Sandy in the UK. Kenneth Williams had also played a series of somewhat closeted, haughty *queens* in numerous *Carry On* films from the late 1950s onwards, alongside Charles Hawtrey, who had specialised in effeminately eccentric characters, coming close to the then visual stereotype of a gay man – weedy and flamboyant. British comedians such as Frankie Howerd, Dick Emery and Danny La Rue followed a tradition based around camp and/or drag personas, which continued well into the 1970s with John Inman and Larry Grayson. However, Julian and Sandy were the only characters who used Polari with any regularity, and their homosexuality was explored much more fully than that of any other homosexual-coded character of the time.

In 1992, an audio compilation of some of the Julian and Sandy sketches was produced by the BBC, and this was followed in 1996 by a second compilation (total running time of both compilations: approximately three and a half hours). Before looking at the sketches themselves, it is useful to consider how they were received by audiences. While the sketches were certainly listened to by gay men and lesbians, the majority of the audience would have been heterosexual: as stated above, the sketches were broadcast on Sunday afternoons, in a popular 'family' time-slot. Therefore, it is likely that both adults and children would have heard them. In the context of the pre-Wolfenden 1960s, homosexual identities and practices were taboo to mainstream audiences. For many gay men who did not live in London or did not have a circle of gay friends, in the 1960s their only exposure to Polari was through listening to *Round the Horne* on the radio.[1] Indeed, at that time, *Round the Horne* was the only programme on the radio or television to base part of its show around homosexuality, albeit in an implicit context:

> Even if you lived in a little village in the back of Hicksville – and you had to be listening to it on the crystal set with the bedroom door locked, and it on very softly, you still had Julian and Sandy giving you courage mon amie.
>
> (Betty Bourne, BBC Radio 4 1998)

> If you farted, little old ladies would come up to you in the street and say 'Oh I hear you farted dear'. [Ipswich] was a very small town. At 4 o'clock all the shops closed and there were balls of weed rolling through the street. I was a keen listener to Sandy and Jules every Sunday afternoon and it was, you know, it was part of the scene.
>
> (Sidney)

> When I was in my really early teens, sort of 12 or 13 or so, living in the middle of nowhere in Yorkshire, and I used to listen to *Round the Horne,* and it was Hugh Paddick and Bill Pertwee and Betty

Marsden and Kenneth Williams and all those persons, and they were coming out with things. And of course I didn't know anything about gay or anything in those days, just that I liked looking at men, you know. But I used to think that it was absolutely wonderful, it was quite advanced for its age.

(Jim E)

So in the late 1960s Julian and Sandy were possibly the only accessible gay identities who were able to provide some sort of clue that, for people living in 'Hicksville' or 'the middle of nowhere', there were others like them who were part of an existing gay subculture.

The camp, outrageous characters created by Barry Took and Marty Feldman were not initially what they envisaged for *Round the Horne*:

We had written two old gentleman, two old actors, they were terribly booming old boys, and in those days it was commonplace for actors to do housework between engagements, and we thought it would be funny for these old theatrical chaps going to Kenneth Horne to do his washing up and the rest of it ... the producer didn't like them – 'they're too sad, make them chorus boys'.

(Barry Took, BBC Radio 4 1998)

So the sketch was modernised, to make the actors younger and more contemporary. Julian was named after Julian Slade, who co-wrote *Salad Days* with Dorothy Reynolds, while Sandy was named after Sandy Wilson, who wrote *The Boyfriend*.[2] Members of The Royal Ballet Company apparently loved Julian and Sandy, possibly recognising themselves in many of the sketches – to them, it was a shared secret.

Almost every sketch had the same premise: Kenneth Horne (playing himself) would find out (usually from a magazine of dubious credentials) about a new business that had just been set up in either Chelsea or Carnaby Street, and his curiosity would take him there. He would knock on the door, ask 'Hello, anybody there?' to which Julian (Hugh Paddick) would always respond, 'I'm Julian, this is my friend Sandy', and Sandy (Kenneth Williams) would follow with a phrase heavily peppered with Polari (usually a variation on 'Hello Mr Horne, how bona to vada your dolly old eke again'). With this introductory routine established, the sketch would begin properly with Julian and Sandy talking about their new business, often leaving Kenneth Horne out of the conversation completely, or trying to get him to try their new product or service. Within this framework there were a number of patterns which came to be expected; for example, Sandy would often reveal or hint at a dark (homosexual) secret of Julian's, causing Julian to hiss 'traitor!' but then eventually be encouraged to 'unburden himself' of the whole story. Each sketch ended rather abruptly, with a quick punchline.

So although the Julian and Sandy sketches are wholly artificial, they were used both as a source of humour and as a source of Polari instruction by gay men of that time. According to David (1997: 199), by the late 1960s Polari had become 'almost extinct' within UK gay subcultures, and the Julian and Sandy sketches provoked a revival.

Gay stereotyping

> The whole point about Julian and Sandy, is the homosexuality is unimportant ... What's so strange about it? ... People don't give a damn about sexual attitudes and behaviour. They know that they themselves have oddities, and they accept other people's oddities.
>
> (Barry Took, BBC Radio 4 1998)

Because of the radio format, language was the most important way that identity was constructed (rather than placing a reliance on visual codes such as dress, gait, posture, facial expressions, gesture etc.). Both Julian and Sandy have stereotypically 'camp' voices, with East London working-class accents (an accent strongly linked to Polari speakers). The roles are played for humour, with a great deal of exaggerated exclaiming, and a good use of comic timing.

Gay identity is therefore constructed via talk, and I would argue that there are two connecting strands or traits which are mainly accessed in order to create Julian and Sandy as gay stereotypes. On the one hand, their homosexuality is associated with stereotypes concerned with femininity, and on the other, they are represented as 'deviant' transgressors, going against the traditional sexual norm of a long-term heterosexual relationship, sanctioned by religion and law.

Julian and Sandy appear to be fond of gossip (a form of discourse traditionally, although often incorrectly, associated with women), while their preferred topics of conversation also contribute strongly to their stereotyping as gay men – common themes include physical descriptions of other men, evaluations of other people's homes and clothing, fear of ageing, and exposure of each other's sad little techniques designed to hide the ageing process:

Sandy: Here, that's never Mr Horne.
Julian: It is!
Sandy: Oooh, he doesn't half look old don't he? I wonder if they're his own teeth?

(Rentachap)

Sandy: Now look at the – vada, Mr Horne, at this garden of yours.
Mr Horne: Right it's through here.

Sandy: Oh, isn't it nasty? Isn't it nasty! I couldn't be doing with a garden like this could you, Jules?

Julian: What!

Sandy: Oh those horrible little naff gnomes. Oh no!

Julian: What! It's a bit like 'Noddy in Toyland' isn't it!

                                                          (Bona Homes)

Sandy: Yeah, we'll be out as soon as Jule's finished doing his riah. Takes him hours combing it so the join don't show.

Julian: Traitor! Traitor! You swore you'd never mention it.

Sandy: You're so vain!

Julian: Oh! Hark who's talking.

Sandy: Mm.

Julian: Puts on hormone cream Mr Horne.

Sandy: Don't listen. Liar!

Julian: Oh yes you do.

Sandy: Liar!

Julian: You do too. And anti-wrinkle cream on your elbows.

                                                          (Bona Christmas)

Gossip, and particularly 'bitchiness', abound in their interactions. Julian and Sandy are often critical of each other, Mr Horne and other men. They are also constructed as physically weak, and trivialising; making much of small matters.

Sandy: He grabbed me by the wrist, he pinned me down, and then he broke it.

Mr Horne: Your wrist?

Sandy: No ducky, me fingernail!

                                                          (Bona Promotions)

Although Julian and Sandy are actors, they are regularly unable to find theatrical work, and therefore take on other jobs to make money: in every sketch they are seen in another line of business. While this allows considerable scope for the development of unique scenarios, this transience implies that they will never settle down to anything permanent – a lack of commitment and respectability which is set up in opposition to the (then) tradition in mainstream society of holding down the same job for life.

Impermanence is also implied by the idea that Julian and Sandy both have dark 'pasts', or many incidents in their romantic lives that they would rather forget about; liaisons which need to be shamefully coaxed from them. As Kenneth Williams said, 'What [they] were doing was making these outrageous characters funny because of the manic insistence of the one making the other confess . . . Life is full of such people' (BBC Radio 4 1998):

Sandy:	Don't mention rugby to Jules! Ooh!
Julian:	Ha! Ha!
Sandy:	Ooh! Don't mention that to him.
Julian:	Ha! Ha!
Sandy:	Ooh! Here, no, here! He's sworn, he's sworn never to touch a pair of rugby shorts again. No listen, no listen ducky. After what happened.
Julian:	Oh! He swore he'd never tell.
Sandy:	Go on, tell Mr Horne about it, go on, tell him.
Julian:	No, no, no.
Sandy:	Go on, let yourself go.
Julian:	No.
Sandy:	Purge yourself! Purge, purge!

(Bona Rags)

Many sketches feature such examples of near-hysteria: the characters seem to flit from one extreme of emotion to another, implying that nothing for them remains stable for long. Such stereotypical, emotional exaggeration is characterised by Rodgers (1972: 11): '[The flaming faggots] overdramatize words to make up for the plainness they find in their own lives; to them life is a stage with all the lights going and the audience constantly clapping for more. It's Vegas every minute!'

Euphemism and innuendo

The fact that homosexuality was illegal at the time gave it an added mystery or frisson because it was naughty. I don't think anyone was shocked by it.

(Sandy Wilson, BBC Radio 4 1998)

The use of the 'double meaning', or saying one thing that can be interpreted in two ways, usually one innocent and one subversive, is a way of being controversial and funny at the same time, obviating the potential amount of offence caused and obscuring the meaning from those too young or innocent to understand. If Julian and Sandy had blurted out 'Guess what, listeners, we've been having anal intercourse!', few people in those days would have found it very amusing, and many would have found it distasteful. But by merely alluding to anal intercourse (e.g. comments such as 'he took his part lovely' in 'Bona Homes'), the writers of the Julian and Sandy sketches managed to create humour from the conflict and interaction between what was said and what was meant. Sexual humour had to be covert if it was not to offend – complaints could be dismissed with something akin to the 'Emperor's New Clothes' syndrome – 'what a dirty mind you must have to make such an interpretation'. Lucas (1994: 104) wonders how the writers of Julian and Sandy got away with it all.

Barry Took's explanation is that most of the people at the BBC either didn't understand it, or they didn't like to admit that they understood it. Also, the programme had a powerful ally in the form of Sir Hugh Carleton Greene, the then Director General of the BBC, who, according to Barry Took (BBC Radio 4 1998), defended *Round the Horne* because he saw nothing objectionable in it. Took goes on to quote a conversation between the two of them in which Greene admitted that, in addition, he 'liked dirty shows'. The following reflexive excerpt demonstrates the foundations upon which *Round the Horne*[3] was based:

Sandy:	We could have been in a railway booking office and I could have said, Jule is checking his departures and looking up his Bradshaw. Haaaa!
Mr Horne:	No, no, no, no, no, oh no. I don't think so. The audience may have seen a secondary meaning.
Sandy:	Them? Secondary meaning?
Julian:	What?
Sandy:	They don't even see the first meaning. Just laugh at anything that might be dirty, don't they. Disgusting!

(No Julian and Sandy)

In the 1960s, innuendo was the dominant form of British sexual humour. For example, the *Carry On* film series contained numerous references to heterosexual intercourse and parts of the anatomy – as mentioned above, Kenneth Williams also played roles in many of these films. So, if heterosexual humour had to be shrouded in innuendo, that went double for homosexuality:

Julian:	here's Cyril, he's **half and half** you know. Half King Charles spaniel. Half fox terrier. We call him a fox cocker.

(Bona Pets)

Sandy:	Isn't he bold? **I've got his number, ducky.** Yes, go on Jules, though. Sorry for that interruption. Go on, it's beginning to sing now, isn't it, yes go on.

(Bona Homes)

Sandy:	I mean you take the Hooded Terror.
Julian:	Hooded.
Sandy:	**He's one of ours.**

(Bona Promotions)

Mr Horne:	I know a bargain when I see one. And where will you dispose of the stuff? To distressed gentlefolk?

Julian: Oh no, no. There's no point in adding to their distress. **We've got a different outlet** Mr Horne.

(Bona Rags)

Sandy: Now look, turn Jule. Watch him Mr Horne. **He's on the turn**. Now that's, yes, that's beautiful, isn't that beautiful, that's fantabulosa.

(Bona Male Models)

Julian: Oh yes, we feel there's a crying need in this country today for **men like us to get out into the open.**

(Lazy Bona Ranch)

While innuendo takes any word or phrase and distorts the meaning by relying on features of the phrase that are ambiguous, euphemism refers to a neutral stock phrase or idiom which is knowingly used to refer to something taboo. Euphemisms can be used for sex, but are also generally found in language surrounding any taboo or uncomfortable subject: *pink slip* (dismissal notice), *collateral losses* (civilian casualties). Euphemisms for homosexuality can often be overlooked as they sometimes occur out of context, when Julian and Sandy are talking about something else, as in their description of a dog as being 'half and half'. Difference and/or belonging are often themes that are used in the creation of a gay innuendo. Phrases such as 'different outlet' and 'half and half' (half male, half female) tapped into common feelings about homosexuality at the time the sketches were written, while 'men like us' and 'one of ours' suggest that, not only are Julian and Sandy labelling someone else as homosexual, but they are also admitting to their own homosexuality at the same time. 'On the turn' is an interesting euphemism, referring to someone whose sexuality is changing – from homosexual to heterosexual, or vice versa, while 'I've got his number' appears several times in the sketches as a Polari phrase, meaning 'I know he's homosexual', but has also survived into present-day English slang usage, now meaning 'I know what you're up to.'

Euphemisms relating more directly to gay sex are very common: the pronoun 'it' is used to refer both to the act of sex, and to particular body parts:

Sandy: Yes, we are the Universal Party, so called because **we're at it** right, left and centre.

(Keep Britain Bona)

Julian: I used to stand there **with it fizzing in me hand**. And I used to say 'I am Swifty, the tonic fruit salts kid.'

(Bona Ads)

The verb 'do' is also used as a euphemism for sex:

> *Sandy*: We're concerned with efficiency, cutting out waste. Take
> when we did the gas board. **We did them** didn't we?
> Julian: Oh, indeed yes.
> Sandy: **We did the gas board**.
>
> (Time and Motion)

However, other types of innuendo have more complex structures. For example:

> *Sandy*: Yes, or there's 'The party's over, **it's all over my friend.**'
> I mean, yes yes, it's lovely, no, it's lovely, that is poignant.
> (Bona Beat Songs Ltd)

Here Sandy is quoting from a song title, and the ambiguity lies in the phrase 'it's all over my friend', which can be interpreted as him telling the friend that the party is over. However, there is a more subversive meaning which translates as Sandy announcing that something, the 'it' of the phrase, is all over his friend, possibly a bodily fluid? The audience understood this, and laughed, prompting Sandy to lapse out of character and 'deny' the double meaning: 'yes, yes it's lovely, no'. The following interchange is a particularly complex example of innuendo:

> *Julian*: [They were] so pleased with us, you know what they
> done?
> *Mr Horne*: No?
> *Julian*: The zoological society **made us fellows**.
>
> (Time and Motion)

Three interpretations can be drawn from the above remark. The innocent meaning translates to Julian and Sandy being made fellow members of the zoological society, while a second meaning would be 'The zoological society turned Julian and Sandy into fellows.' Finally, a third meaning could be 'The zoological society created fellows for Julian and Sandy to take home and keep.' The final two interpretations both refer to homosexuality, in that the former assumes that Julian and Sandy are somehow 'less than men', while in the latter Julian and Sandy want to *possess* men: a reworking of the object cathexis versus identification dilemma which categorises the desire to *have* something with the desire to *be* the same thing (Freud 1977: 135).

Other innuendo devices lie in the employment of words that were commonly known as having secondary meanings in the gay subculture, or were words meaning 'homosexual' in mainstream society. Examples of the former type would be when Kenneth Horne is advised to 'go camping', or 'try cruising' in 'Bona Tours Ltd', or when Julian says he is sick to the stomach on reading the headline 'Queens to be scrapped' (referring to the ships the Queen Mary and the Queen Elizabeth). Names of places also take on gay identification, with 'Queensway', and 'Mincing Lane' both being quoted. Examples of the latter type would be when, describing a cigarette advertisement in which the characters had starred, Julian says 'I'd take a puff and ride off', or in another cigarette-related pun, Julian is upset when 'the government ban fags from TV'. Both *puff* and *fag* have been used as pejorative terms for gay men (in the UK and America, respectively).

Another way in which Julian and Sandy make implicit references to Polari is by their use of names: in 'Bona Books' there are references to Rock (Hudson), Tab (Hunter) and Dorian (Gray). The first two names refer to male film stars who were secretly homosexual. Dorian Gray refers to the title character in the Oscar Wilde novel *The Picture of Dorian Gray*, a character who could be coded as homosexual because of his vanity and close male friendships. There is also the name Pandro Wildebeeste (in 'Le Casserole De Bona Gourmet'), possibly a coded reference to Peter Wildeblood, the journalist whose 1950 autobiography *Against the Law* was a key book in debates over the decriminalisation of homosexuality. Similarly, the character of Gordon (discussed later in this chapter) may have been a reference to the dance 'The Gay Gordons', or to Gordon Westwood, one of the first sociologists to write about homosexuality in the 1960s.

Criminalised and pathogenic identities

As described in Chapter 4, homosexual acts in the UK were criminalised as well as taboo before 1967. Hence, the need for secrecy that Polari afforded. Julian and Sandy's homosexuality put them on the edge of society, and therefore referring to the law, the police or crime became a useful shorthand for indexing homosexuality itself:

Julian: We've got a criminal practice that takes up most of our time.
                                                            (Bona Law)

Julian: Yes, now, erm, could I interest you in a flame red shoulder length wig?
Mr Horne: Well, not me, but you might interest the chief of police.
                                                        (Bona Bouffant)

In 'Bona Law', the criminal practice that Julian refers to is of course both his homosexuality (he is a 'practising homosexual') and the law practice where he is currently employed. Thus Julian manages to straddle both sides of the law at the same time. While in Bona Bouffant, a red wig is enough to suggest criminal deviance to Kenneth Horne.

The sketches also used euphemism to refer to the attitude of some members of the medical profession towards homosexuality in the UK:

> *Sandy*:   Oh hello, Mr Horne, yes, nice to see you, nice to vada your eke. Yes, we're your actual homeopathic practitioners. Yes, yes, **we're not recognised by doctors**.
>
> (Bona Nature Clinic)

While the phrase 'homeopathic practitioners' is a wordplay on the phrase 'practising homosexuals', the next sentence is interesting in that it highlights the ambivalence towards homosexuality of certain doctors[4] in the 1960s and earlier, who believed that gay identities could be cured/erased via drugs or electric shock treatments:

> Throughout much of the 1950s and 1960s, the prevailing opinion of the medical establishment, and certainly the field of psychoanalysis, was that homosexuality was a developmental maladjustment or illness.
>
> (Scroggie 1999: 238)

Therefore, the Julian and Sandy sketches help to represent an *oppressed* gay identity, but in a cheerful, mocking and implicit way, rather than by indexing unhappy, ashamed identities like those in films such as *Victim* (1961), *A Taste of Honey* (1961) and *Boys in the Band* (1970), or the openly politicised identity adopted by members of the Gay Liberation Front movement post-Julian and Sandy.

Julian and Sandy's use of Polari

> We used to hear Kenneth Williams and Hugh Paddick talking like that anyway, and we thought it would be a good idea to incorporate what they did in their private lives into the script.
>
> (Barry Took, BBC Radio 4 1998)

It is likely that the *Round the Horne* version of Polari originally came from the Polari used by the gay and theatrical communities (and others) in London's West End. After leaving grammar school at 15, Barry Took had taken a job at a musical publishers, which led to work as a trumpet player with dance bands, and he eventually became a musical comic in the West End. His choreographer introduced him to Polari (correspondence with Barry Took, 1997).

On the other hand, Kenneth Williams did identify (somewhat ruefully) as homosexual[5] and had a show business background which included the theatre and his days as an entertainer in the Army. According to Barry Took and Marty Feldman,[6] Williams told them the Polari words and their meanings (although not always accurately), and the writers included them in the Julian and Sandy sketches. Table 5.1 shows the Polari words and their frequencies used in the 51 sketches I examined.

The sketches make use of a lexicon of 53 Polari word types (which counts for about an eighth of the words listed in the full Polari lexicon in the Appendix). The total number of times Julian and Sandy use Polari in these sketches (the numbers in the frequency columns added up) is 815. Considering that the total number of words in these sketches is about 33,000, it can be calculated that Polari only counts for about 2.5 per cent of what Julian and Sandy say – the rest is in English.

None of the older Parlyaree-derived terms for numbers (*una, dooey, trey* etc.) are used by Julian and Sandy, nor are the related terms for money (*tosheroon, beyonek, gent*). Also excluded are numerous words related to sex, such as *cartes* (penis), *steamer* (prostitute's client) and *harva* (have sexual intercourse). This is therefore a simplified, 'sanitised' version of Polari – made necessary for the purposes of British media broadcasting in the 1960s. The lack of sexually taboo words can also be attributed to the fact that at least one of the writers didn't want to use them:

Table 5.1 Frequencies of Polari words found in the Julian and Sandy data

Word	Meaning	Frequency	Word	Meaning	Frequency
bona	good	149	cruising	looking for sex	4
vada	see/look	73	irish	wig	4
eke	face	55	nish	no/don't	4
troll	walk	51	strillers	piano keys	3
homi/omi	man	51	thews	muscles (thighs)	3
ducky	endearment	37	cossy	costume	3
bold	audacious	29	order	go	3
butch	masculine	29	trade	casual sexual	3
dear	endearment	28		partner	
palone	woman	27	lau	lay/place	3
lally	leg	26	dishes	attractive men	2
riah	hair	25		(also anuses)	
lattie	house/flat	24	fab	good	2
dolly	good	19	manjarie	food/eat	2
polari	talk	19	omee-palone	gay man	2
nanti	no	17	barnet	hair	1
naff	tasteless	15	treash	endearment	1
fantabulosa	wonderful	14	bods	bodies	1
queen	gay man	12	cod	awful	1
heartface	endearment	11	hampsteads	teeth	1
mince	walk/eye	11	jig	wig	1
drag	clothes	9	lucoddy	body	1
fabe	great	8	plates	feet (oral sex)	1
sheesh	classy	7	scotches	legs	1
bijou	small	6	two and eight	state	1
aris (aristotle)	arse	5	tat	worthless	1
luppers	fingers	5	zhoosh	clothing	1

There were no swear words either. We never used them. We didn't want to, it wasn't in our makeup. Later comedy programmes such as *Steptoe and Son*, and *Till Death Us Do Part* used them, but they were a different generation to us.

(Barry Took, personal correspondence 1997)

The large number of Polari words in existence would have been too complex for the audience to follow, if all had been used (even making the unlikely assumption that the writers knew them all). By concentrating on a core vocabulary, which could be used and reused in a number of different contexts, Polari was made quickly accessible to an audience who hadn't previously been aware of its existence. This accessibility and simplicity made it the dominant version of Polari to exist post-Julian and Sandy (almost all of the words in the Julian and Sandy lexicon were known to the Polari speakers I interviewed). A further aspect of this simplification of Polari was that, in the majority of cases, Julian and Sandy would use it in a way that aided translation – so instead of filling every sentence with incomprehensible Polari, the characters only used the occasional word here and there, sometimes giving translations as they proceeded:

Mr Horne:	Yes, oh I see you've got lallie of lamb on.
Sandy:	Oh yes.
Julian:	Yes, lamb's very nice, or there's your jugged riah. That's erm Polari for hair.[7]

(Le Casserole De Bona Gourmet)

So the sketches cannot be held to represent a typical example of Polari speech, just as textbooks on the English language which rely on carefully constructed, simple, grammatical sentences such as 'John gave Pat the ball' cannot be held up as typical examples of spoken English. However, like language textbooks, the sketches provided a blueprint for learning a basic version of Polari.

The simplest way that Polari facilitated the construction of gay identity in the sketches was by the fact that it was used at all. Considering work on representation by Saussure (1966: 16) and Barthes (1967: 91–2), a sign is made up of two elements, the signifier and the signified. So a Polari word such as *lally* would be a signifier, and the signified would be the mental concept of a leg, or a particular leg depending on the context in which the word is used. This descriptive level, according to Barthes, is the level of denotation, but there is a deeper level of cultural connotation encoded within the word *lally*, which requires the reader (or hearer) of *lally* to understand that the word is being used in reference to a homosexual context. Consider the excerpt below:

| *Mr Horne*: | Could you give me some idea of his act? |
| *Sandy*: | Well he comes on wearing this leopard skin you see. He's a great butch omee, he's got these thews like an oak, and bulging lallies. Ohh! |

(Bona Performers)

In the excerpt, Sandy enthuses about another man's body, saying (translated) that the man has thighs like an oak and bulging legs, and that he's very masculine. It is probably the case that UK family radio audiences in the 1960s would have found it odd to hear a *woman* praise (and sexualise) a man's body, so the idea of a male worshipping another male in this context is unthinkable. Therefore, once again, Polari allows the speaker to say the unsayable. Only part of Sandy's description is in English, and the most important parts of the phrase are in Polari (*lallies, omee, thews, butch*). Not only, then, does Polari work at the level of denotation (as a code for English words), it also works at a connotative level by referring to a gay context, both by the fact that the words can be used to refer to topics of 'male homosexual interest' (men's body parts, sex etc.), and by the fact that it can be recognised as a language variety used by gay men.

Polari, used in recurrent phrases such as 'how bona to vada your dolly old eke!', becomes referenced with the notion of the comedian's catchphrase; a shorthand representation of the comedy identity which is instantly recognisable to audiences, even when decontextualised, and thus able to be appropriated by fans. To audiences, then, the use of Polari in itself is funny – not only because it can obscure taboo meanings, but also because of its *otherness*.

Occasionally, the actors exploit the fact that the audience is not a homogeneous entity when it comes to knowledge about Polari on an individual basis. For example, consider the following excerpt:

Mr Horne:	Well, do the best you can – here's the dishcloth.
Julian:	We couldn't wash up in here. All the dishes are dirty.
Sandy:	Speak for yourself!
Mr Horne:	Well, well, I'm sorry, I'd have washed up if I'd known.

(Rentachap)

The use of the word *dish* to refer to an attractive man (or woman) is a commonly known slang word, which the *Round the Horne* audience[8] would have understood. Their laughter after Sandy's retort confirms that they were able to infer the secondary meaning – Sandy stating that he is both a 'dish', and he is clean. Two stereotypes are accessed here: first, the gay man as vain and appearance-oriented; and second, the gay man who is concerned with cleanliness.

However, in numerous interviews with Polari speakers, *dish* was described as referring to the anus. In this light, Sandy's assertion is taken to a deeper, more sexually-oriented level. It is extremely unlikely that the audience, other than committed Polari speakers, would have been aware of this third meaning.[9]

To give another example, Julian accesses multiple meanings of the word *plates*:

> *Julian*:   [His] scotches may be a bit naff, but his plates are bona.
>
> (Bona Dance)

Plates is a Polari word derived from rhyming slang (plates of meat = feet), but the Polari speakers I interviewed used *plate* to refer to oral sex. Although *plate* can be derived from the rhyming word 'fellate', in *A Dictionary of Rhyming Slang* (Franklyn 1960: 108) lists *plates* as being the stem of both 'plates of meat' and 'plate of ham', which is rhyming slang for *gam* – itself a shortened version of *gamahuche*, which also refers to oral sex. Thus, for Julian to say that someone's 'plates are bona', he could be referring to 'feet', or making a coded reference to oral sex.

According to Barry Took (personal correspondence, 1997) the writers were unaware of these additional 'sexual' meanings of *plate* and *dish*. Took cites *plate* as coming from Army or Navy slang, whereas *dishes* was used in the above sketch initially because of its alliterative function: 'all the dishes are dirty'. Although Took was unaware of the Polari meanings of *plate* and *dish*, that is not to say that Hugh Paddick and Kenneth Williams (the actors who played Julian and Sandy) would not have known them, as both would have had more involvement with the Polari-speaking gay subculture of the time, whereas Took has never claimed to be gay.

Interestingly, in the book *Round the Horne* (Took and Feldman 1974), which features scripts from the series, Sandy's comment 'speak for yourself' is missing, suggesting that it was an ad lib by Kenneth Williams, or was purposefully removed from the script for publication:

> *Mr Horne*:   Well do the best you can – here's the dishcloths.
> *Sandy*:   Ugh! Green and yellow – we can't be doing with that.
> *Mr Horne*:   What's the matter with green and yellow dishcloths?
> *Julian*:   Well, see for yourself, treash. We're wearing blue – doesn't match at all. No anyway, we couldn't wash up in here – all the dishes are dirty.
> *Mr Horne*:   Well I'm sorry, I'd have washed them if I'd known.
>
> (Took and Feldman 1974: 37)

In Williams' diary, he recounts an argument with Barry Took during the recording of *Round the Horne* in 1968, when Took complained that the sketches were becoming too 'rude':

Monday 8 April
'R.T.H.' Barry Took was in a v. funny mood and suddenly got quite
snappy about the show becoming filthy. 'We might as well write a
series called Get Your Cock Out,' he kept crying.

(Davies (ed.) 1994: 324)

It is possible, then, that Williams deliberately used his knowledge about
Polari in order to make controversial jokes that would not have been interpreted by the writers (and the censors), but would only have been
understood properly by well-versed Polari speakers.

While Julian and Sandy were the two 'obvious' homosexual constructs
in the sketches, their sexual identity was not the only one that was referenced. For example, their relationship with avuncular Kenneth Horne was
open to subversion. As the 'straight man' in both the sexual and comedic
senses of the word, Kenneth Horne's fascination with the two characters
was often archly commented upon with suspicion by Julian and Sandy:

Mr Horne:	I take it you're engaged in something pretty exciting at the moment?
Julian:	No, no, not really, we're just standing here with our hands on our heads talking to you.
Mr Horne:	Oh bold, very bold!
Sandy:	I wonder where he spends his evenings?

(Bona Prods)

Although Horne did not claim to be part of the same subculture as
Julian and Sandy, instead being representative of British mainstream
society, he occasionally used a phrase or word that indicated that he knew
what the other two were saying, causing them to gasp and exclaim that
he was very 'bold', a Polari euphemism meaning that he was not afraid
to use the knowledge about the gay community that he had picked up,
thereby implying that he might be gay:

Julian:	We are the Cecil Bs of the 16 De Mille.
Sandy:	Yes.
Julian:	Small budget pictures really.
Mr Horne:	Would I have vadered any of them do you think?
Sandy:	Oooh! He's got all the Polari hasn't he!
Julian:	I wonder where he picks it up?

(Bona Prods)

Horne's character's suspect sexuality and use of Polari is reminiscent of
the cautious gay identities described in Chapter 4, whereby gay men and
lesbians would use occasional Polari words to drop hints about their sexual
availability/orientation.

The stud/queen binary

Although the sketches are essentially a three-hander between Julian, Sandy and Kenneth Horne, a number of their friends are frequently invoked, which afford further constructions of homosexual identity. Most notable are Gordon (who becomes their manservant in one of the sketches), Reynard LaSpoon (a choreographer), Pandro Wildebeeste (a film director) and Jock (a sailor). Julian and Sandy's friends are therefore quite good reflections of the sorts of people who were connected with Polari: musical performers, actors and sailors:

Sandy:	No ducky, no. Reynard LaSpoon, the choreographer, he's a close personal in' he Jules?
Julian:	Oh, close. Very intime.
Sandy:	Very intime. Intimé you mean?
Julian:	Intimé. I mean intimate really.
Sandy:	Yes.
Julian:	Yes.
Sandy:	Lovely person.
Julian:	Get on very well with him. He's your type. He's all butch.
Sandy:	Yes. Mm, but questing.
Julian:	Mm.
Sandy:	Now you must have seen his work, Mr Horne, he does fantastic things on the television.
Mr Horne:	Oh?
Julian:	Yes, you know, they all come trolling on in form-hugging black and do evocative things with chairs and ladders and planks of wood.
Sandy:	Mm.
Julian:	He once did something with a bentwood chair that made Robert Helpmann's eyes stand out like organstops.
Sandy:	True, true, true.
Julian:	Both of them.
Sandy:	It's his own fault for standing so close. Course, course Reynard is classical trained.
Julian:	Oh yes.
Sandy:	Classical trained.

(Carnaby Street Hunt)

Reynard is one of Julian and Sandy's more bohemian and creative friends ('classical trained'), working variously as a female impersonator, choreographer, ballet dancer, advertiser and bar owner. His name is exotic, conjuring up an image of someone French (*renard* is French for the predatory 'fox'). When in drag, he is referred to as Renee LaSpoon. Julian and Sandy claim that he is an 'intimate' friend, euphemistically saying he is 'butch but questing' (curious?). Reynard is described as creative (although possibly pretentious or 'piss-elegant'), inhabiting the world of television and theatre.

While there is never any question of there being anything sexual between Reynard and the other main characters (the relationship being one of gay 'sisters'), a couple of other characters were represented as more masculine objects of desire:

Sandy:	That's Gordon, you see, he helps us out. He's sort of a masseur. He'll give you a good pummelling, I'll tell you!
Julian:	Soon as look at you.
Sandy:	He's a rough diamond, Mr Horne. But underneath, he's a rough diamond, I mean deep down, inside –
Julian:	He's absolute rubbish.
Sandy:	Absolute! Well he's not my friend!
Julian:	Well!
Sandy:	You brought him here.
Julian:	Down on his luck, that's what he said.
Sandy:	Down on his luck, was he?
Julian:	I'm like that. I can't turn a stranger away.
Sandy:	You can say that again. You can't. Yes, and you won't find anyone stranger than Gordon. No, but seriously he is a certified, he is a certified psychopath.
Mr Horne:	Don't you mean osteopath?
Sandy:	We know Gordon better than you do.

(Bona Bodybuilders)

Gordon appears personally once in the sketches, as a menacing man with a working-class accent and gruff voice. Most of the time he is presented as being hyper-masculine – wearing leather jeans, jackets, goggles and a helmet while riding a motorbike, and described as being like 'a kinky AA man' ('Bona Bijou Tourettes'). Gordon's sexuality is thus linked to an aggressive, leather-wearing S&M-practising homosexual identity. Politely, Sandy says that he is a 'rough diamond', whereas Julian is more cruel: 'he's absolute rubbish' ('Bona Bodybuilders'). Gordon's violent tendencies are elaborated on by descriptions of his one-time position as a steamroom attendant at South Mimms Slipper Baths A-gogo ('Bona Tax Consultants'): he's a 'sort of masseur. He'll give you a good pummelling', notes Sandy ('Bona Bodybuilders'). However, he's also a 'certified psychopath'.

Gordon never seems to have much money – and is vaguely associated with prostitution via his job as a 'masseur'. Later, when he is 'down on his luck', Julian and Sandy hire him as a 'gentleman's gentleman' ('Guided Tripettes'), although what his work entails is left largely to the imagination. In the introduction to a Julian and Sandy LP (*The Bona Album of*

Julian and Sandy, 1976), the pair remember how Gordon played the title role in the film *Motorcycle Au pair Boy*; however, Sandy recalls how he had his hand in the till.

Another character, Jock, is described as Julian's special friend. Jock is a WASP (White Anglo-Saxon Protestant) in the Merchant Navy and a 'great butch omee, bulging lallies, eke like a Greek God' ('Bona Rags'). Like his name (jock-strap, football jock), Jock is masculine, good with his hands (he can make ships in bottles), and plays rugby. He also has a disarming generosity which endears him to both Julian and Sandy – every time he comes into port he brings Julian a gift, while on Julian's birthday he presents him with a carafe of the appropriately named 'Merchant Adventurer'.

Jock and Gordon are both representations of 'trade' – ostensibly heterosexual (and often working-class) men who have sex with other men, but do not identify as gay. Gordon and Jock, when contrasted with Julian and Sandy, are good examples of what writers such as Waugh (1996) refer to as the *stud/queen* binary, a defining paradigm of 1960s constructions of queer masculinity. What makes the presentation of this binary in the sketches interesting is that they were not usually associated with Sunday afternoon family radio shows, but were generally found in marginalised, progressive art-forms such as the work of Andy Warhol and Paul Morrissey (particularly in films such as *My Hustler*, *Heat* and *Flesh*), or underground gay pornography: for example, the output from Bob Mizer's Athletic Model Guild in the United States and the drawings of Tom of Finland. Therefore, while it was groundbreaking to represent gay men in the *mainstream* media, even as effeminate stereotypes, to refer to masculine, leather-wearing sexually ambiguous men was exceptionally daring.

Conclusion

In part, it was the popularity of the Julian and Sandy sketches that allowed them to begin to go beyond simple camp stereotypes. Had they not been funny, they would have been dropped, but instead they became the most popular part of the programme, and because of this they were empowered, so they could start to be bolder and more experimental. Also, perhaps the fact that the sketches were in radio format rather than on television or film may have played some part in allowing (what were almost certainly considered at the time) such daring constructions of homosexual identity.

Because they were audio-only, the characters became distanced from the actors who played them. As the characters were merely voices it was up to the audience to create a mental or cartoon image of what Julian and Sandy would look like, rather than have a visual representation imposed upon them, which they may have found overwhelming or shocking. It's not just the Polari that makes Julian and Sandy mysterious, but also the fact that they couldn't be seen. Their radio presence therefore made them less threatening.[10]

While it is easy to dismiss Julian and Sandy as unfortunate, unsympathetic stereotypes who contributed to homophobic prejudice (and as I show in the following chapter, many of the early Gay Liberationists were not comfortable with such representations), I do not believe that it is useful to pass such a judgement, especially from a so-called 'enlightened' position of thirty years later. While, on the surface, Julian and Sandy appeared to kow-tow to the status quo, they were nobody's fools; and, as with the final lines of so many of their sketches, theirs was certainly the last laugh.

And, as well as constructing their own identities, Julian and Sandy subverted everyone. Whenever Mr Horne dropped the odd Polari word into his speech they never tired of asking 'I wonder where he picks it up?' Even the listeners, who over the weeks would have become familiar with the Polari phrases, would be implicated by their understanding of what was being said. Polari ensures that nobody's sexual identity is safe or clearly defined.

The sense of ambiguity surrounding Polari is one of the main themes running through this book. Sexuality can be acknowledged, hidden, subverted, categorised and re-categorised through Polari, never remaining stable, always open to innuendo and counter-innuendo. And related to this ambiguity is a sense of ambivalence. As a language that was used to criticise and eulogise others, there is always the possibility that the Polari speaker may be joking. An adept Polari speaker would litter every phrase with hidden meaning, level upon level of suggestion, designed purposefully to confuse rather than elucidate. It is often difficult to know what the Polari speaker really thinks – every plaudit a potential put-down, every handbag containing a hidden spiked stiletto heel. It is with this sense of ambivalence in mind that we turn to Polari's decline. Chapter 6 continues the story into the 1970s, by which time the 'camp language' was refusing to grow old gracefully, recast not as the risqué toy of repressed 1950's sexuality but as an embarrassing political problem.

6 Decline

Introduction

> I just use *vada*. And *bona* they use. But that's about all you hear
> nowadays. You don't hear a lot now. I don't know anyone who actu-
> ally speaks the whole Polari. Because they can be up-front and open
> about whatever they want to say.
>
> (Freddy Bateman, interviewed for *Word of Mouth*, BBC Radio 4
> 1995)

Polari probably reached its peak of popular exposure with the Julian and
Sandy sketches in the late 1960s. In the 1970s and 1980s there were few
examples of Polari to be found in the media. During the 1970s, one of
the few entertainers to use Polari on television was Larry Grayson,
although this occurred rarely. For example, in a 1976 episode of his
television family quiz programme *Larry Grayson's Generation Game*, he
interviewed a family with the surname of 'Eke', and made a number of
jokes along the lines of 'eke to eke' etc. Hugh Paddick appeared as a
Polari-speaking Robin Hood in the 1971 comedy film *Up the Chastity
Belt* (also starring Frankie Howerd as Lurkalot). Paddick played Robin in
the same way he had played Julian in *Round the Horne*:

Robin Hood:	Well ducky, what do you think of our camp?
Lurkalot:	Oh, I think that's the word for it.
. . .	
Lurkalot:	Robin, I think it's marvellous how you rob the rich and give to the poor.
Robin Hood:	You must be joking!
Lurkalot:	You don't?
Robin Hood:	Course we don't! Keep it all ourselves! How do you think we get all this bona drag?

A few words of Polari were spoken in an episode of the BBC sci-fi
series *Dr Who*, entitled *Carnival of Monsters*, in February 1973, where it
was described as a language used by travelling fairground people:

Vorg:	I bet he understands the Palare! Listen to this, Leta. The Telurian carnival lingo, watch! [To the Doctor] Palare the carny?
Doctor:	I beg your pardon?
Vorg:	Varda the bona palone?
Doctor:	I'm sorry? Erm.
Vorg:	Nanti dinarlì round here yer gills. Ha ha ha!
Doctor:	I must apologise. I'm afraid I do not understand your language.

In Les Dawson's comedy series for Yorkshire Television (also in the 1970s), Roy Barraclough played a cravat-wearing gay man called Mr Bona. Finally, Peter Wyngarde, who had played an effete detective in the programmes *Department S* and *Jason King*, released an album of songs in the 1970s that included a song called 'The Skinhead and the Hippy', which contains the Polari phrase 'troll the Dilly'. However, these are rare exceptions, and tended to be later variations on the comedy *queen* role created by Julian and Sandy.

At the start of the twenty-first century it is difficult to locate people who remember more than a few core words of Polari, and even harder to find those who actually speak it. This waning in popularity was not an overnight process, but one that happened over several decades.

In this chapter, I examine the period from the early 1970s to the late 1980s. As there are few examples of Polari during this time, it is difficult to show how gay men used Polari during this period in relation to their identities. Therefore, this chapter is more concerned with Polari's *lack* of a role in constructing gay identities. By examining the sorts of identities that were becoming popular and more attractive for gay men over this period, and relating them to how Polari came to be viewed, it is possible to hypothesise a number of reasons for Polari's decline. However, it's sensible to back up a little at this point – so far it's been presupposed that Polari wasn't used as much from the 1970s onwards. Before moving on, I will examine the evidence for whether or not this was the case.

Evidence of decline

Popper (Magee 1973: 22–5) states that, while it is possible to falsify an empirical generalisation, it is not possible to verify the same argument conclusively. Therefore, it is much more difficult to 'prove' that something no longer exists than it is to find evidence that it exists. Popper's famous example posits that if a black swan cannot be found then it is not possible to deduce that all swans are white. The same holds true when looking for evidence of Polari's decline. We may search for examples of Polari and find none, therefore concluding that it is no longer spoken. However, it is possible that we have not looked hard enough, or that speakers are unwilling or unable to come forward.

Therefore, it is pointless to claim that Polari was not spoken *at all* during the period under study in this chapter. To be able to assert that Polari has declined, I must be able to state first that I have looked in the right places and offered the right incentives for people to come forward. It should be clear to readers that Polari speakers do still exist – I *was* able to interview small numbers of people who still spoke or remembered Polari. In addition to my own research, during the 1990s the makers of radio and television programmes which examined Polari were also able to locate speakers who were willing to talk about their experiences of using it.

The majority of the speakers interviewed agreed that, during the 1970s and afterwards, Polari was used less than it had been in the 1950s–60s (by those who had had access to gay subcultures during that period). However, there were exceptions. One interviewee said that he still used it as much as ever, and had recently introduced it to several heterosexual work colleagues. Another interviewee asserts that in some informal contexts it is still used:

> There's lots of people in Brighton who know of, and there are still several people who still use it at dinner parties when they get a bit bevvied – you see *bevvied* is another one – getting drunk . . . People do still use it, but only if you're in an age group over 50.
>
> (David A)

This quote is interesting in that the speaker describes the situational context of Polari use as having changed. Compare it to the following quote from the same speaker, describing where Polari was spoken in the 1950s and 1960s: 'It was only spoken in the gay pubs because that was the only context where it would be understood. Basically it was in the pubs' (David A). David intimates that, instead of occurring in a public gay space (gay pubs), Polari is now used in a more private gay space[1] (dinner parties), which is likely to include friends of long-standing. His use of the word 'still' is informative: 'there are *still* several people who *still* use it', indicating that it was something that happened in the past, and the fact that people still use it is notable in itself.

As with David, many of the other interviewees from television and radio talk about Polari in the past tense, placing it firmly as something that had happened, rather than something that continues to happen. Two examples from speakers interviewed in Channel 4's *A Storm in a Teacup* (1993) – David McKenna: 'The sea queen would accentuate or elaborate a lot more on the Polari'; Michael James: I think the difference between the East End Polari and the West End Polari was the West End was fundamentally based on theatre.'

This use of tense could be in response to the way that questions concerning Polari's decline are phrased, e.g. 'When did you use to speak Polari?' already makes the assumption that it occurred in the past. Although

I do not have access to other interviewers' questions, during my own interviews I made clear the distinction between Polari as something that could have happened in the past or could still be happening, by asking questions such as '*If you stopped using Polari, when did you stop? Or do you still use it today?*' And the fact that the television and radio interviews were carried out with the express intention of charting 'gay history' also indicates that Polari is rooted in the past.

Finally, if Polari was still popular after the 1960s, then perhaps we would expect to find it being used regularly in UK gay magazines from the 1970s, 1980s and 1990s. However, examples are rare, especially since the 1980s. Occasional core vocabulary Polari words such as 'bona' appeared in *Gay News* in the 1970s, but in isolated contexts.

In the following section, existing theories of language death and language transmission are considered and placed in relation to Polari, bearing in mind its status as an anti-language. The remainder of the chapter contains an analysis of several possible contributory factors which explain the collective shunning of Polari by the British gay subculture. Then there is an examination of the ways that gay identities began to evolve during the same period, relating this change to Polari's eventual decline.

Language death

The term 'language death' invokes the concept of language being a biological entity – nineteenth-century theories about language considered this to be the case. Jespersen (1922: 65) cites Bopp (1836: 1) as claiming that languages were 'organic natural bodies' which 'develop as possessing an inner principle of life, and gradually die out because they do not understand themselves any longer, and therefore cast off or mutilate their members or forms'.

More recent theories of language death stress the importance of dominant languages. Aitchison (1991: 198) suggests that languages die, not because people forget how to speak them, but because a more dominant language ousts the old one, usually for political and social reasons. McMahon (1994: 285) defines language death as involving a 'transfer of allegiance of part of a population from a language which has been native in the area, to a more recently introduced language in which the indigenous population has become bilingual'. A distinction can be made between language *suicide* and language *murder*. In the former, speakers of an old language gradually begin to use linguistic items from a dominant or prestigious language until the identity of the old language is destroyed. Studies of language suicide tend to focus on situations where a creole is supplanted by its parent, to the extent that McMahon (1994: 287) claims that language suicide is almost synonymous with decreolisation.

Language murder is much more dramatic: the dominant language suppresses and ousts the old one, usually beginning with a decrease in the number of people who speak the language. The change to the dominant language is not a case of gradual borrowing. McMahon (1994: 291) describes the only sort of gradation as being the speaker's loss of proficiency in the declining language, whereas Aitchison (1991: 205) notes that the few speakers who are left tend to be 'semi-speakers': they can speak after a fashion, but forget linguistic items, make errors and use a limited number of sentence patterns. Aitchison (1991: 208) points out that language suicide usually occurs when the two languages in question are similar, while language murder occurs when the two languages are different.

Both Aitchison and McMahon underscore the fact that, in language death, parents cease to 'pass on' a particular language to their children, and as a result it is younger generations who cease to use the language first, instead learning the more prestigious language, usually at school. Parents may be complicit in this, feeling it is better for their children to speak the more prestigious language (Aitchison 1991: 205).

However, low prestige alone is not a good predictor of language death (Ramat 1983). Economic changes can lead to a sociolinguistic 'tip' (Dorian 1981) which can result in the rapid growth of the dominant language, accelerating a community's shift to using it. Aitchison (1991: 209) concludes that language death is triggered by a lack of fulfilment of social needs, and is not due to linguistic deficiencies in the structure of the dead language.

Another distinction in characterising language death is in terms of *sudden* and *gradual* death (Nettle and Romaine 2000: 51–4). In sudden death, a language dies intact as its speakers die out suddenly – for example, following a natural disaster. In gradual death, the process can take several generations, going through a period when it is not used for all the purposes that it was previously. However, Nettle and Romaine (2000: 52) note that it can be difficult to pinpoint the absolute end of any language, and therefore the distinction between sudden and gradual death can be blurred, as I believe is the case for Polari. As with Polari, 'rememberers' may survive the active use of a language, even recalling aspects of a language that they never fully learnt or used. While some of my interviewees can be classed as Polari speakers or ex-Polari speakers, others are perhaps better classed as 'rememberers'.

It is debatable, however, whether Polari can be considered a language. As I concluded in Chapter 1, its aspect of lexical replacement for certain topics, reduced grammatical structure and covert status more readily earns it the label of *anti-language* rather than language. Also, Polari is always learnt as a second language – unlike the languages discussed by Aitchison and McMahon above, it is not passed from parent to child, although there is a tradition of established members of the gay subculture teaching Polari to newer members. Many Polari speakers would have died in the period 1970–90, and notably after 1980, Aids is likely to have contributed to the premature deaths of earlier generations of Polari speakers.

While the death of a generation alone is not enough to ensure that a language variety will die with it, when added to other factors, the inevitable mortality of a small existing set of speakers does become a conclusive reason why the language stops being used. In viewing Polari's decline in terms of language death, it is therefore useful to examine what (if anything) replaced Polari as a language variety used by gay men in the UK. This topic is discussed at the end of this chapter.

Over-exposure

It really became like everything else. Everyone does it. So there's no more mystery about it.

(John, interviewed in Porter and Weeks 1991: 138)

The popularity of Julian and Sandy is perhaps the most obvious factor in Polari's decline. Normally, it would be expected that exposure of words or phrases via the media would result in a marked *increase* in their use (at least in the short term), but I would argue that this would apply more to general slang terminology such as *yuppie*. As Polari was an anti-language, its importance was rooted in the gay subculture, with words and a sensibility that were overtly gay. Therefore, mainstream society's discovery of Polari via the media would not have made it something new and attractive to be incorporated into the mainstream, although, with that said, a few Polari words have at different times crossed over into mainstream slang; the most obvious example being *naff*. Lucas (1997: 88) notes that Polari was exoticised for heterosexual listeners, and as a form of comedy it had a limited appeal to a larger audience. While the mainstream audience may have found Julian and Sandy hilarious for a number of reasons, it is unlikely that their catchphrases would have been integrated into everyday speech.

Another look at the Polari words that were used in the Julian and Sandy sketches is useful in determining its effect on the mainstream audience. As described in Chapter 5, Julian and Sandy used only a small proportion of Polari words (about an eighth of those in the dictionary given in the Appendix) – the Polari:English ratio found within the sketches was 1:41, or one Polari word for 41 English ones.

So, by concentrating on a small, core Polari vocabulary, Barry Took and Marty Feldman were able to make the sketches accessible to a wide audience. Also, importantly, their own knowledge of Polari was not encyclopaedic; Kenneth Williams seemed to be more adept at the language. For example, Took remembers that Williams used to have a long Polari phrase that he'd work into the script:

Sandy: Jule, get on the piano.
Julian: Shall I?

> *Sandy*:   Get on the piano, order lau your luppers on the strillers bona.
> Yes, sit down Mr Horne, we'll give you a sample Mr Horne ...
>
> (Bona Guesthouse)

The phrase 'order lau your luppers on the strillers bona' means 'go and play something good for us on the piano'. When interviewed, Barry Took explained that when Kenneth Williams used to say this, none of the other members of the cast, or the writers used to have any idea what he meant, but they were all far too embarrassed to admit it. So the phrase was allowed to remain.

However, such bursts of concentrated Polari were exceptional, and most of the Julian and Sandy scripts were in English with small, isolated occurrences of Polari appearing occasionally. The following example from 'Bona Guesthouse' illustrates how audiences were 'taught' Polari via a method which almost resembles the cloze tests of language learning: a 'fill-in-the-blanks' game, whereby most listeners would be able to contextualise meanings with ease:

> *Sandy*:   [singing] I dream of Jeannie with the light brown riah.
> *Julian*:   Yes, then there was [sings] Bless this lattie, butch and stout.
> *Sandy*:   Or what about our duet?
> *Julian*:   Oh yes.
> *Both*:   [singing] We'll troll beside you through the world today.
> *Sandy*:   Lovely!
> *Julian*:   Tears to the eyes.
> *Sandy*:   And the –
> *Julian*:   And the big finish –
> *Sandy*:   The big finish.
> *Julian*:   Yes.
> *Both*:   [singing] Some day she'll troll along. The palone I love.
>
> (Bona Guesthouse)

If the writers of *Round the Horne* had been aware of Polari words for numbers, money, sex etc., they had to choose with care the ones they used. Polari originated from a variety of backgrounds, and its lexicon tends to reflect this, having words that would be relevant and frequently used in context by the various groups who contributed to it – thus tramps would use words concerning money, food, lodgings etc., sailors would use words related to their profession (taken from Lingua Franca), prostitutes and homosexuals would use words related to money or sex, and show business or circus people would use the entertainment-related words. Julian and Sandy changed professions every week (although they tended towards the service industries), and so they could not be bound by words that would relate to one type of trade. Words directly indexing sex would have also been taboo, which perhaps demonstrates one of the strongest differences between *Round the Horne*'s use of Polari and the way it would have been spoken by real-life homosexual men and lesbians. The *Round the Horne* version of Polari is sanitised and simplified – necessarily so, for the demands and sensibilities of the 1960s British radio audience.

It is also likely that the words related to money and numbers would have been too complicated for audiences to learn – in any case, Barry Took was unaware of any Polari words for numbers or money. The large number of Polari words in existence overall would have been too complex for the audience to follow. By concentrating on a core vocabulary, which could be used and reused in a number of different contexts, Polari was made quickly accessible to the radio-listening British public who had not previously been aware of its existence. Even if viewers were not able to understand what all of the words meant, translations were provided in a *Round the Horne* annual (Took and Feldman 1974: 12).

So Julian and Sandy ensured that those who had no access to the UK gay subculture would have become aware of Polari, albeit at a most basic level. Even if they were not able to comprehend exactly what was being said, it is likely that they would have recognised Polari for what it was: some sort of secret code used by homosexuals. And similarly, within the gay subculture, those who were not 'in' on the joke would gradually have become aware of it. There was no prestige in talking Polari when the *naffs* who lived next door were imitating Julian and Sandy's 'bona to vada your dolly old eek'. Something that had once been delightfully obscure and special was now public property. Polari, initially attractive to its users because of this obscurity, would have become publicised out of existence.

However, while Julian and Sandy may have made Polari too popular for the original speakers to use it, the newer set of speakers who had just started to pick it up could have just as easily let it go again. One interviewee, John E, cites the decline of Polari as being related directly to the fact that, by the beginning of the 1970s, *Round the Horne* had *stopped* making new episodes. With the demise of its last two champions, Julian and Sandy, Polari had become another fad on its way out.

The Wolfenden Report and the 1967 Sexual Offences Act

> I think it [Polari] stopped when the gay scene became so open. It changed incredibly ... People do still use it, but only if you're in an age group over 50. When you're at dinner parties and that'll come out. 'I've had a bona day!' or theatrical people who are like that.
>
> (David A)

In 1967 (the same year that *Round the Horne* was at its peak, winning an award for best comedy radio programme), the legal situation for the average gay man improved with the implementation of the Wolfenden Report's recommendations of ten years earlier. The Sexual Offences Act was passed under Harold Wilson's Labour government on 4 July 1967 and received Royal Assent on 27 July 1967. The Act legalised homosexual acts in private between consenting adult males over the age of 21.

With the partial decriminalisation of homosexuality, for the first time in centuries being homosexual would not lead to arrest. Fred Dyson, a miner, describes how he was on a bus with a friend when he heard the news:

> I got hold of him and I give him a great big kiss and everybody on the bus were looking but I weren't bothered. I just kissed him. I said: 'You can all look, it's legal now.'
>
> (Jivani 1997: 149)

From that point on, being openly gay became slightly easier, and with this new freedom, there was less of a need for secrecy. John F notes that the change allowed breweries to open pubs and bars legally, specifically for gay people. Such businesses often proved to be lucrative:

> The gay culture suddenly became more open. There were established gay pubs and bars. Some of the big brewers actually stuck by and kept them open because they brought in revenue, the violence level was low ... so it wasn't an encumbrance or embarrassment or a burden to them. There were plenty of straight landlords, particularly women, who were quite prepared to run them, because they loved all the gay guys ... The actual culture of staying in this in-built language suddenly died out because there was nobody actually living it.
>
> (John F)

As Harris (1997) argues, capitalism helped to propel homosexuality into the open. The 'secret subculture' had been reinvented as the 'gay scene'. However, the existing stigma of homosexuality was not eradicated overnight, nor did the Sexual Offences Act give homosexual men the same rights as heterosexuals. Warner (1982: 84) points out the inconsistency in logic over the male age of consent:

> having dismissed the 'seduction theory', the [Wolfenden] committee opted for 21 because to fix the lower age would lay young men 'open to attentions and pressures of an undesirable kind'. And yet, four paragraphs earlier, the committee had commented, 'there comes a time when a young man can properly be expected to "stand on his own feet" and we find it hard to believe that he needs to be protected from would-be seducers more carefully than a girl does', clearly implying 16 was the appropriate age.

The Act did not apply to members of the armed forces, merchant seamen, residents of the Channel Islands or the Isle of Man.

As a result of this half measure, and taking the lead from the Stonewall riots in New York which led to the formation of the Gay Liberation Front (GLF), David (1997: 225) dates Britain's first gay rights movement march as taking place in November 1970. The GLF created a new vocabulary – 'gay' became widely used to describe people who were attracted to their own sex, replacing the derogatory 'queer' or clinically neutral 'homosexual'. While 'gay' had been used in the US since the 1950s, in the UK at least, it had previously been associated with the upper classes and up-market drinking establishments (Weeks 1977: 190). Concepts such as 'coming out' and 'gay pride' were also developed by the GLF.

As well as being a movement of human sexual liberation, gay liberation was also connected to, influenced by, and in some ways paralleled the civil rights and students' movements of the 1960s, and the women's liberation movement of the 1960s/1970s (McIntosh 1997: 234). The traditional view of gender was linked to homo/hetero roles, in that men were supposed to love women, and vice versa. Hegemonic masculinity and femininity were related to loving members of the opposite sex. Young (1972: 7) put gay liberation as being a 'struggle against sexism' – the belief/practice that sex(ual orientation) gives the right to privileges/powers/roles to some. Sexism was seen as responsible for the creation of homo/hetero and masculine/feminine identities which place heterosexual men in a position of privilege, at the expense of others (i.e. for heterosexual men to maintain their position of power, other identities such as 'female' and 'gay' must be constructed as being less powerful). For Young, gay liberation was going to enable people to break free of their narrow roles and express their bisexual, androgynous nature in equal relationships and social bonds.

With the introduction of GLF politics, many people *wanted* to be as open as possible about being gay. This openness would have meant that Polari's protective status in maintaining the closet would have appeared less attractive. But by this time Polari wasn't just about secrecy, it also allowed the performance of a camp sensibility, and that should still have given it some currency. However, camp itself was under attack – from within gay ranks.

The backlash against camp

> Because it hasn't been used in the last ten years that much. I think nowadays people tend to think that it's too camp. They think it's silly, *naff* – that's another one [Polari word] isn't it?
>
> (David A)

As a result of new gay rights movements, there was a backlash against a number of established notions of gay identity which had developed over the 1950s and 1960s. Up to the 1970s, the most well-known 'homophile' movement in the UK had been the Campaign for Homosexual Equality

(CHE). Beginning in 1954 as the North-Western Committee for Homosexual Law Reform, the CHE had similar goals to the 'respectable' hat-and-tie-wearing Mattachine Society in America. Jivani (1997: 164) describes the CHE model for gay men as a 'distorted reflection of the heterosexual family', or respectability. Differences between the CHE and GLF are well-documented (see Figure 6.1 below). While the CHE have been positioned as desiring assimilation into mainstream society and the GLF were supposedly concerned about community building around the notion of gay identity, both groups tended to have converging views around the 'problem' of camp, effeminate men.

Camp identities were seen by some activists as being about as far removed from politics as possible, and therefore useless in the struggle for equality. In a now-famous essay titled 'Notes on "Camp"', Susan Sontag argued that camp sensibility was 'disengaged, depoliticized or at least apolitical' (1966: 277).[2] Britton's critique of Sontag (1979: 12) is harsher, describing camp as an anaesthetic, 'allowing one to remain inside oppressive relations while enjoying the illusory confidence that one is flouting them'.

In pre-Queer politics, certain aspects of camp were seen as degrading, both to gay men, and to women – the belief appears to have been that gay men, by acting like women, were degrading women as well as themselves. The Gay Liberation Front's *Manifesto* (1971, revised 1979: 9) complained that many gay men and women had restricted their lives by compulsive role-playing of 'butch' and 'femme'. While they viewed gay people as being outside the boundaries of the mainstream gender-role system, the imposition of gender roles on themselves and each other was seen to be 'bad'. 'Butch' was therefore an oppressing identity, while 'femme' was constructed as being oppressed, as expressed in the Gay Liberation Front's *Manifesto* (1971, revised 1979: 9): 'those gay men and

Figure 6.1　Dissenting adults

Lunch magazine issue 45 (Bone (ed.) 1972: 19)

women who are caught up in the femme role must realise, as straight women increasingly do, that any security this brings is more than offset by their loss of freedom'.

So with the arrival of gay liberation in the 1960s and 1970s, a number of gay men and lesbians began to show a growing disapproval of camp gay identities. An anonymous letter to *Gay News* in 1976 spoke out in disgust about Quentin Crisp and 'camp':

> [Quentin Crisp] has set the 'gay' world back twenty years . . . As far as I am concerned, being 'gay' means that I am perfectly normal, with one slight difference – I prefer to see another man. I can . . . see no point in trying to ape a female. There are a great deal like me. Our local has a good number of 'affairs' and although in the 'Camp' life it would be boring, our lovers chat about food, clothes and the men about cars, television etc, just as normal couples do . . . There is no need to slap us and the hets in the face with 'high camp' . . . Quentin, keep it to yourself. No need to write books about it, have it on the box. Who wants to know?
>
> (Higgins 1993: 208)

As Sidney (one of the Polari speakers I interviewed) noted: 'people were recoiling from effeminacy'. Another reason for the rejection of camp is that it was seen as being sexually unattractive. American gay magazines from the 1950s onwards, such as *Physique Pictorial*, consisted mainly of black-and-white photographs of muscular, working-class young men posing nude or in jockstraps. By the 1970s, these images were beginning to be enshrined as ideals of authentic masculinity and sexiness. A letter to 1970s gay magazine, *Quorum*, complained about a spate of models who were deemed unsatisfactory:

> There are 14 nudes in [issue] No. 1, and few of them have any great appeal for me. And why so many with women's hairdos? A true homosexual prefers to look upon a virile physique with a clean-cut aspect of a real man in every respect – not a male body with a top-heavy head of feminine hair.
>
> (S. H. quoted in Baker 1972: 38)

Mainstream camp entertainers such as John Inman (from the television comedy *Are You Being Served?*) and Larry Grayson (from *Larry Grayson's Generation Game*) were loved by mainstream audiences, who found them to be harmless and funny. Such entertainers echoed Julian and Sandy from the previous decade: '[Julian and Sandy] were no threat – they weren't going to steal your husband or demand equality' (Maureen Lipman, BBC Radio 4 1998).

However, attitudes towards blatantly effeminate men were not viewed so tolerantly by gay liberationists in the 1970s. In the book of the television series *Are You Being Served?*, David Walker, a campaigner for gay rights since 1969, remarks on John Inman's camp role:

> When this flamboyant image screamed across the screen, it was like a nail in the coffin of what we were trying to achieve. The majority of people saw gay men as being very waspish, skipping around the place with limp wrists, and that's exactly what they saw on *Are You Being Served?*. Of course there were protests, because if you want a large section of the community to be accepted, sending them up like that does no end of damage.
>
> (Rigelsford *et al.* 1995: 29)

The *Daily Express* reported on a campaign to have Inman removed from the series:

> Are you being unfair? Actor John Inman – 'I'm free' – has angered homosexuals with his portrayal of the limp-wristed shop assistant, Mr Humphries, in the B.B.C. TV series 'Are You Being Served?' Members of the Campaign for Homosexual Equality plan to picket his concert appearances in protest over the mincing high-pitched voiced Mr Humphries. They began their protest at Brighton by handing out leaflets before his show at the town's Dome Centre Hall. A campaign official said yesterday 'He is contributing to the television distortion of the image of homosexuals.' They complained that he depicts homosexuals as . . . sexually obsessed, too extravagant in manner and too keen to dress up in drag.
>
> (Wigg 1977: 5)

As well as Inman and Grayson, other 'camp' comedians such as Frankie Howerd, Charles Hawtrey and Dick Emery also came under attack. Apart from the limp-wristed mannerisms, the outrageous clothing and mincing walk, it was the language of such men of which campaigners disapproved. Writing in *Lunch* (a CHE-based gay magazine of the 1970s) in 1972, Mary McIntosh sums up what many gay rights campaigners were starting to think about 'camp' language:

> camp is a form of minstrellisation . . . parlare is a product of a culture that is deeply ambivalent and even while it celebrates effeminacy, 'obviousness' and casual promiscuous sexuality (precisely the elements that the straight world most abhors) [it] can never really accept that these are good . . . The terms of address that are distinctively gay are always used in a negative mocking way: 'Ooh, get you Duchess'.
>
> (McIntosh 1972: 8)

Although McIntosh herself did not seem to be against Polari, she acknowledged that many of the new liberationists were uncomfortable with 'jokes' about straight values from the gay ghetto, preferring to dig them out and defuse them:

> In doing so they become very self-conscious about language, aware that if the way people see the world is to be reformed then language, the means by which we share our understanding, must be reformed too ... In some groups there is a reluctance to abstain altogether from parlare ... new language ... affirms new ideas.
>
> (McIntosh 1972: 9)

In a response to McIntosh's article published in a later issue of *Lunch*, Jonathan Raban was more openly critical of Polari, foreshadowing Burton's sentiments (1979: 23) that Polari did not help to hide one's sexuality but instead paraded and ghettoised it. Raban warned that such 'toys' would lead to 'little freedom for anyone':

> Gay slang[3] is a means of group self-advertisement; like full drag or the one-piece leather suit, it is a succinct way of putting one's propensities on show. In large cities ... we all have to do this to some extent; we have to communicate with others with brevity and speed, in an instant code of badges and symbols. But the obvious trap facing any member of a recognisable minority is that his symbols will consume him; that his identity will disappear into the narrow funnel of his clothes and slang. He will become no more than a shrill mouthpiece for a sectarian lobby, determined, in the case of the homosexual, by a language of body parts and fucking ... Isn't it time for everybody to tidy their toys away, to put the old uniforms in the trunk in the attic, or donate them to Oxfam, and to take a few, at least, of the bricks out of the walls of the ghetto?
>
> (Raban 1973: 17)

In addition, there were concerns about certain Polari words which can be viewed as sexist or racist. Just as some scholars have argued that gay male drag is misogynist, resulting in an exaggerated and mocking female impersonation (or performance) (e.g. Frye 1983, Tyler 1991, White 1980) Polari's appropriation of female pronouns and names begged the question 'What place do "real" women have in the Polari speaker's world-view?' In parodying women, gay men could be seen to be mocking them. The word *fish*, used disparagingly to refer to women, suggested a particularly unpleasant answer. Additionally, words that categorise people according to the colour of their skin or nationality (such as *chinois* and *schvartzer*) were deemed as containing a distinctly racist flavour:

> although gay slang is the vocabulary of people who are themselves outcasts from the straight culture, it is also sexist, classist and racist,

and the existence of terms that reflect such attitudes binds us to the same value system that makes us outcasts.

(Stanley 1974: 386)

Sagarin (1970: 41) describes how the more 'manly', well-adjusted homosexuals established 'role distance' between themselves and the 'exhibitionistically effeminate screaming' *queens*. Blachford (1981: 189) claims that one of the reasons why these 'deviant' homosexuals were rejected for not fitting into a prescribed pattern of masculine behaviour was because of their use of language:

their slang ties them to the dominant order and offers no challenge to a society which labels all homosexuals as deviants and oppresses them as such, although effeminate homosexuals are more likely to be singled out for the brunt of any attack because of their visibility.

(Blachford 1981: 190)

Finally, there is a sense of discrimination or objectification within the Polari-speaker's world, not only relating to race and gender, but also to age and attractiveness, which can be deemed to be against the humanist philosophy of gay liberation. It could be argued that the word *chicken* sums up the gay male attitude towards attractive younger males – to be consumed sexually, like food. Not only are young and/or attractive people objectified and sexualised within the context of Polari gossip and cruising, but older and/or unattractive people are reviled or ignored. Such discrimination was addressed by the Gay Liberation Front's *Manifesto* (1971, revised 1979: 9):

gay men are very apt to fall victim to the cult of youth – those sexual parades in the 'glamorous' meat-rack bars of London and New York, those gay beaches of the South of France and Los Angeles haven't anything to do with liberation . . . these gay men dread the approach of age, because to be old is to be 'ugly' and with their youth they lose also the right to love and be loved, and are valued only if they can pay.

Stanley's (1974) solutions to the conflict within the gay subculture involving slang were either to reject the gay slang value system completely, or to embrace and redefine such words to give them newer, positive meanings, in the same way as words such as 'black' have been embraced by African-Americans. While it may have been possible to reclaim some words – and reclaiming of words such as *queer* has occurred – the problem with Polari wasn't just its lexicon but the gossipy, evaluative way in which it was often used. With hindsight, it's clear that getting rid of Polari hasn't stopped some gay men from practising the art of bitchiness, but it was a convenient enough scapegoat at the time.

The generation gap

After the 1970s, many of the original speakers of Polari had died, as several of my interviewees intimated. However, as with all forms of language, would it not be expected that the older speakers would have passed the language down to younger gay men? After Wolfenden, it should have been easier than before to join the gay subculture. If anything, there should have been more potential users of Polari in the 1970s and 1980s. However, this was not the case: 'It was ... Polari was an old person's language I think' (Sidney). Sidney points out another aspect of Polari that was deemed to be unattractive: it was used by a group of men who were gradually ageing. The newer generation of gay men, who had grown up in a relatively more liberal political climate than the older Polari users, were simply not that interested in associating with this group, who were considered unfashionable:

> A lot of younger people didn't want to associate with older people, which to some extent I can understand, because I went to discos, when I was 20, 22, 23, I didn't want someone who was 50 or 60 there. It was all right in a pub, but you wanted to let your hair down and go ... But when you've got some old chap who's greatly overweight, with 15 double chins, he's got a naff haircut and is half bald, in green leather trousers and Hush Puppies and a white shirt, it doesn't work, and ... it's like sitting next to a family in an airport when the children are screaming, you might be going first class but it ruins the whole flight. These things do make a difference.
>
> (Jim E)

The Gay Liberation Front was strongly linked to youth – for example, being linked to the student protest movements of the 1960s. Camp, as discussed in the previous section, was seen as 'yesterday' as well as being linked to middle-aged gay men. So Polari had been over-exposed in the media, made unnecessary by Wolfenden, criticised by the liberationists as one of the prime components of camp, and finally viewed as 'naff' by younger gay men. It was clear that talking about someone's *bona lallies* did not fit in with the new type of gay identity that was on offer – an identity that was about as far away from Polari as possible.

New masculine identities

> The American West Coast was Mecca for European queens in the 1970s; American-butch the dominant gay style.
>
> (Gardiner 1997: 148)

Camp was not completely eschewed during the 1970s. British pop stars such as David Bowie and Mick Jagger typified the androgynous, makeup-wearing, strutting, sexually ambiguous identities that were popular with both straight and gay audiences, and were eventually incorporated into the rebellious punk look of the mid–late 1970s. However, while a proportion of straight men were beginning to explore their 'feminine sides', a significant number of gay men had begun to move to a diametrically oppositional performance of gender, that of hyper-masculinity or 'butch-ness', as signified by the 'Marlboro Man' used in cigarette advertise-ments (Bronski 1998: 97). So, although camp identities never went away completely, during the 1970s and 1980s a compelling 'butch' alternative was offered, coming typically from America, where the introduction of cheap flights to New York by Freddie Laker allowed British gay men to consume the new culture for themselves:

> People were wearing hard construction helmets and cut-off jeans and work boots with rolled down socks and skimpy T-shirts in Scotland, in a climate which even in the summertime is pretty appalling . . . We felt international, we felt being gay was a passport to anywhere in the world . . . I don't think that he [Freddie Laker] knows how many young gay guys he flew virginally across the Atlantic to America to be absolutely stunned and astonished by the scene they saw over there. They brought back from the States a lot of the music and a lot of the attitudes, a lot of the politics and a lot of the social dynamics of the American gay scene.
>
> (Derek Ogg, quoted in Jivani 1997: 173–4)

Jivani (1997: 174) explains that the American gay subculture, being more advanced, complete and self-promoting than the British gay subculture, provided a political and cultural template for British gay men. The Americans had shown that, in uniting, they were beginning to achieve economic and political power – for example, gay men and lesbians were winning political office. However, as Spencer (1995: 373) notes, the over-riding social ethic of the time was for sexual self-fulfilment. With gay liberation, the concept of homosexuality as gender deviance was weak-ened, provoking a sense of pride and masculinity in gay men.

Much of this identity was focused around the adoption of what Blachford (1981: 192) calls *expressive artefacts* and *concrete objects*. Clothes were the most common means of expression: button-up Levis, tight jeans, chaps, leather, handle-bar moustaches, cropped or short hair, uniforms, work boots and checked shirts. The word *clone* was introduced into gay vernacular, referring to a uniformly masculine gay identity: butch, muscular, good-looking and 'well hung'. With minor modifications, the clone identity still exists today. Going to the gym became a popular pastime. Gardiner (1997: 162) points out that, by the 1980s, the London leather scene had become increasingly popular among gay men, with the opening of a specialist shop and a members-only club. Other gay identities, relating to clothing (rubber), physical appearance (bear – see below), or sexual practice (S&M, CP (corporal punishment), water-sports) were becoming more acceptable (at least within the gay subculture) and were presented as alternatives to effeminacy, although they were generally reworkings on the theme of the masculine male. A good proportion of gay pornography since the 1970s has presented images of 'heterosexual' masculine men having gay sex. David (1997: 253) describes the change to masculinity as the result of 'burgeoning self-confidence' which 'ineradicably replaced the simpering Julian and Sandy stereotype'. Rather than emulate 'Jules and Sand', gay men tended towards other characters from the sketches: gruff Gordon, the 'kinky AA man' and Jock, the disarming, rugby-playing Scottish sailor. Most importantly, by the 1970s, ideas of the types of men who could find each other attractive within the gay subculture had changed. The stud/queen binary of the 1960s and earlier (Waugh 1996) was replaced by the notion of 'real men' who were attracted to other 'real men'. The camp homosexual lost ground, becoming barred from the landscape of gay imagery.

The descriptive codes that functioned within Polari – useful for describing sexual preferences and people – have since been replaced. For some, handkerchief codes became popular – gay men would wear a coloured handkerchief in their pocket, on the left side usually signifying 'active' and on the right meaning 'passive'. Keys worn on the right or left side would also carry the same significance. Different coloured handkerchiefs corresponded to a variety of sexual preferences: green: prostitution; light blue: oral sex; pink: orgies etc. More recently, on the Internet there are various codes that gay men can use as e-mail signatures to reveal their appearance, personality and sexual preferences. These are known as *twink* or *bear* codes. Attractive, young, muscular gay males are known as twinks, after the twinkie bar, a sweet American snack, whereas older, hairy, tubby gay men are referred to as bears. The codes appear as a series of letters and/or numerals which stand for various attributes, so 'k' means kinky. Addition and subtraction symbols after each letter would indicate to what extent this attribute is true of a particular person. For example, the bear code B4 k++ s+ c– t– w++ r– p would signify a bear with a mostly full beard, extremely sexually open, acts like a 'bear cub' but isn't, is small, very fat, prefers indoor activities and has some idiosyncrasies.

Bronski (1998: 102) categorises the appearance of new codes as an 'intense need and willingness to construct a new visible, unavoidably blatant language of masculinity'. However, where Polari was primarily a language variety that was used for secretly exposing *others* (via gossiping about those nearby to friends), handkerchief and twink codes exposed the *self*, by advertising preferences to those who knew the code. While Polari could also be used discreetly in order to 'fish' for a suspected gay identity, the new codes focused on distinctions between numerous possible gay identities or practices.

A non-verbal code was also an easy means of constructing masculinity. Anonymous silent sexual encounters could be facilitated, where each participant could project the illusion of masculinity on to the other, without having to say anything that might conflict with the outward physical appearance. Butch clothes can be donned, bodies can be exercised into masculine shapes, but the voice is harder to change. But, like the makeup worn by Quentin Crisp and Peter Burton, for Spencer (1995: 375) the 'butch imagery' was equally artificial – the result of gay men caricaturing a society that still excluded them.

Conclusion: changing identities

Although Polari is better categorised as a language variety rather than a language, it appears that its decline followed the pattern of language murder more closely than that of language suicide. Its demise was relatively rapid, and it was not the case of a new language gradually taking the place of an old one. Initially, Polari had been viewed as a prestigious language variety by its speakers. However, as it came to be seen as less prestigious there was a shift back to English – but, unlike the cases of decreolisation that are typical of language suicide, Polari speakers did not have to learn English gradually and begin to incorporate it into their speech – English was already familiar to them. Many of the remaining speakers of Polari are 'semi-speakers' – remembering words with difficulty, and prone to errors.

While this chapter has discussed a number of possible reasons for Polari's decline, it is possible to link each factor to the gradual change in how gay identity was perceived, both by the gay subculture and by mainstream society. For example, Polari's over-exposure (and subsequent redundancy) to mainstream heterosexual society as a result of the Julian and Sandy sketches would not have been possible had the British public been unready to 'accept' two boisterous gay men visiting them via their radio every Sunday. The growth of tolerance, and the partial discrimination of homosexuality in the UK, led to a reworking of homosexual identity as gay identity within the subculture. Polari was associated with secrecy, repression and effeminacy. It was also viewed at best as apolitical, and at worst as disrespectful towards other identities.

By embracing an alternative masculine identity, some gay men emulated what they found to be most attractive in heterosexual males. There was belief that acceptance would come more readily if camp identities were suppressed. And the new gay masculine identities originated in America – where Polari was barely known. As a curiously British phenomenon, Polari was one of the first casualties of gay globalisation.

The gay subculture still retained a few unique words – a number of the original Polari words had been borrowed from, or originated alongside, a more standard and well-known 'homosexual slang', and these words: *trade, chicken, cruise, cottage, butch, camp* etc. remained in this general gay vocabulary. Many Polari words had mainstream English counterparts (*riah, bona, eke, vada*), but the words that survived tended to have no real English equivalents within mainstream society. The major difference between these and many of the Polari words that had been derived from homosexual slang was that the latter were more useful in defining gay experience (e.g. relating to sexual acts between men), and were unlikely to have exact equivalents in English. They were not translations of existing concepts, but rather descriptions of phenomena that were unique and important mainly to the gay subculture. Such words were retained by the gay subculture and many are known and continue to be used by gay subcultures in the UK. Interestingly, some of these surviving words are also used by (or initially derived from) American gay subcultures – *butch, camp, cruise* and *trade*. The definition of such words as 'Polari', 'gay slang' or both was always tenuous, even at the height of Polari's popularity. With Polari's decline, these words shifted back into the category of 'gay slang'.

With hindsight, it's easy to understand why Polari was considered passé, politically incorrect or silly in the 1970s and 1980s. The new liberationists wanted to distance themselves from old camp habits, whereas masculinity offered a chance at 'normality', as well as appearing sexier. The secret was no longer a secret in any case, and in general the younger gay men were more interested in impressing one another than in learning a discredited way of speaking from their unfashionable elders. While it was easy for the gay subculture to distance itself from Polari, for a time it was only remembered for its negative aspects. However, over the 1990s that began to change – Polari is now being reappraised, and while it certainly isn't the case that people have begun to speak it again, it is possible to talk of a revival of interest in Polari. The following chapter examines how this revival relates to the continuously changing identities of gay men.

7   Revival

Introduction

> The Robert Burns Centre in Dumfries is holding a monthly lesbian
> and gay film screening. The night is called Bona Vada and takes place
> on the first Thursday of each month.
>
> (Gay Times 2000: 69)

While it is not the case that Polari will ever be as popular as it was in
the 1950s–60s, from the mid-1990s onwards there has been a small but
notable resurgence of interest in it, which, when compared to the dearth
of information available in the 1970s and 1980s, is in itself remarkable.
I begin this chapter by suggesting possible reasons for this change of
interest, relating them to the recent rise of a gay community or culture
(as opposed to a subculture) in the UK. Moving on from that, I spend
some time looking at the different ways that Polari is being rediscovered
and redeployed by new generations of gay men.

Increased tolerance

Politically, the Conservative government under Margaret Thatcher accom-
plished little that was of any benefit to gay men and lesbians, and in some
cases actively opposed them. For example, the introduction of Clause 28
in 1988 stated that a local authority should not 'promote homosexuality
or publish material for the promotion of homosexuality . . . promote the
teaching in any maintained school of the acceptability of homosexuality
as a pretended family relationship by the publication of such material or
otherwise'.

However, as the 1990s progressed, UK law slowly became more tolerant
of homosexuality. The age of consent for gay men remained at 21 (it was
16 for heterosexuals) until 1994, when it was reduced to 18. Tony Blair's
Labour government, which came to power on 21 July 1997, lifted the
ban on openly gay men and lesbians serving in the armed forces on
27 September 1999, as the result of a ruling by the European Court of

Human Rights. On 30 November 2000 the government equalised the age of consent to 16 for homosexual and heterosexual sex, despite opposition from the House of Lords, which had rejected the measure three times. Although, politically and socially, gay and lesbian activists would argue that much remains to be achieved,[1] popular opinion about homosexuality has begun to change. For example, David (1997: 270) notes that there was not a single complaint to the BBC after it screened a gay kiss on the prime-time soap opera *EastEnders* in 1994. Table 7.1 shows one measure of attitudes towards male and female homosexuality over the 1980s and 1990s. Negative attitudes towards homosexuality apparently *increased* from 1983 to 1987, the period coinciding with the initial impact of the arrival of Aids. Unsurprisingly, Clause 28 was passed in 1988, just after hysteria around homosexuality had reached a plateau. However, in the 1990s attitudes swung towards tolerance.

While increased tolerance from mainstream society in itself has done little to make Polari of interest to anyone, it has paved the way for the growth of a UK gay community, which, as I argue below, has led indirectly to a revival of interest in Polari.

A defined, self-sustaining gay community

In the 1950s and 1960s, a UK homosexual subculture existed, but it remained hidden from the public view, and even within its confines members had to self-monitor themselves closely, lest they appeared obviously 'homosexual' or 'lesbian'. By the 1990s, this situation had changed. In large cities, gay-run businesses (shops, bars, clubs, cafés, gyms, saunas, insurance brokers, taxi-firms) began to appear, often located close to one another, and mirroring on a smaller scale the model of San Francisco's Castro area. The two most famous examples of this are Old Compton Street in London and Canal Street in Manchester. The term 'gay village' was used to describe these commercial clusterings, although the less affirmative term 'ghetto' could also be used by those who were in favour of an integrated society (Levine 1979: 182–3). Being relatively free from raids, such legitimate businesses became known as 'safe spaces' or 'gay spaces' (Hindle 1994: 11) for gay men and lesbians. These streets also attracted those who didn't self-identify as gay, because they were quickly

Table 7.1 Percentage of respondents answering 'always wrong' to the question, 'What about sexual relations between two adults of the same sex?'

Year	1983	1984	1985	1987	1989	1990	1995	1998	2000
%	50	54	59	64	56	58	55	38.5	37.5

Data derived from *British Social Attitudes 9th, 13th, 16th and 17th Reports* (Jowell *et al.* 1992: 124; 1996: 39; 1999: 348; 2000: 112)

established as being alternative and fashionable. Yearly events such as Gay Pride and Summer Rites in London and the Manchester Mardi Gras also became popular, attracting up to 40,000 participants in the mid-1990s (David 1997: 268). The concept of the 'Pink Pound' – the idea (rather than the reality) that gay men have large disposable incomes – may also have played a role in their increasingly accepted status, at least as consumers.

A 'gay media' also became established in the UK. Since the early 1970s, gay magazines had existed, some of which were run by political groups, such as the Campaign for Homosexuality's *Lunch*, or the Gay Liberation Front's *Come Together*. Others had a lighter tone: *Jeffrey*, *Line-up*, *Quorum*, *Man to Man*, *Play Guy* and *Q International*. The most popular was *Gay News*, founded in 1972 as a newspaper and relaunched in 1983 as a magazine. In 1985, it was incorporated into *Gay Times*. Launched in the early 1990s, *The Pink Paper* and *Boyz* were free weekly newspapers available from gay establishments, the former focusing on news and politics, while the latter was more concerned with lifestyle and popular culture. The 1990s also saw monthly magazines such as *Gay Times* and *Attitude* beginning to be stocked in High Street shops. The mainstream media began to take gay issues more seriously, and started to be more careful about the ways in which they were reported. In the late 1980s, Channel 4 launched *Out on Tuesday*, a weekly gay documentary television programme (later called *Summer's Out*, or *Out*), while BBC2 followed a few years later with the more populist *GayTime TV*. In 1999, Channel 4 launched a gay drama serial, *Queer as Folk*.

While it is tempting to paint a rosy picture of a gay subculture happily coexisting alongside, or integrating with, mainstream culture, it is not the case that homophobia ceased to exist in the 1990s. For example, the bombing of the Admiral Duncan pub in Old Compton Street in 1999 highlights the fact that violence is still committed against gay men and lesbians. The fact that the concept of a 'safe space' has to exist at all, and that such places must be designated, suggests that for many gay men and lesbians the rest of the world is not so safe. And in many parts of the country gay men are still arrested for cruising in parks, woodland areas and lay-bys.

Therefore, while the profile of gay men and lesbians is perhaps higher than it has ever been before, and the message in the media is generally more positive than in the past, this has not always translated to tolerance of homosexuality in everyday situations. A recent survey (Mason and Palmer, 1996) found that one in three gay men and one in four gay women had experienced violent attacks because of their sexuality. Thirty-two per cent of those interviewed had been harassed (persistent threatening abuse, possibly including violence) and 73 per cent had been verbally abused. A defined, self-sustaining gay community may exist, but it is not one that has been completely accepted by the mainstream.

Historical and linguistic interest

While increased visibility and tolerance for UK gay communities have been beneficial for people on an individual basis, it appears odd that, under these circumstances, interest in Polari has grown. There is less of a need for the gay subculture to have a 'secret' language, although, as discussed earlier, some of the old Polari terms which refer to gay experience continue to be useful to the gay subculture.

However, the expansion of UK gay communities has resulted in a fascination with 'gay history' or the documentation of the lives and experiences of gay-identified men and lesbians from the past. Many gay men and lesbians do not procreate, and some may have found their sexuality has alienated them from their families – there is a sense that the gay community is a surrogate family: 'a community is an idea as well as a group of people. Those who form a community have a sense of togetherness, or belonging' (Weightman 1981: 107). Therefore, gay people from earlier times, although unrelated to today's gay men and lesbians, may be viewed as ancestors, or at least pioneers. Until fairly recently, only small amounts of information have been available. Even in books such as *Mother Clap's Molly House* (Norton 1992), a great deal of evidence is taken from sessions papers and newspaper reports – reports not written by gay men, but about them, and from an antagonistic perspective.

The lack of (positive) representation of homosexuality in history has therefore resulted in a need for the gay subculture to redress the balance, both as part of the political process of gaining equality, remembering the injustices of the past, and as a matter of curiosity in itself. The rapid pace of social change in the twentieth century implies that current gay and lesbian experiences are likely to differ significantly from one decade to the next.

While some histories focused on gays and lesbians who had lived extraordinary or high-profile lives (Porter and Weeks 1991, Gardiner 1997), others were more concerned with the lives of 'ordinary' people (Hall-Carpenter Archives 1989, David 1997, Jivani 1997) and included testimonial-style quotes about the personal histories of gay men and lesbians. Most of these books contained a couple of paragraphs about Polari, which always appeared briefly in sections linked to Julian and Sandy or the 1950s. Channel 4's *A Storm in a Teacup* documentary (1993) was instrumental in putting Polari back into the consciousness of the gay community, while a handful of linguists and queer studies theorists began to take an interest in Polari as an interesting language variety (Hancock 1984, Lucas 1997, Cox and Fay 1994).

The release by the BBC of two Julian and Sandy audio compilations, as well as a number of *Round the Horne* tapes, has helped to revive interest in Polari among people who may have forgotten about it, and has also introduced it to a new set of younger listeners. In the late 1990s,

Polari workshops became popular. Generally run by gay men, they were used to describe and teach Polari to those who were unfamiliar with it. The following description was sent to me by a Polari workshop organiser:

> The workshops I ran were for the Stonewall Youth Group in Edinburgh, which has an under-18 and an under-26 age group. I was asked to run a workshop (I've run previous training days for them on self esteem, mental health and other topics) and decided to teach the group some basic Polari. I talked a bit about the origins of Polari through Julian and Sandy (oooh, magic luppers he has, yes. He's a master of the cottage upright Mr Horne!) and into the disapproval of Polari in the 1970s, while at the same time many of the words were finding themselves in common usage – *naff, manky, camp, butch, glossies, closeted, come out* etc. One of the exercises involved pinning up a big poster of a man, handing round an envelope filled with Polari words for body parts and asking the members to draw a word and guess where they thought it should go on the body. We then pinned the word onto the correct part of the body. I also gave the group a handout with some of the basic words – *vada, eek, riah, cartes, jubes, omi, palone, omipalone, ajax* etc.
>
> (Craig)

From Craig's description of the workshop, Polari was used as a way of teaching young gay men and lesbians about gay social history and the changing shape of gay identity over the twentieth century. While the purpose of the workshop was not to encourage people to start speaking Polari again, it aimed to provoke an interesting topic for discussion, while the body-naming game was intended to be fun. It also gave young people the opportunity to consider alternative historic gay identities, and the reasons for their unpopularity.

Polari, as a language variety which was mainly associated with an older generation of gay men and lesbians, was also revived in 1993 as the name of a support group in London which aims to raise the visibility of older lesbians and gay men. An information leaflet about the group describes their history:

> The love that dared not speak its name. Polari ... The organisation was set up in 1993, choosing the name Polari for its associations with older gay people. (Polari was used as a covert gay language before the decriminalisation of homosexuality in 1967) ... Firstly: Polari is actively seeking the views of older lesbians and gay people on how they want to be represented. Secondly: Polari is noting these diverse views and identifying the gaps through which people 'disappear'. Thirdly: Polari is producing leaflets about a range of social care and

housing issues to different types of inquirers. Fourthly: Polari aims to encourage older lesbian and gay people to speak directly to housing and social care providers through a programme of education and training.

(Polari leaflet, London)

Other gay businesses and groups have used Polari in naming themselves – a short-lived gay tabloid-style magazine of the early 1990s was called *Bona*, a community theatre group based in Manchester is called *Vada*, while a UK gay commercial website goes by the name of *bonaport.co.uk*. In Australia, a doctor has named his medical practice after Polari:

Polari may be alive and well among Australian drag queens. I have two friends from Sydney, one of whom was 'raised' by drag queens when he first came out and they were the ones who first told me about the language. In fact, I liked the idea of a gay language so much that I decided to name my medical practice, catering largely to gay men and lesbians, Polari. You should see the looks I get when I actually explain to someone what it means.

(Howard)

Growth of the Internet

The Internet is also being used effectively to disseminate information about Polari. The development of the World Wide Web in the 1990s, coupled with the popularity and availability of personal computers (PCs) has led to a large increase in the number of people who are able to access information via a computer and a modem link. While the Internet has allowed gay men to socialise via e-mail or chatrooms, buy the latest gay fashions online or browse 'adult-themed' galleries in any of the commercial gay websites, it has also given a platform to thousands of individual gay men and lesbians who have used it to present their personal interests and opinions.

A number of (mainly British) websites[2] have recently appeared, which usually include Polari lexicons, taken from older sources such as Julian and Sandy, or from magazine articles such as those described in this book. Most of these sites give a brief description of Polari, referencing Julian and Sandy. It is usually the case that the creators of these websites are not people who learnt Polari in the 1950s or 1960s, but younger men who had learnt about it relatively recently.

Because access to the World Wide Web is cheap (or in many cases free), it is possible to quickly find and download large amounts of information (such as those contained in lexicons). As many Polari-based web pages are parts of larger gay websites, it is possible that they will be stumbled across by gay men and lesbians who were not looking for them specifically. And, importantly, Polari's wilderness years have forced it back into the obscurity that made it so desirable in the first place. No longer the over-exposed, mediated fad of the late 1960s, or the passé, politicised outcast of the 1970s, anyone who expressed interest in Polari during the 1990s has been able to delight in the rediscovery of a forgotten secret.

Polari now comes with academic credibility. Its historical roots have turned it into a grand old dame and it is potentially more accessible than ever before. While it is unlikely to be as popular as it once was, the diversification and continuing reflective nature of the gay scene has ensured that Polari is unlikely to ever become completely extinct.

Historic gay identity via media shorthand

As stated above, the recent interest in 'gay history' has resulted in a number of books, television and radio programmes which, while not usually focused especially on Polari, have mentioned it briefly. While often featuring interviews, these sources have also included re-creations of Polari as it was spoken in the 1950s and 1960s. As with the Julian and Sandy data, this form of Polari shouldn't be confused with how it was spoken in reality – indeed, these more recent types of scripted texts are another step removed from Julian and Sandy, which, although scripted, was at least performed at a time closer to the period when Polari was actually used. Occurring thirty years after Julian and Sandy, the reconstruction of a Polari-speaking gay identity is bound to be different from the original ones, although without the presence of naturally occurring data it is difficult to verify this.

However, what these recent scripted texts do reveal is how such 'historic' Polari-speaking gay identities have recently been reconstructed, within the context of today's gay culture. Although such texts can be classed collectively as mediated, it is not always possible to attribute the same set of motivations to each author (or more usually, group of authors).

A Storm in a Teacup

In 1993, Channel 4 showed, as part of their *Summer's Out* television series, a programme about gay life in London in the period 1940–70. Given the title 'A Storm in a Teacup', the programme contained three scripted Polari dialogues set on a London bus going through Piccadilly Circus. These sketches are particularly interesting as they consist of almost the only case of Polari being spoken at length on British television (other than excerpts from Julian and Sandy). The first sketch features two sailors and a bus conductor (all male) and is set in the Second World War. A and B are sailors. C is the bus conductor. The setting is the top floor of a London bus, circa 1945.

A: Vogue us up ducky. Your mother's a stretcher case.

B: That's because mother takes her gin on a dripfeed.

A: What was I like in that club?

B: Like Mae West only balder and with big tits. How far have we got to go?

A: A mere powder compact's throw from here heartface. And a bona little lattie, stocked with gin. Faster driver!

B: Take it easy will you. We don't want any trouble with betty bracelets.

A: Keep your riah on. We're immune. We're girls in uniform. 'Wrens on shoreleave' starring Deanna Durbin and Gracie Fields.

B: Shut your mouth will you.

A: I should be in Hollywood. Carmen Miranda eat your hat out.

C: Fares.

A: We'll take two of your finest tickets to Camberwell, conductor. And er, do give my best to the little woman and the nippers.

C: And whose little boy are you then? Is he with you? Gawd help us.

A: Wait a minute. I know you. You're Boris Karloff's big sister and I claim my five pounds.

B: Stop will you.

A: Do you think she's on the team?

B: Who?

A: The omee in the bijou capella.

B: You don't fancy him do you?

A: Well I'm not sure. Bona brandy on it. Dolly drag too.

B: Shut your screech. He's coming back.

A: Tell me officer. My friend and I was just wondering.

C: Yes.

A: What time do you get off?

C: I beg your pardon.

A: Do you work in shifts?

C: I generally find them more comfortable.

The second sketch is a conversation between two women and is most probably set in the early 1960s.

A: Did you see that butch number with the big martini on her? She said I had the look of Lena Horne.

B: Lena Horne, you? Kenneth Horne more like.

A: Jealous.

B: Me, jealous. Honestly, one compliment from a palone going as Cliff Richard and you go all femmie.

A: She did not look like Cliff Richard. She was much butcher.

B: Anyway, I thought she was married to that piece in the cashmere and crimplene.

A: What, George? You must be joking. He makes Liberace look like a lumberjack. Anyhow, she was too busy smooching with that one in the skin-tight lucoddy suit. I didn't get a look in.

B: No, neither did I tonight. Mind you, some nights I don't mind just looking. All those lovely lallies.

A: Tall ones, short ones.

Both: Some as big as your hat!

The final sketch features the same actors who played the sailors, although now they are dressed in 1970s fashions.

A: Bona dolly rave down that shutzy bar de nuit the other night. Up to me pots in gin ducky.

B: Full drag?

A: Toto.

B: Fantabulosa.

A: Vada well: zhooshed riah, the shyckle mauve, full slap, rouge for days, fake ogle riahs, fortuni cocktail frock and mother's fabest slingbacks.

B: Freeman, Hardy and Willis?

A: Mais oui ducky. Then la tout ensemble. Gert with a macintosh.

B: Look Tom, you can't be too careful. The place is crawling with orderly daughters down there.

A: Ooooh!

B: Honestly Tony you are so self-oppressed. All this camp bitchy chat is so sexist like. It really puts down women and gay men.

A: It's called Polari. Words like camp and gay, fab and groovy – they've entered the language.

B: Just listen to yourself. 'Entered' – that is a revolting metaphor. You are a slave to phallocentric discourse without even realising it.

A: Oh that's just the madcap fun-loving Stalinist in you ducky.

These three examples represent idealised interactions in Polari. They contain a high proportion of Polari lexical items, and are presented in the context of gay subculture – the characters in the dialogues are talking about clubs, their appearance and potential sexual partners. Polari does not seem to be employed in the cloaking of gay identity, only to make hidden the precise details of the conversation. In two of the sketches, B is uncomfortable and tells A to exercise caution when speaking Polari: 'Look Tom, you can't be too careful.' There is perhaps a contributory factor to this: the other speaker is talking loudly and excitedly, drawing attention to himself.

Bearing in mind that the sketches above are scripted, giving a stylised/idealised rendition of Polari, how are gay identities constructed in the three *A Storm in a Teacup* sketches? The sailors in the first sketch make use of feminine nouns and pronouns when referring to themselves ('We're girls in uniform'), each other ('Like Mae West'), other suspect gay males ('Do you think she's on the team?') and the police ('*betty bracelets*'). The sailors describe themselves as '*wrens*', one of the names for females in the Navy. Interestingly, during one of the few times when one character refers to another as male it is again in terms that subvert identity – 'And whose little boy are you?' Calling someone a 'little boy', when they are a grown man could refer to the youth (and attractiveness) of the target, or to the fact that he is an 'undeveloped' man.

In the second sketch, which features a conversation between two lesbians, *male* identities are presented for discussion: Liberace, a flamboyant gay (yet closeted) pianist and Cliff Richard, something of a 1960s lesbian icon. When one character compares herself to female singer Lena Horne, the other character suggests that she is more like Kenneth Horne (the bald host of *Round the Horne*). One person under discussion is called George, and referred to as he, but it is difficult to tell if George[3] is male or female. Although 'he' is described as being feminine, it might be the case that this is something which makes 'him' an unsuitable lesbian partner, when 'butchness' is valued.

As well as using feminine identifiers, labels referring to familial relationships are also employed: 'Your mother's a stretcher case.' The use of the family metaphor is employed ironically by one character to the bus conductor: 'Give my best to the little woman and the nippers.' In implying that the bus conductor is married (and thus heterosexual), the speaker is drawing attention to the fact that he is being ironic, and that he suspects the conductor of being homosexual.

References to cinema are also used to flavour Polari. The characters are creating an alternative reality to the one on the Piccadilly bus, which is populated by glamorous and/or larger-than-life female film stars, of whom the speakers are able to assume the identities, or compare themselves to: Carmen Miranda, Mae West, Deanna Durbin and Gracie Fields. On the other hand, insults can also be drawn from the movie genre: the bus conductor is claimed to be the big sister of horror film actor, Boris Karloff. One speaker says 'I should be in Hollywood.'

There is also an emphasis on clothing and physical appearance. In the male sketches, gay identity is referenced by the use of female symbols: the '*bona lattie*' is described as being 'a powder compact's throw' away; policemen are '*betty bracelets*' – the bracelets referring to handcuffs; whereas in the third sketch, one character gives a full description of everything he was wearing previously – all involving female apparel. In order to index a gay identity at the end of the first sketch, the bus conductor changes the meaning of the phrase 'work in shifts' so that 'shifts' does not refer to his timetable, but is used in the sense of female undergarments. The phrase 'What time do you get off' makes use of innuendo in a way which echoes Julian and Sandy.

Thus the main way that these sketches construct gay and lesbian identities is through the use of gender or sex subversion – male to female, or female to male. This is mainly marked by employing alternative pronouns or proper nouns, or by referring to clothing and makeup. By refusing to obey gender codes (e.g. the implication of wearing shifts to work) the speakers are differentiated from mainstream society. Meanwhile the social aspect of gay identity is addressed by the creation of nominal family constructs, whereas a fantasy element has the glamorising effect of changing the drab surroundings of the bus into a Hollywood movie set, where the speakers are the stars.

The writer or writers of the sketches were clearly familiar enough with Polari to be able to lay claim to some degree of authenticity, but they have *constructed* a set of twentieth-century gay identities for a British 1990s gay (and gay-friendly) audience. While the characters are not as stereotypically camp and 'obvious' as Julian and Sandy, as the above analysis reveals, gender-switching, gossip, speculation over the sexual identity of others, and the overlay of a glamorised Hollywood existence are all indexed in the texts.

Finally, in another way, the sketches are used to address a number of common issues concerning the perception of gay (male) identity during this period. This can be seen in the first and third sketches, where the less flamboyant character feels uncomfortable with his companion's loud and outrageous behaviour, especially when others might overhear. The third text in particular suggests B's unease with the A's camp Polari-speaking performance, referring to it as 'sexist', and 'put[ting] down women and gay men'. In this sketch, B is dressed in black clothes and a beret, which appear reminiscent of the stereotypical garments worn by radical political pressure groups of the 1960s–70s, e.g. the Black Panthers. It is likely that he was written in to signify the growing distancing from camp of members of the gay liberation movement. The phrase 'slave to phallocentric discourse' in effect parodies and exaggerates what Hayes calls Radical-Activist GaySpeak (1976: 51).

Who's a Pretty Boy Then?

The book *Who's a Pretty Boy Then?* (Gardiner 1997: 123) gives a mainly pictorial history of gay life in the twentieth century. It includes a short Polari monologue, which is reproduced below:

> 'So sister', I polaried. 'Will you take a varder at the cartz on the feely-omi in the naf strides; the one with the bona blue ogles over there polarying the omi-palone with a vogue on and the cod sheitel.' Well, she schlumphed her Vera down the screech at a rate of knots, zhooshed up the riah, checked the slap in the mirror behind the bar, straightened up one ogle fake riah that had come adrift, and bold as

brass orderlied over as fast as she could manage in those bats and, in her best lisp, asked if she could parker the omi a bevvy. Shook me rigid, I can tell you. Normally my sister is a regular Miss Mouse. Not for nothing is she called The N. P. P., the nanty-polare-palone. 'Nantoise,' the omi polaried back, 'But if you fancy tipping the velvet, we could orderly to my bijou latty just down the street.' Well, if you could have vardered the eke on the omi-palone in the sheitel: the screech dropped open; the vogue fell out; she even dropped her bevvy with a crash that prompted some butch polone-omi to yell, 'There goes another aunt nelly fake.' 'Did you varda that bold omi-palone?' she polaried to my friend Gordon, who was propping up the bar next to her, all the better to show off her rather bona dish and distract attention from the cod eke and chronic pots. Shame really, as she's quite bona vardering, even if she does cake the eke in half an inch of slap which she thinks no-one notices. Doesn't really go with her big tattooed navvy's marts which she waves around a lot to show off her groins, and the size twelve plates, squashed into bats a size too small 'cause she's conscious of them. She used to be quite butch when she first came in here, but that was back in the year blob. Now she's the living, breathing truth that today's trade is tomorrow's competition.

Polari, in this text, is used to describe and evaluate people – their body parts and their clothes. The context is a gay bar, and the narrative is concerned with sexual competition, beginning with two gay males each trying to procure a younger male, and ending with a description of the author's friend Gordon (possibly another nod to Julian and Sandy). Pronouns in the extract are at times left vague, with the definite article replacing *his* or *her*: '*the* size twelve plates', 'she does cake *the* eke in half an inch of slap', 'zhooshed up *the* riah'. At other times, and more frequently, feminine pronouns and terms of address are employed when talking of (gay) male subjects: '*she* schlumphed *her* Vera down', 'in *her* best lisp asked if *she* could parker the omi a bevvy', 'my *sister* is a regular *Miss* Mouse'.

The description of Gordon concentrates on his gender as being a complex mix of masculine and feminine. He has big tattooed hands and size twelve feet, and was once considered 'trade', yet he wears a lot of rings, cakes his face in makeup and squashes his feet into shoes a size too small because he's self-conscious about them.

An analysis of the narrator of this sketch is revealing. It is impossible to say whether any of the other characters ever speak Polari, or whether this is simply an interpretation laid over their speech by the narrator. The narrator plays no part in the story, but instead acts as an interested observer who knows and notices everyone.

The narrator is critical of the other people in the bar; in particular, their clothes, their bodies and the way that they act. One sentence about Gordon is especially interesting: 'She used to be quite butch when she first came in here, but that was back in the year blob.' While this suggests that masculinity can somehow be compromised by association with gay non-masculine men, the speaker is also referring to Gordon's age: the year blob implies that Gordon has been coming into the bar for years and is therefore ancient. However, for the narrator to know this, it is likely that he (or she) would also have to have been coming into the bar since 'the year blob' too. Therefore, implicitly, the Polari-speaking narrator is represented negatively, as a watchful, possibly ageing, critical, gay man.

Other uses of Polari in the media

Several other books, plays and films feature gay characters who use Polari briefly. For example, the novel *Sucking Sherbert Lemons* (Carson 1988), which was discussed in Chapter 4, and the play *Cleo, Camping, Emmanuelle and Dick* (Johnson 1998), which focuses on the interplay between Sid James, Barbara Windsor and Kenneth Williams (who all appeared in the long-running series of British *Carry On* films) during the 1960s and 1970s. The first few words from Williams contain some basic Polari (*vada* and *eke*). Apart from connecting Williams to the role he played in *Round the Horne*, it also established the character as gay, but for the rest of the play, the Williams character does not use any Polari.

Similarly, in the films *Love is the Devil* (1998), a biography of the gay painter Francis Bacon, and *Velvet Goldmine* (1998), based around the glam-rock movement of the 1970s, gay characters again use Polari briefly. In *Velvet Goldmine*, a music company is called 'Bijou Offices', and in the following excerpt from the film script Polari is used by two characters in a nightclub:

> Int. Sombero Club – London – Night – 1971. A Drag singer lip-syncs with the song, on a small club stage draped in silver spangles . . .
> Cecil sits with two middle-aged gay friends at a table . . .
> *Friend 1:* Ooo, varda Mistress Bona! (Subtitle reads: 'Say, have a look at "Miss Beautiful"!')
> *Friend 2:* Varda the omie palome! (Subtitle: 'Have a look at the homosexual!')
> *Friend 1:* A tart, my dears, a tart in gildy clobber! (Subtitle: 'A slut, mates, a slut in fancy clothes!') . . .
> [Cecil rises to go to talk to the 'omi palome']
> *Friend 1:* She won't be home tonight. (Subtitle: 'He won't be home tonight')
>
> (Haynes 1998: 34–6)

The subtitling of the final line in this text is clearly unnecessary (for the purposes of audience comprehension) and, like many other scripted instances of Polari, is used for comedic effect. As before, Polari is used to evaluate and criticise: the first speaker's use of 'Mistress Bona' should be considered as sarcasm rather than praise, especially in light of the later remark, 'a tart in gildy clobber'. Interestingly, this is the only use of *palome* (rather than *palone*) that I am aware of. While it may be the case that there were some speakers in the early 1970s who used this pronunciation, it is more likely an error, revealing one of processes through which gay reality has been filtered to 1990s audiences.

These more recent uses of Polari in the media are therefore important in establishing context and characterisation (as gossipy, camp or flamboyant) in portrayals of the gay subculture of the 1950s–70s. While only a few words at most are needed, Polari is used in such productions as a shorthand message: the core Polari words *bona*, *vada* and *eke* are used as quick and easy signifiers of gay identity in the same way, for example, that a pair of flared trousers and a glitter ball summarises the disco movement of the 1970s, or a swastika represents Nazi Germany. As well as helping to furnish recreations of recent historical gay subculture, a Polari word spoken by a character immediately identifies that person as being a gay effeminate stereotype.

For the sake of audience comprehension, only a few obvious Polari words are used. As indicated, *Velvet Goldmine* employs a tactic to ensure that even those who are unfamiliar with Polari are able to understand what is being said – a subtitled English translation appears at the bottom of the screen, giving humorous credibility to the notion of Polari as a 'language'.

Klub Polari

So far, the examples of recent Polari usage under discussion in this chapter have been media constructions, usually to show how it was spoken in various historical contexts. While Polari is clearly not spoken now as much as it was in the 1950s, it appears to be the case that it has not been completely forgotten by gay men. However, as has always been the case with Polari, the newer ways of using it reflect other influences – Polari continues to evolve, as the following quote from a 40-year-old gay man who works in the media suggests:

> on the London club scene I use 'Klub Polari' with my mates . . . use loads more words than are in the Internet word lists . . . dad was a cockney born in central London (like me) and was o-fay with cockney rhyming slang, backslang, guttersnipe and NavyArmyAirForce (NAAFI) slang so I had a good base!
>
> (Tony, via e-mail, 2001)

Tony's use of Klub Polari, which he also calls 'Klubspeak' or 'Klubari', suggests that it has remained on the gay scene, notably in London and connected to gay clubs such as Heaven and G.A.Y., although its usage has now been combined with various clubbing slangs:

> Klubspeak . . . it's like . . . Bangra, Parlaree/Panarly, Indy, Techno, Cockney rhyming backslang with the emphasis on Polari, hell lets name it 'Bungalo P'. I've clokt it here and there since the mid 90s but more so lately . . . I don't club as much as I u-star-doo but it seems to be in some club circles more than others, more the sort of clubs that have a mix of youths or 'stars' (*young-'stars'*) or skinheads (*bolleds*) and older guys (*yadad*) so praps some elements do come from the older grey boys, tru-say, mostly men, mostly gay or gay acting roughnecks, mostly West End, Soho or central London, now it seems to be travelling out to the sticks though with the Essex boys (*Vikings*) who come in from the fens for a bat on Sat . . .
>
> (Tony, via e-mail, 2001)

So, although Tony uses the older Parlyaree words and some Cockney rhyming slang, his Polari has been influenced by lexicons connected to particular clubbing scenes, which are not necessarily associated with homosexuality. Bangra is a fusion of British and Indian music which became popular in the UK around 1995. Indie music is broadly defined as music played by bands who have signed to independent labels (as opposed to major record companies such as EMI, Universal etc.). Techno (derived from technical or electronic) is music created by non-classical instruments such as synthesisers. However, not all forms of Polari are spoken in a clubbing context today. David G, a doctor in his late fifties, describes how he uses it:

> My mates and I speak a fruity mixture of Polari, Tok Pisin from Papua New Guinea and various invented expressions of our own. Most of the words we use are our own invention, although Polari plays a part.
>
> (David G)

In comparing his present-day use of Polari, to how he sees it being used in the 1950s and 1960s, David notes:

> It strikes me as having been a very camp, rather bitchy, perhaps mis-ogynist mode of communication, born of a need to be invisible, whereas for us it is much more a fun tool for bonding, the cosy exclusiveness of knowing that no one else has any idea what we are talking about . . . we enjoy any kind of ridiculous banter, and Polari helps contribute to that.
>
> (David G)

So, for David, Polari has become divorced from its associations with campness, bitchiness and repression and is instead used for bonding –

however, the exclusivity (and exclusion) afforded by using a secret language is still present. What's interesting in both David and Tony's cases is that Polari is only one component of their slang, which has been influenced by contact with other (non-gay) language varieties. However, for both men, the secret language is used in familiar contexts – as part of the gay clubbing scene or privately among groups of gay men. For a more contemporary, and overtly postmodern, take on Polari, which completely recontextualises its form and function, we need to examine a group of British gay male nuns.

High Polari – the Sisters of Perpetual Indulgence

The London Order of the Sisters of Perpetual Indulgence, founded by Mother Ethyl Dreads-A-Flashback in 1990, use High Polari during their rituals and blessings. A complete understanding of the political goals, history and workings of the Sisters is beyond the scope of this book; below is a short description.

Describing themselves as gay male nuns, the Order was founded in America in the 1970s. The Order spread to the UK in the 1990s (there are now Orders in Canterbury, London, Manchester, Nottingham, Newcastle, Oxford and Scotland). The Sisters can be viewed on several levels – as drag queens, as spiritualists, or as political activists who wish to parody, question or reclaim traditional notions of 'virtue'. They have carried out rituals such as the canonisation of Derek Jarman, house-blessings and marriages, in a paradoxical mixture of solemn and camp.

Many organised religions in the twentieth-century UK were not well-known for their positive attitudes towards gay lifestyles (the Metropolitan Community Church and the Quakers being important exceptions). Despite the fact that, for some gay men, a profession in the Church is attractive, phrases such as 'love the sinner, hate the sin' or 'we don't want to know what you get up to' are typical of the attitude of some religions. On the other hand, the mainstream gay scene has been criticised for downplaying spirituality. The Sisters of Perpetual Indulgence redress this imbalance for gay men, by placing an overtly gay twist on religion – mocking and questioning hegemonic religious forces, but at the same time creating a religious arena for gay men which is tolerant of male–male desire, camp, and is able to meet the different spiritual needs of individual gay men.

In the UK, the Sisters have collected and revived Polari words, through conversations with older gay men. Lucas (1997), in his description of one of the ceremonies of the Sisters, gives words from Julian and Sandy (*thews, lucoddy, riah, lally*) with more overtly gay slang words (*trade, cottage, mince*), and includes a number of words from Parlyaree (*carsey, charver, strillers*) and Cant (*badge cove, farting crackers, hearing cheat*). This borrowing from old and new sources is in keeping with Polari's ideology (and with postmodernism), although the Order's use of reclaiming offers the most extreme and all-encompassing examples of cross-over lexicalisation to date. One of the Sisters I interviewed described why the decision was taken to use Polari in their religious ceremonies:

> Dolly [one of the Sisters] was concerned that, because camp is unfashionable with the younger gays and radical queers, Polari would just be lost. The other motivation was that the Sisters of Perpetual Indulgence were thinking of conducting their ceremonies in Polari, mirroring mass being conducted in Latin. Ultimately, we decided that having ceremonies that no one but the celebrants understood wasn't helpful (just as the Church had done!). We do use a little Polari in ceremonies, for the exotic feel, but we're careful to make sure people can get the meaning from context.

Below is an excerpt from one of their ceremonies, the canonisation of Derek Jarman.

> Sissies and omies and palonies of the Gathered Faithful, we're now getting to the kernel, the nub, the very thrust of why we're gathered here today at Derek's bona bijou lattie. The reason being that Dezzie, bless his heartface, is very dear to our heart. Look at him, his little lallies trembling with anticipation, heart of gold, feet of lead, and a knob of butter. So, perhaps we could take a little time to reach out and touch, to handle for a moment Dezzie's collective parts.
>
> (Lucas 1997: 91)

The following excerpt is taken from a website[4] run by Sister Muriel of London:

> May all our dolly Sisters and Brothers in the order receive multee orgasmic visitations from the spirit of Queer Power in 1998,
> May you have multee guilt free charvering from now until 'The Victory To Come',
> May our fight against homophobia and in-bred stigmatization bring forth a new millennium of love & freedom,
> May our blessed Order of Perpetual Indulgence continue to breed new and delicious acolytes across the world,
> May we never forget our nearest & dearest who have been lost to us by HIV/AIDS,
> May we not forget those who are living with it day by day,
> May we as Sisters encourage all those with the fear of opening the closet door to have the courage to get their hands on that door-knob,
> May we all continue to bring joy to the gathered faithful when we manifest together on the streets,

May Perpetual Indulgence always be our aim, and may the blessings
of this beloved Celtic house be upon you and your happy parts
now and forever.
Ahhhhh-men!

High Polari is different from older versions of Polari. It is ceremonial,
sermonising and ritualistic. Like the Polari spoken by Julian and Sandy
it is scripted, with feminising and sexualising elements employed: gender
terms are subverted, and phrases like 'knob of butter', 'touch . . . Dezzie's
collective parts' and 'hands on that door-knob' are used as innuendo.

Despite these elements, where older versions of Polari (both in the media,
and in real life) were used socially, consisting of ad-libbed conversations,
High Polari takes the form of a structured, well-prepared monologue, stated
in mock-seriousness, although the underlying attitude of subversion and
humour remains the same. By using Polari, the Sisters are indexing the older
gay identity from the 1950s and earlier. Therefore High Polari at once pays
tribute to gay ancestry and camp, and connects contemporary gay identities
with it. The importance of Polari as a religious 'tool of the trade', something that is touched on above, is described by Lucas:

> Polari . . . was also treated as one of the structuring elements of the
> ceremony; it helped formalize responses between the Sister Celebrant
> and the Gathered Faithful. In this sense, it helped define the event
> itself. Responses were conditioned and directed through the formal
> use of Polari . . . For those members who were unsure about the
> sincerity of the canonization, the use of Polari offered a refuge, a
> semi-comprehensible sanctioning and mystifying of the Event.
>
> (Lucas 1997: 90)

Although Lucas describes Polari as semi-comprehensible, the Sister I interviewed noted that there was no intention of using Polari to confuse or
hide their message. In this way, Polari is redefined, not as a secret language,
but one which, like Julian and Sandy's Polari, is *intended* to be understood by a mass audience. The dilution of Polari into English is most
noticeable in Sister Muriel's website blessing, where only the words *dolly*,
multee and *charvering* are used.

As discussed in the previous chapter, although some gay rights activists
of the 1970s had viewed camp as apolitical, and Polari as a narrow
language, creating a restrictive, ambivalent identity that would not lead to
freedom, by the 1990s camp had been reassessed. Medhurst (1997: 281)
points out that, despite the masculinisation of Western gay subcultures in
the 1970s, camp has proved to be difficult to banish:

> Camp . . . was weaned on surviving disdain – she's a tenacious old
> tigress of a discourse well versed in defending her corner. If decades

of homophobic pressure had failed to defeat camp, what chance did a mere reorganization of subcultural priorities stand?

Far from being apolitical, some campaigners for gay rights, reacting to inadequacies in political responses to the Aids crisis, recognised and rede-ployed camp strategies in a political stance that was difficult to ignore, by using equal amounts of humour and outrage to disseminate its message, e.g. the way in which camp is deployed at funerals of gay men who have died of Aids, mixing outrage with celebration. Medhurst (1997: 283) argues that camp has a place in a society where 'gender hierarchies still persist'; Polari, as one of the tools of camp, has always carried the potential to question and resist gender hierarchies.

The Sisters' use of High Polari is one of the best examples of the re-definition of camp as a subversive political tool. Sister Muriel's blessing contains numerous political messages – mentioning guilt-free gay sex (*charvering*), the fight against homophobia and stigmatisation, remem-bering those who have been lost to or have HIV/Aids, and encouraging people to be open about their sexuality. While earlier versions of Polari were merely used to be funny, or to pass the time away in gossip, it appears that Polari has finally succumbed to Dynes' (1990) comment that camp takes serious things frivolously, and frivolous things seriously. Polari, a frivolous thing, is now being used to make a serious point by some members of the gay community.

New millennium: old attitudes?

> Bona: 'old sixties gay-coded slang to signal something good or impressive, e.g. "Bona Eek" (nice face), "Bona Lallies" (nice legs), "Bona Drag" (nice Morrissey album). Only use this word if you're weird.'
>
> (*The Gay to Z of Queer Street*, BBC Online 'gay' dictionary 2000)

While small groups of people (academics and male nuns) continue to rediscover and celebrate Polari, is this reflected by the attitude of the gay scene as a whole? Or, as the above quote suggests, is there still a prevailing belief that Polari is something to use only if you're 'weird'? In June 1999, over the course of several weeks, a number of people took advantage of the telephone feedback service in *Boyz* (a free weekly UK listings maga-zine catering for young gay males) to make their feelings known about Polari. *Boyz* transcribed and printed a selection of the responses to the telephone service, and published a short response article about Polari. The debate ran for three issues and is useful to analyse, as it reveals a number of interesting attitudes about how contemporary gay men view Polari speakers, as well as how they view gay men collectively. While it's impor-tant to frame this debate as occurring within a magazine (and therefore possibly being subjected to editing practices and constraints of space), it reveals attitudes at a grass-roots, non-academic level. Because *Boyz* is available in gay shops, bars, nightclubs, health clubs etc., it is also highly accessible.

It should be noted that the small number of respondents (all of whom were *Boyz* readers) should not be considered to be representative of the collective opinions of the 'gay community', but they are useful in shedding light on a range of possible modern representations of Polari-speaking identities. Although the debate began with a single complaint about Polari, other aspects of camp gay identity were also brought in, including clothing and musical taste. However, as the debate focused on Polari, it reveals the importance that the gay culture still attaches to language as a key indicator of identity.

The responses to the *Boyz* hotline are shown below (note that response 9 was an article written by the members of the *Boyz* editorial team and, unlike the other responses, is not a telephone transcript:

Response 1
Isn't it about time camp words and gay phraseology such as 'lallies', 'trade', 'bona' (need I go on?) were consigned to the annals of gay history. Like a limp wrist, they are neither useful, relevant or reflect the queer society we live in today. Okay, 50 years ago, such words were contrived as a language code by suppressed homosexuals, who found their freedom of choice difficult to express, but hang on ... we're approaching the new millennium, and frankly, such words now just seem an embarrassment. It seems ludicrous that we, as a liberated society, should still be carrying the suppressed baggage of our forebears. Surely it's time to close the closet door once and for all, and move forward and integrate.

(Boyz 1999: issue 408)

Response 2
About that palare thing – too fucking right. Get rid of that bollocks and drag, and Kylie and little tight-arsed queens in T-shirts that don't reach down to their waist. I mean, some of them'd be half decent looking if they wiped all that shit off their faces and put away the feather boas. John Inman's bastard love children they are. It's 1999 for God's sake – are we really going into the millennium as overly-eager-to-please 70s sitcom characters, or as modern-thinking and behaving men?

(Boyz 1999: issue 409)

Response 3
[In response to Respondent 1] Lighten up mate! Children talk childish things, politicians talk gibberish, and gays talk our own camp language.

It's all just fun. *Boyz* mag regularly provides us with new words to slip into our conversation; some work, some don't. Why should we forget the days when gays were suppressed into using gay sign talk? It's part of our history.

The only word we should all lose is 'queer' – it's offensive, and 'gay' is much better. So stop getting your lallies in a lather and find yourself some bona trade. Thank God that's all you have to moan about, as recently some people got blown to bits for being in a gay pub.

(*Boyz* 1999: issue 409)

Response 4
[The Respondent in 1] who says that we should forget about words like 'lallies' and 'trade' from 50 years ago needs a damn good slap in the face. Or should I say slap in the 'eke'. It's part of our heritage, and it was a language that was made up by gay men that were closeted so that they could communicate. Why should we turn our back on that? We should respect and remember them. Silly old faggot!

(*Boyz* 1999: issue 409)

Response 5
About that palare thing; is it not coincidental that the two guys who want to keep palare live in the sticks?

(*Boyz* 1999: issue 410)

Response 6
On the palare thing. Remember, those who don't remember the past are forced to repeat it.

(*Boyz* 1999: issue 410)

Response 7
What's wrong with being gay? We have a trend for straight-looking and straight-acting gay males. Now you're suggesting straight-talking as well? What next? If you're afraid or ashamed of being gay, and can't accept everything that goes with it, then get off the gay scene and leave the proper, fun-loving easy-going gays alone. We don't want to be straight. We want to be gay and proud, not clones of straight people.

(*Boyz* 1999: issue 410)

Response 8
I'm just replying to [Response 2]. I feel sorry for queens like you who've got nothing better to do than bitch about what gay guys

wear. Let them wear crop tops if they want to – they're young and they'll grow out of it. Get your head out of the 1970s and into the 21st Century.

(*Boyz* 1999: issue 410)

Response 9
Beginner's Guide: Palare
What is it?
Causing a bit of a controversy in the *Boyz* backchat column right now.
Readers' knickers in a twist.
Vada those knickers, doll.
Eh up, that's a bit 50s and a bit round the horn[sic], isn't it?
Eek! Slap my screech! You might be right.
What relevance does it have in the year 2000?
Well, that quite amusing song about Piccadilly rent boys by Morrissey aside, absolutely none. It's just an attempt to play the benign, neutered, eager-to-please comedy 'poof' for acceptance in the straight world.
But isn't that all over now?
Well, if you live anywhere credible, like away from farmland or the kind of town where a trip to Woolworth's is seen as going posh. The odd worthless scum aside, homosexuality is okay by us and okay by most of them now.
So why do people still speak in this way?
Some elderly gay gennelmen [*sic*] find it comforting amidst the hurly-burly of the modern age. They also find bananas quite unusual as they never had them in their day.
Will it ever die out?
One day it will be akin to those Benny Hill re-runs on cable where he 'does' a Chinaman – we'll laugh in outrage and wonder how we ever allowed it to happen.
Isn't this intra-community bitching self-defeating?
No, palare is evil. Lisping with a limp wrist and 'kicking up your lallies' to old hi-nrg [music] isn't being 'zhoosy' or an act of agit-prop defiance, it just upsets your mother and makes you deeply unattractive to most other gay men.
But what about live and let live?
Absolutely. Spout your palare all you like, but live somewhere far, far away from us ... like 1954.

(*Boyz* 1999: issue 410: 3)

The responses construct several possible versions of gay identity, which are linked to current attitudes towards Polari. Respondents 1, 2, 5 and 9 want to abandon Polari, while respondents 3, 4, 6, 7 and 8 are in favour of it.

By looking at how individual speakers construct gay identity in these texts, the most striking feature is the lack of neutrality: many of the speakers reveal prescriptive attitudes about what is a 'good' gay man and what is a 'bad' gay man.

'Little queen'

Respondent 2 links Polari to several other attributes of a particular gay identity, including clothing choices: drag, tight trousers, T-shirts that reveal the midriff, makeup (described as *shit*), and feather boas. A liking for Kylie [Minogue] also forms part of this identity – Kylie Minogue, an ex-soap actress turned pop star is especially popular among teenagers and some gay men. A historical reference to the effeminate character John Inman played in the 1970s sitcom *Are You Being Served?* is also made. Rather than ascribing this taboo, non-conforming gendered performance as being against the norm, or confrontational to mainstream subculture, the respondent associates it with being 'overly-eager-to-please'. For the respondent, the preferred gay identity involves being seen as a 'man', rather than a 'little . . . queen'. His use of swearing ('too fucking right', 'bollocks', 'bastard', 'shit') enhances his own identity as being masculine and/or working-class (Queen 1997: 240). Respondent 1 points out that Polari is 'like a limp wrist', and that both are 'neither useful, relevant or reflect the queer society we live in today'. Respondent 9 also refers to 'lisping with a limp wrist', and builds upon the existing effeminate stereotype of the Polari speaker by describing him as '"kicking up your lallies" to old hi-nrg'.

Respondent 9 agrees that Polari speakers are performing a 'benign, neutered, eager-to-please comedy "poof"' identity and that speaking Polari makes you 'deeply unattractive'. Finally, speaking Polari is seen as non-political: '[it isn't] an act of agit-prop defiance'.

Interestingly, Respondent 8, who puts forward a more lenient view of what young gay men should and shouldn't wear, returns one of Respondent 2's insults by referring to him antagonistically as a 'queen'. While Respondent 2 uses *queen* to refer to a certain type of gay man (effeminate), Respondent 8 uses the word more inclusively, to refer to all gay men, even those who complain about effeminacy.

Finally, even Respondent 3, who is in favour of Polari, implies (though somewhat ambivalently) that it is 'silly', by comparing it to the language of children and the gibberish of politicians (lines 1–2): 'Children talk childish things, politicians talk gibberish, and gays talk our own camp language.'

'Elderly gentlemen'

A number of those involved in the debate, both for and against Polari, make references to the millennium or the twenty-first century, which have the effect of positioning the years 1999/2000 as an important cut-off point for a changing direction in gay identity. Respondent 2 views the millennium as a time for 'modern-thinking men', while describing Polari speakers as being typical of the 1970s. Respondent 1 worries that such words are an 'embarrassment' as we approach the new millennium, and that it is time to 'move forward'. Respondent 9 asks 'what relevance does it have in the year 2000?' noting that current speakers of Polari tend to be 'elderly gentleman' who find the modern age to be too much for them ('hurly-burly') and also find bananas unusual, a reference to the UK in the Second World War, when fruits were scarce.

However, Respondent 8 also refers to the new millennium, with the imperative 'Get your head out of the 1970s and into the 21st Century'. 'Bitching' about 'what gay guys wear' is viewed by this speaker as dated (1970s). However, the speaker also voices ambivalence towards this performance, rather than approval: 'let them wear crop tops if they want to – they're young and they'll grow out of it'.

'In the sticks'

Respondent 5, on the other hand, rather than ascribing Polari to a camp/ effeminate or old/old-fashioned identity, notes that it is none the less an unfashionable feature of living 'in the sticks'. The *Oxford English Dictionary* (1994) cites this as being 'a remote, thinly populated, rural area; the backwoods; hence, in extended (freq. deprecatory) use, any area that is off the beaten track or thought to be provincial or unsophisticated'. To live 'in the sticks' is viewed by Respondent 5 as being neither progressive or fashionable. This attitude is echoed by Respondent 9, who notes that Polari is no longer used 'if you live anywhere credible, like away from farmland or the kind of town where a trip to Woolworth's is seen as going posh'. By necessity, many gay men and lesbians have relocated to cities; both respondents view non-urban spaces as being unimportant to and unrepresentative of the current gay subculture.

It is interesting that the derogatory comment 'a trip to Woolworth's is seen as going posh' implies that Polari speakers live in deprived regions (and therefore non-Polari speakers are more sophisticated and wealthier). The linking of Polari to non-urban gay men is also peculiar, considering that Polari flourished in cities such as London in the 1950s and 1960s, although the implication may have been that trends begin in cities and by the time people 'in the sticks' have caught hold of them, they have become unfashionable, or that elderly gay men who once lived in cities have since retired to the countryside.

'Historically relevant'

One strategy used by the proponents of Polari during the debate is concerned with focusing on Polari as an important and historically relevant gay identity, as discussed earlier in this chapter.

Both Respondent 3 and Respondent 4 use similar rhetorical questions with inclusive first person plural pronouns to put forward their argument: Respondent 4 – 'Why should we turn our back on that?'; Respondent 3 – 'Why should we forget the days when gays were suppressed into using gay sign talk?'

The words *history* (Response 3), *heritage* (Response 4), *respect* (Response 4) and *remember* (Response 4) are used in arguments for historical relevance. Respondent 3's referral to a recent bombing of a gay pub (the 'Admiral Duncan' in Soho) links modern gay identity with the oppression of the gay Polari speakers in the 1950s. Respondent 6 notes that those who forget the past are forced to repeat it, which is, again, ambiguous: it could be taken as a negative evaluation of Polari (we don't want to be forced to repeat history), or its message could be that Polari should not be forgotten.

'*Fun-loving, proud and easy-going*'

Respondent 7 makes a distinction between 'proper fun loving, easy-going gays' who like Polari and are 'proud, not clones of straight people', and the 'straight-acting, straight-looking . . . straight-talking' gays who are 'afraid and ashamed' and 'can't accept everything that goes with' being gay. Such a view accuses the detractors of Polari of internalised homophobia. Like Respondents 3 and 4, this respondent employs questions: 'What's wrong with being gay?', 'What next?' as part of his rhetoric. This respondent uses an inclusive we: 'we don't want to be straight', 'we want to be gay and proud' suggesting that he is speaking for persons other than himself.

Respondent 3 points out: 'gays talk our own camp language. It's all just fun'. The use of the possessive first person plural pronoun ('our') positions this respondent as laying claim both to the 'fun-loving' gay identity, and to the 'camp language'. The word 'own' strengthens the connection (compare 'our camp language' to 'our own camp language'). Respondent 3 also hints that Respondent 1 is sexually repressed, advising that he finds himself some 'bona trade' in order to 'stop getting his lallies in a lather'. Interestingly, while Respondent 3 uses Polari 'lallies in a lather', he also refers to Respondent 1 as 'mate', a term that constructs both the speaker and the hearer as being masculine. Polari is therefore mixed with another, more masculine register.

'*Suppressed and evil*'

Respondent 1 argues a different line, that Polari was 'contrived as a language code by suppressed homosexuals' and is part of the 'closet'. As a 'liberated society', Respondent 1 says that it is time to 'integrate'. Polari is seen as being part of 'suppressed baggage' from 'homosexuals, who found their freedom of choice difficult to express'. While Respondents 3 and 4 note that Polari is relevant historically, Respondent 1 argues that it is neither 'useful' nor 'relevant'.

Respondent 2 also uses the adjective *tight-arsed* in reference to the 'little queens'. The *Oxford English Dictionary* (1994) gives the following meaning of 'tight-assed' (listing 'tight-arsed' as a variant spelling of the same word): 'a. of a woman . . . b. Unwilling to relax or enjoy oneself, full of inhibitions or constraints . . . stingy, mean.' It is possible that Respondent 2 is using *tight-arsed* to suggest another association with femininity, but it could also be that he views his 'little queens' as inhibited or sexually repressed in some way.

Respondent 9 compares Polari to reruns of a 1970s comedy series starring Benny Hill, which can be viewed by today's standards as racist and sexist, and claims 'Palare is evil'. Respondent 9's advice, 'Spout your palare all you like, but live somewhere far, far away from us . . . like 1954', effectively constructs Polari as an unpleasant form of communication. The verb *spout* means 'to speak or utter in a strident, pompous or hackneyed manner; declaim' according to the *Longman Dictionary of the English Language* (1984: 1450).

Conclusion

For both sides of the debate, a common 'enemy' is the mainstream heterosexual community, and comparisons to heterosexuals are viewed by everyone as detrimental. So Respondent 7 accuses those who dislike Polari of trying to emulate heterosexual people ('straight-looking and straight-acting'), as do Respondents 2 and 9, with their comments that Polari speakers are 'overly eager to please' or 'eager to please'. Although they do not make the link to the heterosexual mainstream society explicit, it is implied that this is who they think Polari speakers are trying to please.

Although Polari is argued against explicitly by the writer of the *Boyz* article (Respondent 9), it could also be read as humorous exaggeration. The article includes a number of Polari words (*vada, screech, doll, eek, slap, zhoosy, lallies*) and at one point includes a coded Polari reference that many readers would not understand: 'it just upsets your mother', an embedded usage of first person pronoun: *your mother*.

While in the debate above, the gay media can choose to have the last 'say' about Polari's worth,[5] it is clear from the issues raised in the debate that Polari's future is far from established. Although it may be classed as a 'dead' language by many, or a language best forgotten by a portion of the gay subculture, there are others who view it as historically important or fun.

The *Boyz* debate over Polari suggests that gay identities continue to be fragmented. From the initial 1960s media representations of effeminate, camp, gay men, through to the hyper-masculine alternatives created by the gay subculture, the 1990s saw a resurgence and reappraisal of both identities. As Blachford (1981: 197) notes: 'Masculinity and femininity are just roles to be donned or shunned at different times.' However, the donning or shunning of such roles can be equally problematic, and perceived transgressions (e.g. donning a role perceived to be inappropriate) can be penalised by societies.

The debate also highlights the ongoing ambivalence of the gay subculture towards the ways that gay men 'do' their gender. Despite attempts to politicise camp by groups such as Act-Up, Queer Nation and the Sisters of Perpetual Indulgence, for most people it continues to be viewed as apolitical, and effeminate men are viewed as unattractive by a sizeable proportion of gay men. In 1968, one of the characters in the play *The Boys in the Band* (Crowley 1968: 88) remarked of the effeminate Emory: 'Why would anyone want to go to bed with a flaming little sissy like you?' and the general consensus has not changed radically since then. Effeminacy is still seen by many gay men as weak, unmanly and unsexy. While Queer Theory argues from a postmodern perspective that gender and sexuality are fluid concepts, the use of phrases such as 'little tight-arsed queen' reinforce old stereotypical and homophobic boundaries of gender and sexuality.

However, masculine gay identities are equally open to similar criticisms: the 'butch' masculine gay male can be viewed as somehow fake, or an attempt to appease heterosexual mainstream society by trying to emulate heterosexual gender norms:

> the butch imagery and the semblance of masculine normality was as artificial a pose as the frock that had been worn before ... trying to create a social niche in a society which still negates you forces caricatures of that society upon you.
>
> (Spencer 1995: 375)

The term 'straight-acting',[6] which Respondent 7 uses in reference to masculine gay men is one in which the 'performance' aspect is crucial. 'Straight-acting' mirrors the term 'drag act', in that both are implicitly unreal – underneath there must be a 'true identity'. Finally, butch identities can be viewed as stripping individuality (the word *clone* implies sameness), which can be equally as ghettoising and isolating as the older, camp Polari-speaking identities.

To end this chapter, I present the results of a Polari poll carried out on the UK website www.outintheuk.com. This is essentially a website database of gay men living in the UK, but it also has features such as message boards, chatrooms, e-mail, and facilities to display personal information and photographs. The website contains a daily poll, suggested by its users. I suggested a poll to examine attitudes to Polari. This poll appeared on 6 November 2000 and received 816 responses. The question asked was:

'What's your opinion of the old "gay language", Polari?' I chose a number of possible responses which were in part based on my analysis of the *Boyz* data. The selection of responses, and results, were as follows:

It's absolutely bona, and it's due for a revival: 7%.
It's an interesting piece of gay heritage: 23%.
It's just a bit of harmless nonsense: 10%.
It's very old-fashioned and encourages men to act camp so it should never
    be brought back: 10%.
I've never even heard of it: 50%.

While half of the people who responded to the poll were unaware of Polari's existence, about a quarter believed it was an 'interesting piece of gay heritage'. However, 10 per cent believed it should never be brought back, and only 7 per cent wanted a Polari revival. Clearly, opinions on Polari continue to be divided in the present-day gay subculture. It is with this thought in mind that we reach the concluding chapter.

8 Conclusion

Tension and change

In reference to Polari, I have also had to consider the question 'What is a language?' carefully. Although some speakers used Polari in a complex, creative way that meant it was mutually unintelligible to outsiders, others merely employed it as a limited lexicon, relying to a greater extent upon an English base. Even people who knew it very well would be hard-pressed to extend their knowledge of Polari to communicate as effectively as they could in English. For these reasons, Polari cannot be called a language in the same way that English, French, Italian etc. are languages. Therefore, early in this book I considered classifying Polari in other ways: *dialect, language variety, sociolect, creole, pidgin* etc. Halliday's term *anti-language* appeared most useful in describing Polari's function in relation to its users. Anti-languages can provide (multiple) lexical items for concepts considered important to a particular 'anti-society' – they allow the anti-society to remain hidden, the shared language acts as a bonding mechanism and means of identification, and, most importantly, the anti-language allows its users to construct an alternative social reality and alternative identities for themselves.

Looking at the ways in which Polari was used, I have found evidence of all of these aspects of anti-language being employed. However, as Halliday (1978: 171) notes, the difference between anti-language and (mainstream) language can be measured as a function of the tension between the anti-society and (mainstream) society. The changes in how Polari was viewed and what it was used to do can be related to the changes in society and anti-society over time. So, typically, the 1950s are remembered as a repressive time for homosexual men, and the statistics of arrests for homosexual-related 'offences' bear this out. Interviewees recalled using Polari in this period for maintaining secrecy and other-identification. The repressive sexual climate led to numerous public homosexual scandals, widely reported in newspapers, which in turn were partly responsible for the subsequent Wolfenden Report. As a result, homosexuality, while still taboo, at least became the subject of scrutiny by mainstream society. From being something that wasn't talked about, homosexuality changed its status over the 1950s – it was brought into the public consciousness.

During the course of the 1960s, Polari's role in constructing gay identity appears to have shifted. The 1967 Sexual Offences Act partially legalised homosexuality, while the Julian and Sandy sketches in *Round the Horne* brought the concept of a secret homosexual language to a wider audience, perhaps even 'cracking the secret code' for those not associated with the theatre or the homosexual subculture. The tension that Halliday refers to was lessened, and Polari was no longer useful in maintaining secrecy. Instead, flamboyantly 'out' queens could use it as part of a more aggressive gay identity, terrorising heterosexuals (and each other) with a bitchy lexicon designed to pick out the physical flaws of others, while, within the gay subculture, Polari enabled the uptake of camp identities, acted as a cruising shorthand and served as an initiation rite for younger gay men.

While a tension still existed between the gay subculture and mainstream society in the 1970s, the social status of gay men had improved since legislation in the late 1960s. The start of the Gay Liberation movement signalled a move towards sexual freedom – to be openly gay was a political statement. This led some members of the gay scene to reject Polari as being ghettoising and associated with earlier oppression. Camp became stigmatised, and hyper-masculine identities, typically coming from America, were adopted by some parts of the gay subculture. It was during this period that Polari appeared to have become moribund, so that by the 1980s it was more forgotten than remembered.

However, by the mid-1990s there was the idea of a 'revival' of Polari. The form of this revival was important – and again could be related to the idea of a tension (albeit of a different kind) between the gay subculture and mainstream society. It was not the case that gay men had adopted Polari as an anti-language in the sense that it was used in the 1950s and 1960s. The form of revival was more concerned with historic or academic interest. Polari is now viewed as part of a shared 'gay heritage' and is reconstructed nostalgically via plays, documentaries and films about gay life in an earlier era. The Sisters of Perpetual Indulgence use High Polari as part of their politicisation of camp, while also reclaiming it retrospectively in the name of gay history. The sense of tension between gay culture and mainstream culture is much lessened (although still in existence). The gay scene of the 1990s and beyond is a visible, vibrant place, often openly influencing the tastes of the mainstream. The gay scene is also a consumer culture, with its own literature, films, clubs, art, insurance brokers etc. While integration between homo- and hetero- has occurred to some extent, the concept of a distinct gay culture is perhaps stronger than ever. And it is this sense of a reified gay identity, which spans decades of history (and oppression), that has led to Polari's revival, at least in theoretical if not practical terms.

So Polari offers a much less static view of anti-language than Halliday originally conceived. By following its development throughout the decades (from underground 'language', to a media phenomenon, to a 'dead language', and to what was considered by some to be an 'important part of gay heritage'), and relating this development to changes within the gay subculture, Polari served multiple functions of anti-language at different times. In the case of its 1990s revival of interest, Polari is still serving to create an alternative view of reality, but it is an alternative view of *historical* reality – history from the point of view of gay men.

This preservation of Polari, in order to index historic identities, is also missing from theories surrounding language death. Language death occurs when a dominant language gradually ousts an older language. From one perspective, Polari was ousted by English, with a few Polari terms being retained in the subculture as 'gay slang'. However, this view places English and Polari on an equal footing from the outset, which was not the case. Polari is an anti-language rather than a language, and arose in relation to English. Its use occurred in specific contexts, between particular groups of people. It was not the case that the people who constituted the gay subculture ceased to exist – a theory which could be used to explain Polari as a case of language murder. Rather, there were changes within the gay subculture, and its relationship to mainstream culture. These changes had a number of consequences – the removal of a need for a secret language, the politicisation of the subculture, and, ultimately, the unmasking of Polari via Julian and Sandy. So, rather than undergoing language death, Polari suffered from *anti-language over-exposure* – in the case of anti-languages, what is perhaps guaranteed to finish them off is their public (media) identification. Society had changed sufficiently to allow the Julian and Sandy sketches to be broadcast via the radio. So, although there are several routes available in explaining Polari's 'death', they all point back to theories surrounding changes in the tension between the gay subculture and the mainstream culture.

Identity and ambivalence

It appears that Polari contributed to a specific type of gay identity, which involved effeminacy or camp. However, it should be clear that there was no single 'Polari-speaking' identity. Just as Polari appeared to be slightly different to each user or group of users, then it was used to construct different types of identity, depending on a number of factors surrounding situational context, speaker and audience.

Polari allowed its users to rename themselves, their friends and outsiders in terms of their own standards. Some of these words had been appropriated from homophobic slang and it is not easy to say whether they were used in a positive 'reclaiming' sense, or whether they retained an element of their derogatory status, even when used within the gay subculture.

In my analysis of Polari's link to conceptions of gay identity, I have therefore continually found a sense of *ambivalence* – the existence of 'simultaneous and contradictory attitudes or feelings (as attraction and repulsion)' (Merriam-Webster 1993: 36), or an internal conflict between two opposite states.

For example, Polari's relationship to the closet reveals this ambivalence. On the one hand, Polari could be used as a way to conceal sexuality. The use of a carefully-placed word could hint at one's sexuality, but in a way that only those who were also gay would understand. When talking with gay friends, Polari allowed speakers to 'out' themselves privately in public spaces while essentially allowing them to remain in the closet. However, in other cases, Polari could be used aggressively to reveal a non-closeted identity. As Burton (1979: 120) notes, Polari would act as a contributory factor to a flamboyantly 'out' performance, resulting in a redundancy of easily interpretable signs (e.g. mincing gait, camp voice, flamboyant clothing, use of Polari) to outsiders. So, while Polari could be used to protect gay men and lesbians from outsiders, it could also be used to attack.

Similarly, within the 'safe' space of private bars and pubs, Polari acted as identity 'glue' – attaching a social identity to a group of people who were likely to have come from different backgrounds, united by their 'deviant' sexual status. However, while Polari helped gay men to reaffirm their subcultural membership, it could also be used against each other, in order to be insulting and aggressive. The fact that Polari had different variants with different degrees of complexity (e.g. East End and West End) suggests a hierarchy within the private gay space, unsettling the notion of a simple shared identity. And in analysing the words, many of them appear to be focused around sexual evaluation and conquest. While Polari enabled gay men to unite in secrecy, it then gave them a language by which they could sharpen their critical wits on each other.

The secretive, playful way that Polari could be used raises many rhetorical questions. As with drag, when a gay man calls another man 'she', is he insulting women, or does he suggest an affinity and identification with women, or both? Is Polari misogynist and racist, or is it simply ironic and liberating? Is there a sense of a 'reclaiming' of words like *fairy* or *sissy*, or are they being used in a mocking, repressive way? Was Polari a form of 'positive politeness', or a form of rudeness?

Polari was originally both a weapon and a shield against the repressive social atmosphere in the 1950s, but by the 1970s it was viewed as trivialising or limiting. Its eventual demise was partly the result of the ambivalence of the gay subculture towards it.

As the analysis of the attitudinal Polari data in the *Boyz* telephone debate (see Chapter 7) has shown, two extreme oppositional forms of gay gender identity (camp and butch) are both open to criticism from within the grass-roots gay subculture. A paradox is created, whereby feminine identities are viewed as 'unmanly' or insulting to women, while masculine identities are viewed as an 'act' – a self-conscious attempt to mimic heterosexual males. This is 'gender performance' at its most self-conscious.

So, if each alternative can potentially be viewed as problematic, perhaps the implication is that an unself-conscious identity that does not involve 'copying' someone else is therefore the ideal. In this way, gay identities, when seen in relation to heterosexual identities, will be viewed as flawed because they appear to be studied replications of heterosexuality. An 'ideal' male identity would be one that is masculine *and* heterosexual, and therefore unattainable for gay men. Such a notion echoes Quentin Crisp (1968: 62) who writes about the impossible fantasies of gay men: 'they set out to win the love of a "real" man. If they succeed, they fail. A man who "goes with" other men is not what they would call a "real" man.'

Some subcultural theorists (e.g. Blachford 1981) have pointed to the limitations of subcultures in solving problems: 'there is no sub-cultural career for the working-class lad' (Clarke *et al.* 1975: 47). From the *Boyz* debate about the usefulness of Polari to modern gay identities, it appears that, for some, the problems surrounding conceptualisations of gay identities still remain. While the modern gay subculture in the UK is self-sufficient enough to 'solve' some problems (for example, plenty of 'subcultural' careers exist within the gay subculture, thanks to its commercialisation), effeminate identities still continue to be perceived negatively, while masculine identities are seen as unreal.

Although some aspects of gay men's unease with each other's identities can be put down to the interaction between subculture and mainstream culture, it is perhaps also due to the fact that the gay male subculture is overwhelmingly concerned with standards of sexual attractiveness. Effeminacy, like ugliness and old age, has a low sexual currency for gay men, while masculinity has a long association with male heterosexuality, both inside and outside the gay subculture. While gay men continue to be stigmatised in dozens of ways by mainstream society, then their identities will continue to be seen as problematic, contested and somehow 'less' acceptable than their heterosexual counterparts.

Concluding remarks

This book is not a 'definitive' work on Polari. At the most basic level, I don't believe that any researcher can reach a stage where the meaning and usage of every Polari word has been 'discovered', and this was never my intention anyway. Similarly, with almost every interviewee that I found, I heard different perspectives surrounding how and why it was used. It was not easy to make contact with Polari speakers from the 1950s and 1960s, and as time progresses the task is likely to become even more difficult. However, the revival of interest in Polari suggests that new generations of gay men will at least be familiar with some aspects of it. One task for future researchers would be to analyse how attitudes and use of Polari continue to change as the twenty-first century progresses, and how these factors relate to the tensions between the gay subculture and mainstream society. It could be the case that the current revival of interest is merely a fad, or perhaps the amount of academic discourse surrounding Polari will have a lasting effect on the way that it is perceived and used by future gay subcultures. Will attitudes continue to change, or will the results of the poll discussed at the end of Chapter 7 be replicated 10 or 20 years on? The status of gay men in the UK continues to shift – for example, the ban on gay men in the armed forces has recently been lifted, and the age of consent for gay men has been lowered to 16. As homophobia within mainstream society ostensibly decreases, will effeminacy eventually come to be viewed as a desirable alternative to traditional masculinity both within and outside the UK gay scene, will it vanish altogether, or will it remain but simply cease to be regarded at all?

It is also the case that gay subcultures in countries other than the UK have implemented anti-languages. In the case of South Africa, the anti-language *Gayle* shares some lexical similarities with Polari (Cage 1999). A comparative study which looks at common elements or differences between 'gay languages' on a global scale would also be useful. One of the possible reasons for Polari's decline was the effect that the gay subculture of America had on the British gay subculture. Is it the case that globalisation has influenced the notion of individual gay languages? Do gay subcultures in other countries undergo similar stages of development in terms of their relationship to mainstream culture? Does partial assimilation always result in a decline of the anti-language? Do the anti-languages of other gay subcultures also eventually cause political controversy within the subculture, or eventually become associated with notions of 'heritage' or historical gay identities? Is it always the case that gay 'languages' are mainly used by effeminate working-class gay men, with masculine or middle-class gay men eschewing them? And are they used for similar purposes?

Finally, this book has placed an emphasis on the construction of gay male Polari-speaking identities, perhaps to the exclusion of other types of people. The relationship of Polari to lesbians is something I have only touched upon briefly. Also, Polari was initially used in the theatre, and according to one e-mail exchange I had, Polari is still being used by dressers, makeup and wardrobe people within that context. The use of Polari by heterosexual speakers within the theatre is worth examining, and would possibly yield different results from those described here.

My research on Polari has examined perhaps one of the most dynamic half-centuries in the development of gay identities in the UK. My interviewees recalled incidents from the 1950s where their sexuality could lead to them being blackmailed, arrested or attacked. While there is still progress to be made in obtaining true 'liberation' for gay men, their legal status and the ways that they are viewed, and see themselves, have altered considerably since the 1950s. By examining how gay men and wider mainstream society oriented to Polari over the second half of the twentieth century, I have begun to make more sense of this process.

For gay men, Polari did much more than enable them to communicate – it also allowed them to create the world as they saw it. With this book, I have been able to uncover a valuable piece of gay heritage, which no longer needs to be kept secret as it was in the 1950s, or dismissed as unimportant or retrogressive as it was in the 1970s, but can now stand as a testament to the gay men and lesbians who lived through times very different from our own.

Appendix: Polari dictionary

It is unlikely that any Polari speaker would have used or even known all of the words listed in this section. And, as discussed earlier in the book, a Polari word can possess multiple spellings, meanings, origins and in some cases pronunciations, due to the secretive, unstandardised, constantly-changing nature of the lexicon. Many of the words which are derived from acronyms (e.g. *TBH, vaf*) and the words derived from proper names (e.g. *jennifer justice, manly alice*) could be written as either lower-case or with upper-case initial capitals.

Each word is presented in the following order: The word (alternative spellings); phonetic pronunciation; grammatical category; meaning(s); etymology; other notes; examples of use; and related words.

As Polari was a spoken language variety first and foremost, attempts to write it down have generally being phonetic. The pronunciation guide (see Table A.1) should be useful in interpreting the phonetic spelling of each word:

Numbers

½	medza
1	una, oney
2	dooey
3	tray
4	quarter
5	chinker
6	say
7	say oney, setter
8	say dooey, otter
9	say tray, nobber
10	daiture
11	long dedger, lepta
12	kenza

Table A.1   Explanation of phonetic symbols used

	Consonants			Vowels
b	ball	i:		sheep
d	draw	i		busy
dʒ	judge	ɪ		ship
f	fall	e		let
g	give	æ		bat
h	help	ɑ:		heart
j	yes	ɒ		cod
k	cold kite	ɔ:		ball
l	like tall	ʊ		bush
m	man	ʌ		shut[1]
n	nice	u:		boot
ŋ	thing	ɜ:		bird
p	pin	ə		colour the[2]
r	ring	eɪ		make
s	sit	aɪ		bite
ʃ	shoot	ɔɪ		boy
t	to	əʊ		note
tʃ	cheat	aʊ		crowd
θ	thing teeth	ɪə		here
ð	then teethe	eə		there
v	vow	ʊə		poor
w	win			
z	zoo			
ʒ	measure			

Notes:
[1] This sound is generally pronounced as /ʊ/ in northern English
[2] This sound (called *schwa*) tends to be a generic soft vowel sound that occurs at the end of many words that end in a vowel

A

ac/dc /eɪ si: di: si:/ 1 *noun*: a couple; 2 *adjective*: bisexual.

acting dickey /æktɪŋ dɪki/ *noun*: temporary work.

active /æktɪv/ *adjective*: butch or bull in trade.

affair, affaire /əˈfeə/ *noun*: someone with whom a (usually same-sex) sexual/emotional relationship is shared, of any length of time, i.e. ten minutes to ten years. From French.

ajax /eɪdʒkz/ *preposition*: nearby. Perhaps from a truncation of the English *adjacent*.

alamo /æləməʊ/ *vocative*: 'I'm hot for you'. Derived from the acronym 'Lick Me Out'.

almond rocks /ˈɑ:mənd rɒks/ *noun*: socks. From rhyming slang.

and no flies /ənd nəʊ flaɪz/ *vocative*: honestly! I'm telling the truth! Also *and no mogue?*

antique h.p. /æn'tiːk eɪtʃ piː/ *noun*: old gay man (the *h.p.* part stands for *homee palone*).

aqua, acqua /ækwə/ *noun*: water. From Parlyaree, after Italian *acqua*.

aris /'ærɪs/ *noun*: arse. Via a chain of Cockney rhyming slang and Parlyaree. 'Arse' rhymes with 'bottle and glass' so 'bottle' is the rhyming slang word for 'arse'. However, 'bottle' also rhymes with 'aristotle' which can be truncated to 'aris', almost taking us back to the original word 'arse':

Sandy: Oh, anything else, Jules?
Julian: One moth-eaten Shetland tweed. Ooh! Look, he's got a baggy old aris!
Sandy: I'll say he has.

(Bona Rags)

Mr Horne: Well that's my holiday taken care of and I'm looking forward to it, so for the next few weeks I shall be swotting up my Greek philosophers, studying my Plato, brushing up my Copernicus, and if I can manage it I shall make a point of looking up my Aristotle.

(Bona Tours Ltd)

arva, harva /ɑːvə/ *verb*: sexual intercourse. Probably a truncation of *charva/charver* from Parlyaree. Also *noun*, e.g. *to have the arva*. Anal intercourse was referred to as *the full harva*.

aspro, aspra /æsprəʊ/ *noun*: prostitute. From Parlyaree via truncation of English *arse pro(stitute)*.

auntie /'ɑːnti/ *noun*: older gay man.

aunt nell /'ɑːnt nel/ 1 *verb*: to listen; 2 *imperative*: be quiet!

aunt nells /'ɑːnt nelz/ *noun*: ears.

aunt nelly fakes /'ɑːnt neli feɪks/ *noun*: earrings.

B

B-flat omee /biː flæt əʊmi/ *noun*: fat man. From rhyming slang.

back slums /bæk slʊmz/ *noun*: back-rooms or dark-rooms in gay bars or bath-houses where sex occurs. Originally the term referred to gambling dens or a district where the houses and conditions of life were of a 'wretched character'.

badge cove /'bædʒ kəʊv/ *noun*: pensioner. From Cant.

bagaga, bagadga /bæˈgædʒə/ *noun*: penis. From Italian *bagaggio*: baggage?

balony, balonie /ˈbəˈləʊni/ *noun*: rubbish. Possibly from *bolonga* (sausage). US slang.

barkey, barkie, barky /ˈbɑːki/ *noun*: sailor. From Italian *barca*: boat? First recorded in early eighteenth century.

barnet /ˈbɑːnɪt/ *noun*: hair. From nineteenth-century Cockney rhyming slang – Barnet Fair:

> *Julian:*   You got your blue rinse, you got your grey rinse, you can have any colour to match your barnet.
>
> (Bona Pets)

barney /ˈbɑːni/ *noun*: fight.

bat, batts, bates /bæts/ /beɪts/ 1 *noun*: shoe; 2 *verb*: shuffle or dance on stage.

batter /ˈbætə/ *noun*: prostitution. To go *on the batter* was to walk the streets as a prostitute.

battery /ˈbætəri/ *verb*: to knock down. From Italian *battere*.

battyfang /ˈbætɪfæŋ/ *verb*: to hit and bite.

beak /biːk/ *noun*: magistrate. From pedlar's French.

beancove /biːn kəʊv/ *noun*: young person. From Cant. See *bencove*.

bedroom /ˈbedruːm/ *noun*: any place where men can have sex. Generally used to refer to a toilet cubicle in a *cottage*, but can also apply to lock-up 'rest-rooms' in saunas.

beef curtains /biːf ˈkɜːtɪnz/ *noun*: flaps on a woman's vagina.

ben, bene /bene/ *adjective*: good. From Italian *bene*.

benar /benɑː/ *adjective*: better.

bencove /benkəʊv/ *noun*: friend. From the Cant *benecove*, literally 'a good fellow'.

beone, bianc, beyonek, beyong /biːjəʊni/ *noun*: shilling. From Parlyaree.

betty bracelets /ˈbeti ˈbreɪslətz/ *noun*: police.

bevvy, beverada, bevie, bevois /bevi/ 1 *noun*: drink (especially beer); 2 *noun*: public house. Survived into common slang usage. Also *bevvied* (to be drunk). From Italian *bev-*.

bevvy omee /bevi əʊmi/ *noun*: drunkard.

bexleys /beksli:z/ *noun*: teeth. From rhyming slang: Bexley Heath.

bibi /bibi/ *adjective*: bisexual.

bijou /bi:ʒu:/ *adjective*: small. From French. Although *bijou* means 'small', it is also used to indicate a positive evaluation towards something – small is good, e.g. 'I've got a bona bijou flatette just up the road from Shepherd's Bush'. An earlier meaning of *bijou*, dating from around the thirteenth century, means finger-ring, and can also be applied to any kind of jewel, trinket or gem.

billingsgate /'bɪlɪŋsɡeɪt/ *noun*: bad language. The name of one of the gates of London, and hence of the fish market established there. The seventeenth-century references to the 'rhetoric' or abusive language of this market are frequent, and hence foul language is itself called '*billingsgate*'.

billy doo /bɪli du:/ *noun*: love letter. Derived from the French *billet doux*.

bimbo /'bɪmbəʊ/ *noun*: dupe.

bimph /bɪmf/ *noun*: toilet paper.

binco /'bɪnkəʊ/ *noun*: kerosene flare. From Italian *bianco*: white.

bins /bɪnz/ *noun*: spectacles.

bit of hard /bɪt əv hɑ:d/ *noun*: sexual partner (male), especially **trade**.

bitaine /bɪteɪn/ *noun*: prostitute.

bitch /bɪtʃ/ 1 *noun*: feminine man; 2 *verb*: to complain. Used as early as 1000 BC in the form of *bicce*, the word originally referred to a female dog, and began to be applied to women in about the fifteenth century.

blag /blæɡ/ *verb*: make a sexual pick-up.

blasé queen /blɑ:zeɪ kwi:n/ *noun*: used to describe an 'up-market' homosexual.

blocked /blɒkd/ *adjective*: high on drugs. From 1960s drug-users' slang.

blow /bləʊ/ *verb*: to give oral sex. Truncated version of *blow-job* from US slang.

BMQ /bi em kju:/ *noun*: acronym for *Black Market Queen* – someone who hides his homosexuality.

bod /bɒd/ *noun*: body.

bodega /bɒd'eɪdʒə/ *noun*: shop. From Spanish.

bold /bəʊld/ *adjective*: 1 *bold* has a rather specific meaning in *Round the Horne*, where it is used to mark reference to homosexuality. Whenever

Mr Horne interprets a double entendre in its rude sense, or when he uses Polari himself, Julian and Sandy immediately label him as bold:

Sandy: Would you like us to lay on a turkey?
Mr Horne: Well, I hadn't planned on a cabaret.
Sandy: Oh, he's bold.

(Bona Caterers)

As well as meaning brave, fearless and stout-hearted, the *Oxford English Dictionary* (1994) lists a secondary meaning of *bold* – an audacious or shameless person, which is perhaps associated with the meaning Julian and Sandy had in mind. Because of the need to keep references to homosexuality hidden, only the brave, or careless, would dare to use the euphemisms and innuendoes that would reveal their true natures. To be bold, in the Julian and Sandy sense, is to be homosexual. Even to use the word *bold* is to be linked to homosexuality, as it shows an understanding of a subtext that would not be available otherwise.

2 *bold* could also be used to imply that someone wasn't very pleasant – e.g. *bold palone of the latty*, when the landlady wasn't being very co-operative.

bolus /'bəʊləs/ *noun*: chemist. Originally a seventeenth-century word referring to any form of medicine that came as a rounded pill.

bona /'bəʊnə/ 1 *adjective*: good. From Italian *buono*; Lingua Franca *bona*:

Julian: How bona to vada your dolly old eke.

(Bona School of Languages)

2 *adverb*: well:

Julian: Order lau your luppers on the strillers bona.

(Bona Guesthouse)

bona nochy /'bəʊnə nɒʃti/ *vocative*: good night.

bona vardering /'bəʊnə vɑ:dərɪŋ/ *adjective*: attractive. Literally 'good looking'.

(the) bones /bəʊnz/ *noun*: the boyfriend.

boobs /bu:bz/ *noun*: breasts. Originally US slang.

booth /'bu:θ/ *noun*: room, especially bedroom.

bowl brandy /bəʊl brændi/ *noun*: faeces. See **brandy**.

box /bɒks/ *noun*: posterior.

boyno /bɔɪnəʊ/ *vocative*: hello.

brads /brædz/ *noun*: money. From Cant.

brainless /'breɪnləs/ *adjective*: good.

brandy /brændi/ *noun*: posterior. From rhyming slang 'brandy and rum' = bum.

brandy latch /brændi lætʃ/ *noun*: toilet (lock-up).

bugle /bjuːgəl/ *noun*: nose. Originally used to refer to buffalo or oxen, the term occurs in connection with military instruments of brass or copper used as signal-horns for the infantry. To be 'bugle-browed' is to have horns like a wild ox. The connection of *bugle* with the nose may be to do with the shape of the nose, or the noise it makes.

bull /bʊl/ *noun*: masculine female.

butch /bʊtʃ/ 1 *adjective*: aggressively masculine. *Butch* is most probably taken from early-twentieth-century US slang; the crewcut hairstyle was also known as a *butch-cut*. It is also a colloquial abbreviation of *butcher* – itself seen as a masculine, aggressive trade. The nickname 'Butch' was given to tough men as early as 1902, e.g. 'Butch' Cassidy. *Butch* can be applied to both males and females (a butch woman is usually a lesbian) but it is a positive evaluatory term when Julian and Sandy use it on other men, or one another:

Sandy: There! Look, Mr Horne. Look, vada that great butch lucoddy. No, ripple your muscles Jules.

(Bona Bodybuilders)

Like *naff*, butch has followed a similar pattern of evolution, passing from America in the early twentieth century across the Atlantic to become a commonplace word in the British gay subculture. It has since become more widely used in mainstream slang. Innes and Lloyd (1996: 11), in their discussion of lesbian *butch*, note that:

'butch' is an important word in the gay male lexicon, with multiple meanings. Employed as a campy adjective, 'Oh isn't Brian looking butch today!', the word has a light-hearted tone; on the other end of the spectrum are the gay men who take their butch identity very seriously, labouring endlessly to achieve and maintain the most masculine physique, bearing and overall presence.

2 *noun*: a *butch* can be used to refer to a masculine-acting man or lesbian.

buvare /bjuːˈvɑːreɪ/ *noun*: something drinkable. From French *buv-*, stem of boire: to drink.

C

cabouche /kəˈbuːʃ/ *noun*: car. Derived from *caboose*, which was originally eighteenth-century Navy slang referring to the kitchen of merchantmen on deck. By the nineteenth century the word was used in the US to refer to a van or car on a freight train. By the early twentieth century, the Canadian usage of the word referred to a mobile hut or bunk-house, moved on wheels or runners.

cackle /'kækəl/ *noun*: talk . From seventeenth century slang: 'cut the cackle'.

cackling fart /kæklɪŋ fɑːt/ *noun*: egg. From Cant.

camisa, commission, mish /kæmiːsə/ *noun*: shirt. Parlyaree. Seventeenth-century, derived from the Italian *camicia*.

camp /kæmp/ *adjective*: flamboyantly effeminate, original, amusing, homosexual, affected. Originally used at the beginning of the twentieth century. Possibly derived from the acronym *KAMP*: 'Known As Male Prostitute'.

capella, capolla, capelli, kapella /kæ'pelə/ *noun*: hat, cap. From Parlyaree after Italian.

carnish /kɑːnɪʃ/ *noun*: meat, food. From Italian *carne*.

carnish ken /kɑːnɪʃ ken/ *noun*: eating house.

caroon /kəruːn/ *noun*: crown piece.

carsey, karsey /kɑːsi/ 1 *noun*: house; 2 *noun*: toilet; 3 *noun*: brothel. From Italian *casa*.

cartes /kɑːts/ *noun*: penis.

cartzo /kɑːtzəʊ/ *noun*: penis. From Italian *cazzo*: thrust.

catever, kerterver /kætevə/ *adjective*: bad. From Parlyaree after Italian *cattivo*.

cats /kætz/ *noun*: trousers.

cavaliers and roundheads /kævə'lɪəz ən raʊndhedz/ *noun*: uncircumcised and circumcised penises.

caxton /kækztən/ *noun*: wig.

chant /tʃɑːnt/ *verb*: to sing.

charper /tʃɑːpə/ *verb*: to seek. From Parlyaree after Italian *cereare*.

charpering carsey /tʃɑpərɪŋ kɑːsi/ *noun*: police station. Parlyaree.

charpering omee /tʃɑːpərɪŋ əʊmi/ *noun*: policeman. Parlyaree.

charver /tʃɑːvə/ *verb*: to fuck. Parlyaree.

charvering donna /tʃɑːvərɪŋ dɒnə/ *noun*: prostitute. Parlyaree.

chaud /ʃəʊd/ *noun*: penis.

chavvies /tʃæviːz/ *noun*: children. Parlyaree.

chemmie /tʃemi/ *noun*: shirt or blouse. Probably from *chemise*.

cherry /tʃeri/ *noun*: man's virginity.

chicken /'tʃɪkən/ 1 *noun*: attractive man (usually aged under 25); 2 *noun*: young boy.

chinker, chickwa /tʃɪnkə/ *numeral*: five. From Parlyaree after Italian *cinque*.

cleaning the cage out /kliːnɪŋ ðə keɪdʒ aʊt/ *verb*: cunnilingus.

cleaning the kitchen /kliːnɪŋ ðə kɪtʃɪn/ *verb*: oral/anal sex (see **rim**).

clevie /klevi/ *noun*: vagina.

clobber /klɒbə/ *noun*: clothing.

cod /kɒd/ *adjective*: bad. Possibly derived from a usage of the word which originated in the fourteenth century, meaning 'scrotum' (itself from the earlier definition of 'bag'), which is perhaps best known from the term 'cod-piece'. However, from the seventeenth century onwards it became a slang word which could be applied to people, having a number of different meanings including fool, honest man, old man (perhaps an abbreviation of *codger*), or drunken man. By the beginning of the twentieth century, *cod* was also slang for a joke, hoax or parody. One could speak of the 'cod' version of something, 'cod Victorian decorations' for example. The Polari meaning of *cod* is slightly different from this; having taken and distilled the negative connotations from *cod* meaning 'hoax', *cod* as Polari simply means something bad:

Sandy:　Right, right, well I'll just open the wardrobe. Oh, here, look – his wardrobe. Haaaa!

Julian:　Haaaaa! Oh, what a naff lot!

Sandy:　It is a bit cod, isn't it?

(Bona Rags)

coddy, cody /kɒdi/ 1 *adjective*: bad, amateurish. Elaboration of *cod*; 2 *noun*: body. Truncation of *lucoddy*.

cods /kɒdz/ *noun*: testicles.

cold calling /kəʊld kɔːlɪŋ/ *verb*: walking into a pub looking for company.

colin /kɒlɪn/ *noun*: erection.

coliseum curtains /kɒlə'siːəm kɜːtɪnz/ *noun*: foreskin.

(the) colour of his eyes /kʌlə əv hɪz aɪz/ *noun*: penis size.

corybungus /kɒrɪbʌŋdʒəs/ *noun*: posterior.

cossy /kɒsi/ *noun*: *cossy* occurs once as a Polari word in *Round the Horne*. It is a truncation of *costume*, and appears to be fairly commonly known as the slang word *cozzy* or *cozzie* today, frequently heard in Australian soap operas and used to refer to 'swimming costume'. However, if it were not for Julian explicitly noting its Polari status, it would not have been included here:

Julian: Oh dear, I wonder if he's with BBC2? What cossy did they say?
Mr Horne: Cossy?
Julian: Costume. Polari for costume.
Mr Horne: Oh yes, they said a dinner-suit.

(Bona Studios)

cottage, cottaging /'kɒtɪdʒ/ *noun*: public lavatory or urinal. *Cottage* first started being used to mean toilet at the beginning of the twentieth century. In British parks, the 'facilities' provided tended to look like miniature country cottages, with a sloping roof and windows, and gay men started to refer to them as such. Just as *camping* and *cruising* can be used as double entendres, so could phrases that involved *cottaging*: 'I'm just back from a lovely cottaging holiday in the Lake District.'

crimper /'krɪmpə/ *noun*: hairdresser.

crocus /krəʊkəs/ *noun*: doctor. Possibly derived from the Latinized surname of Dr Helkiah Crooke, author of a *Description of the Body of Man* (1615).

cruise /'kruːz/ *verb*: look for sex. *Cruise* originated in the sixteenth century and was first used in connection with the movement of ships in the sea. By the end of the seventeenth century, its meaning had generalised to other types of movement, including people:

'Madam, how would you like to cruise about a little': Farquhar, *Love and Bottle*. 1698.

(Cited in *Oxford English Dictionary* 1994)

However, the Polari meaning of *cruise* comes most probably from twentieth-century America, where it was used to mean walking or driving around, either aimlessly, or to look for casual sexual (especially gay) partners:

Sandy: Well, what else is there, let's see, you could go cruising. We have your cruising. We often go cruising, don't we Jules?
Julian: You speak for yourself!

(Bona Tours)

In *Tearoom Trade* (1970), Laud Humphreys describes how cruising was a popular activity for gay men, as a result of the popularity of the automobile and the installation of a comprehensive water system across American towns, which preceded the creation of a number of public conveniences in secluded areas in parks.

As well as the 'movement' use of cruise, it can also be used to describe the intense, interested way that a man looks at a potential sexual partner: 'I've been cruised at least five times since leaving the house this morning.'

cull /kʌl/ *noun*: 1 mate; 2 fool. Cant, Molly slang. *Culls* is also used as a shortened version of *testicles*.

D

dacha, daiture, deger /deɪtʃə/ *numeral*: ten. From Parlyaree after Italian *dieci*.

daffy /dæfi/ *adjective*: to be drunk on gin. Daffy's Elixir was a medicine given to infants, to which gin was often added.

dally /ˈdæli/ *adjective*: sweet, kind. Possibly an alternative pronunciation of **dolly**.

dash /ˈdæʃ/ *verb*: leave quickly.

deaner, deener, dener, diener /diːnə/ *noun*: a shilling.

dear, dearie/dɪə *noun*: used as a friendly yet rather patronising personal term of address. To be called *dear* may imply that someone is unable to remember your name.

delph /delf/ *noun*: teeth.

dewey, dooe, dooey, duey /ˈdjuːɪ/ /ˈduːɪ/ *numeral*: two. From Parlyaree after Italian *due*.

dhobie, dohbie /ˈdəʊbi/ *verb*: to wash; *noun*: washing. From nautical slang, although the word originally comes from the Hindi *dhobi*: an Indian washerman.

diddle /ˈdɪdəl/ *noun*: gin. A *diddle-cove* was the keeper of a gin or spirit shop. In the US the word meant liquor.

(the) dilly /ˈdɪli/ *noun*: a shortened version of *Piccadilly Circus*: a part of central London that was a popular hangout and pick-up place for Polari-speaking male prostitutes.

dilly boy /ˈdɪli bɔɪ/ *noun*: a male prostitute.

dinarly, dinarla, dinaly /dɪnɑːli/ *noun*: money. From Spanish *dinero*; Italian *denaro*.

dinge /dɪndʒ/ *adjective*: black. A *dinge queen* was a gay man who sought out black partners.

dish /dɪʃ/ *noun*: 1 anus; 2 attractive man. The original meaning was associated with food – terms to do with food are often used metaphorically to imply sex or attractiveness, e.g. *chicken, beefcake*. A more recent gay (but not Polari) use of *dish* as a verb means to tell someone what you think of them.

dish the dirt /diʃ ðə dɜːt/ *verb*: talk things over, gossip.

dizzy /dɪzi/ *adjective*: scatterbrained.

do a turn /duː ə tɜːn/ *verb*: have sex. Most likely derived from theatrical slang, but also used among gay men in the Merchant Navy.

do the rights /duː ðə raɪts/ *verb*: seek revenge.

dog and bone /dɒg ən 'bəʊn/ *noun*: telephone. From rhyming slang.

dolly /dɒli/ 1 *noun*: a smart or attractive woman. Can also be used as a term of address: 'It's ages since I've seen you, dolly!' 2 *adjective*: attractive (e.g. dolly-bird):

> *Sandy*: Oh yes, we're filling in as photographers between acting engagements on the telly. We just done this one where I'm all dragged up as a Sultan squatting on me cushion. All surrounded by these dolly little palones.
>
> (Studio Bona)

3 *noun*: penis. Bruce Rodgers (1972: 65), in his American-based gay lexicon, translates *dolly* as meaning 'penis', as well as 'attractive'. However, it is not certain if this would have been known by the *Round the Horne* writers, who used the word in its adjectival sense.

Dolly most probably began as a pet-name for Dorothy, and as early as the seventeenth century was being used to refer to a drab, a slattern or useless woman. By the early twentieth century, its meaning had changed to refer to a pleasant, attractive woman. By the 1970s, *dolly* could be used about men as well as women – for example, a gay porn magazine of the 1970s was called *The Dolly Male*.

dona, donner, donah, doner /dɒnə/ *noun*: woman. From Parlyaree, probably after Italian.

don't be strange /dəʊnt biː streɪndʒ/ *imperative*: don't hold back.

dorcas /dɔːkəs/ *noun*: term of endearment, 'one who cares'. The Dorcas Society was a ladies' church association in the nineteenth century, which made clothes for the poor.

dowry /'daʊri/ *quantifier*: a lot.

drag /dræg/ *noun*: 1 any type of clothing; 2 women's clothing when used by a man, or vice versa. Used in the nineteenth century to refer to a party or dance attended by men wearing feminine attire.

drag queen /dræg kwi:n/ *noun*: one who wears women's clothes.

drag up /dræg ʌp/ *verb*: to wear women's clothes.

drage /dreɪʒ/ *noun*: drag.

dress up /dres ʌp/ *noun*: a bad (as in unconvincing) drag queen.

drogle /drəʊgəl/ *noun*: dress.

dubes, doobs, doobies /du:bz/ *noun*: 1 pills; 2 marijuana cigarettes.

duchess /'dʌtʃəs/ *noun*: rich or grand gay man.

ducky, duckie /dʌki/ *noun*: term of address, used in a similar way to *dear*. In the sixteenth century, *ducky* was used to refer to a woman's breast, but by the nineteenth century it was used as a term of affection.

dyke, dike /deɪk/ *noun*: lesbian. Possibly 1940s US slang.

E

ear fakes /ɪə feɪkz/ *noun*: earrings.

ecaf /'i:kæf/ *noun*: face. Derived from backslang (the backwards spelling of 'face').

eek, eke /i:k/ *noun*: face. Truncated and more familiar form of *ecaf*, thanks to Julian and Sandy:

Julian and Sandy:	He flies through the air with the greatest of ease.
	The daring young ome on his flying trapeze.
Sandy:	His eke is so bona.
Julian:	All polones he does please.
Both:	And my love is stolen away!
	(Bona Christmas)

efink /i:fiŋk/ *noun*: knife. From backslang.

eine /aɪn/ *noun*: London.

emag /i:mæg/ *noun*: game. From backslang.

esong /'i:sɒŋ/ *noun*: nose. Derived from backslang.

F

fab /fæb/ *adjective*: great. Original truncation of 'fabulous'.

fabe /feɪb/ *adjective*: great. Most probably an expansion of *fab*.

fabel /feɪbəl/ *adjective*: good. Possibly a blend of *fab* and *belle*.

fabulosa /fæbju:'ləusə/ *adjective*: wonderful. A play on 'fabulous'. The *-ulosa* ending links the word to Italian. Also from the Spanish *fabuloso*.

fag /fæg/ *noun*: gay man. Abbreviation of US slang word 'faggot'.

fag hag /fæg hæg/ *noun*: female friend of a gay man.

fairy /feəri:/ *noun*: effeminate homosexual man.

fake /feɪk/ 1 *noun*: an erection; 2 *verb*: to make; 3 *adjective*: used as a stem to imply that something is false or artificially constructed in some way. From Italian *faccio*: to make.

fake riah /feɪk 'raɪə/ *noun*: wig.

fakement /feɪkmənt/ *noun*: 1 thing; 2 personal adornments. Derived from *fake*.

fambles /fæmbəlz/ *noun*: hands. Also *famble cheat*: a ring; *fambler*: a glove. Sixteenth-century slang. The original sense of the word most likely meant to grope or fumble.

fang carsey /fæŋ kɑ:zi/ *noun*: dentist's surgery. Also *fang crocus*, *fang faker*: dentist. Fangs were teeth.

fantabulosa /fæntæbju:'ləusə/ *adjective*: wonderful. Most probably derived from 'fantabulous', a blend of 'fabulous' and 'fantastic', occurring in the late 1950s. The *-ulosa* ending gives it the Italian/Polari sound.

farting crackers /fɑ:tɪŋ krækəz/ *noun*: trousers.

fashioned /fæʃənd/ *adjective*: synonym of the adjectival use of *fake*.

fashioned riah /fæʃənd 'raɪə/ *noun*: wig.

fatcha /fætʃə/ *verb*: shave, apply makeup. From Italian *faccia*.

feely, feele, feelier, fellia /fi:li/ *noun*: young person, child. From Italian *figlie*: children.

femme /fem/ *noun*: 1 female; 2 feminine lesbian. US slang.

ferricadooza /fɜ:i:kædu:zə/ *noun*: a knock-down blow. The stem *ferri-* refers to something made of iron, while *caduca* means 'fall' in Italian.

filiome /fi:liəumi/ *noun*: 1 young man; 2 under-aged sexual partner. Made from a combination of *feely* and *omee*. From Italian (see **feely**).

filly /fɪli/ *adjective*: pretty.

fish /fɪʃ/ *noun*: woman (derogatory).

flange /'flændʒ/ 1 *noun*: vagina. One of the original eighteenth-century uses of *flange* refers to a projecting flat rim, collar or rib, used to strengthen an object, to guide it, to keep it in place or to facilitate its attachment to another object. 2 *verb*: to walk along.

flatties /flæti:z/ *noun*: men (especially those who make up an audience). The female equivalent is *gillies*. The term *flattie* is slightly derogatory, originally meaning one who is ignorant of the ways of professional thieving, and therefore a dupe.

flowery /'flauəri/ *noun*: lodgings, accommodation. A *flowery dell* is nineteenth-century rhyming slang for prison cell.

fogle /'fəugəl/ *noun*: handkerchief or neckerchief (usually silk). A *fogle-hunter* was a pickpocket.

fogus /fəugəs/ *noun*: tobacco. Seventeenth-century slang, derived most likely from the word *fog*, which was used to mean smoke.

foofs /fu:fs/ *noun*: breasts.

fortuni /fɔ:tʃu:ni/ *adjective*: gorgeous.

frock /frɒk/ *noun*: female attire.

frock billong lallies /frɒk bɪlɒŋ læli:z/ *noun*: trousers. Adapted from Tok Pisin, where the word 'billong' means 'belonging to'.

fruit /fru:t/ *noun*: gay man. Originally US or prison slang.

full drag /fʌl dræg/ *noun*: completely decked out in women's attire, e.g. 'Betty's got the full drag on tonight!' See **drag**.

full eek /fʌl i:k/ *noun*: wearing makeup. See **eek**.

fungus /'fʌŋgəs/ *noun*: old man.

funt /fʊnt/ *noun*: a pound.

G

gajo /gædʒəʊ/ *noun*: outsider. From Romany.

gam /gæm/ *verb*: 1 to have oral sex. Shortening of the French *gamahuche*. 2 leg. Possibly coming from 'gamb' or 'gambe', the northern form of 'jambe' which means the 'leg of an animal represented on a coat of arms' or simply a leg.

gamming /gæmɪŋ/ *verb*: oral sex. From **gam**.

gamp /gæmp/ *noun*: umbrella. After Mrs Sarah Gamp, a nurse in Dickens' *Martin Chuzzlewit*, who carried a large, cotton umbrella.

gardy loo /gɑ:di lu:/ *vocative*: look out! Originally used when the contents of a chamber pot were thrown out of a window. From pseudo-French *gare de l'eau* 'beware of the water' (the correct version would be *gare l'eau*).

gay /geɪ/ *noun*: noisy homosexual. 'Gay' has an illustrious etymology, with one of its earliest meanings being 'disposed to joy and mirth', or, of a horse, 'lively, prancing'. In the seventeenth century, a 'gay dog' was a man given to revelling or self-indulgence. Poetry was called the 'gay science' in the early nineteenth century, while, when used about women, it was first an epithet or praise. In the nineteenth century 'gay' had come to mean an immoral woman who lived a life of prostitution. By the late nineteenth century in the US it had come to mean someone who was over-familiar or impertinent. A 'gay tail' was an erect dog's tail. By the early twentieth century, 'gay' was applied to homosexuality, although in the 1950s UK it was mainly only used by upmarket *queens*. By the early 1970s, the Gay Liberation Front helped to publicise *gay* as a word with positive connotations.

gelt /gelt/ *noun*: money. Most probably from German.

gent /dʒent/ *noun*: money. Variant pronunciation of *gelt*, or perhaps from the French *argent*.

gildy /gɪldi/ *adjective*: fancy. Used in the film *Velvet Goldmine*: 'A tart in gildy clobber' – 'A slut in fancy clothes'.

gillies /dʒɪli:s/ *noun*: women (especially those in an audience). From Parlyaree.

girl /gɜ:l/ *noun*: term of address, similar in meaning to *ducky*, *dear*, *heart-face* etc. These words are often used as a kind of full-stop at the end of every sentence: '. . . dolly ecaf, girl!'

glory-hole /'glɔ:ri həʊl/ *noun*: hole between two stalls in a toilet or *cottage* – usually big enough to poke things through. Smaller holes which are only big enough to look through are generally referred to as *peep-holes*. It's likely that this word originated from Navy or Army slang. In the Navy, a 'glory-hole' was any of the various compartments on a ship, or one or more rooms used as sleeping quarters for stewards (of whom a significant proportion were homosexual, at least in the Merchant Navy). In Army slang, a 'glory-hole' was an expression for any small billet or dug-out.

glossies /'glɒsi:z/ *noun*: magazines. US slang.

goolie /'gu:li/ *adjective*: black.

goolie ogle fakes /'gu:li əʊgəl feɪks/ *noun*: sunglasses.

got your number /gɒt jʊə nʌmbə/ *verb phrase*: if you've 'got someone's number' you know what they're up to, or you know they're gay. A favourite of Julian and Sandy:

Mr Horne: Now if you're referring to Miss Fifi La Bootstrap.
Julian: Yes, we are.
Mr Horne: She's a talented cabaret artiste.
Sandy: Oooh!
Mr Horne: Yes, I was helping her with her career.
Sandy: Oooh! Helping her, that's alright ducky, we've *all* got your number!

(Bona Tax Consultants)

groin, groyne /grɔɪn/ *noun*: ring.

groinage /grɔɪnədʒ/ *noun*: jewellery.

gutless /gʌtləs/ *adjective*: either very good or very bad.

H

hambag, handbag /'hæmbæg/ *noun*: money.

hampsteads /'hæmpstəds/ *noun*: teeth. Rhyming slang from 'Hampstead Heath'.

harris /hærəs/ *noun*: arse. Likely to be derived from *aris*.

head /hed/ *noun*: toilet. Military slang.

hearing cheat /hi:rɪŋ tʃi:t/ *noun*: ear. From Cant – literally, 'a hearing thing'.

heartface /'hɑːt feɪs/ *noun*: term of address. Used in a similar way to *dear*. These terms of address can be used sarcastically or ironically – *heartface*, for example, when used on an old or unattractive man can be quite insulting. Julian and Sandy were big advocates of *heartface*:

Julian: Now how can we help you visage de coeur?
Sandy: That's French for *heartface*!

(Bona School of Languages)

hilda handcuffs /hɪldə 'hænkʌfs/ *noun*: the police.

h.p. /eɪtʃ pi:/ *noun*: gay man. Derived from the initial letters of *homee-palone*.

husband /'hʌzbənd/ *noun*: male lover, usually more than just a one-night stand, but can be used to refer ironically to any short-term sexual partner. See also **wedding night**.

I

importuning /ɪmpɔː'tʃuːnɪŋ/ *verb*: street 'trading'. Ironic and often bitter use of legalese.

in the life /ɪn ðə laɪf/ *adjective*: euphemism for *homosexual*.

irish /aɪrɪʃ/ *noun*: wig. From rhyming slang – Irish jig.

it /ɪt/ *pronoun*: used to refer to a short-term sexual partner.

J

jarry /dʒɑːri/ *verb*: to eat. Derived from the Parlyaree word *munjaree*. It is especially used to refer to eating something sexually, e.g. 'jarry the cartes' (to fellate).

jennifer justice /dʒenəfə dʒʌstɪs/ *noun*: police.

jew's eye /dʒuːz aɪ/ *noun*: anything of value. From sixteenth-century slang.

jim and jack /dʒɪm ən dʒæk/ *noun*: back. From rhyming slang.

jogger, jogar /dʒɒgə/ *verb*: 1 play; 2 sing; 3 entertain. From Italian *giocare*: play/game.

joggering omee /dʒɒgərɪŋ əʊmi/ *noun*: entertainer.

joshed up /ʒuːʃd ʌp/ *adjective*: looking your best. See **zhoosh**.

jubes, joobs /dʒuːbz/ *noun*: breasts (female). Also pectorals (male).

K

kaffies /kæfiːz/ *noun*: trousers.

kapello /kæ'peləʊ/ *noun*: cloak. From Parlyaree. Also from Italian *capello*.

ken /ken/ *noun*: house. From Cant.

kenza /kenzə/ *numeral*: twelve.

kerterver cartzo /kɜːtɜːvə kɑːtzəʊ/ *noun*: venereal disease. Literally 'bad penis'. *Kerterver* is a variant of *catever*. From Parlyaree after Italian.

kosher homie /kəʊʃə həʊmi/ *noun*: Jewish man. From Hebrew.

L

lady /leɪdi/ *noun*: homosexual male.

lag, lage /læg/ 1 *noun*: convict or prisoner. 2 *verb*: to urinate.

lallie, lally, lall, lyle, /læli/ *noun*: leg. A favourite of Julian and Sandy. Also *lally-pegs* (possible rhyming slang for 'leg').

lally-covers /læli kʌvəz/ *noun*: trousers.

lally-drags /læli drægz/ *noun*: trousers. Also *vally-drags*, although this may be a misspelling.

lamor /læˈmɔː/ *noun*: kiss. From French.

lappers /læpəz/ *noun*: hands.

large /lɑːdʒ/ *superlative*. See **mental**.

lattie /ˈlæti/ *noun*: house or flat. From Parlyaree, where its original meaning referred to the lodgings used by itinerant actors.

lattie on water /ˈlæti ɒn wɔːtə/ *noun*: ship. Literally 'a house on water'.

lattie on wheels /ˈlæti ɒn wiːlz/ *noun*: car, taxi. Literally 'a house on wheels'.

lau /laʊ/ *verb*: to place or put. Used in the Julian and Sandy phrase 'order lau your luppers on the strillers bona'.

lav /læv/ *noun*: word. The phrase *bona lavs* can be used as a sign-off to a letter, meaning 'best wishes'.

lell /lel/ *verb*: to take.

lepta /leptə/ *numeral*: eleven.

letch water /letʃ wɔːtə/ *noun*: pre-cum.

letties /ˈletiːz/ *noun*: lodgings. From Italian *letto*: bed.

letty /ˈleti/ 1 *noun*: bed; 2 *verb*: sleep. From Italian *letto*: bed.

libbage /lɪbɪdʒ/ *noun*: bed, or any sleeping quarters. Cant. *Lib* was sleep.

lills /lɪlz/ *noun*: hands.

lily, lilly /lɪli/ *noun*: the police. From *lily law*.

ling grappling /lɪŋ græplɪŋ/ *noun*: sex. Originally, to *ling* was to stick the tongue out of the mouth.

lingo /lɪŋgəʊ/ *noun*: foreign language.

lippy /ˈlɪpi/ *noun*: lipstick.

long dedger /lɒŋ dedʒə/ *numeral*: eleven.

lucoddy /luːkɒdi/ *noun*: body. Cockney rhyming slang.

lullaby cheat /lʊləbai tʃiːt/ *noun*: baby.

luppers /lʊpəz/ *noun*: fingers.

M

mais oui /meɪ wiː/ *vocative*: of course. French.

manky /mæŋki/ *adjective*: bad, poor, tasteless. From 1950s UK slang. Possibly influenced by the French *manqué*.

manly alice /mænliː ælɪs/ *noun*: masculine gay man.

maquiage /'mæki:ɑ:ʒ/ *noun*: makeup. From French *maquiller*: to make up one's face.

maria /mæriːə/ *noun*: sperm.

mart covers /mɑːt kʌvəz/ *noun*: gloves.

martini /mɑːtiːni/ *noun*: ring (jewellery).

marts, martinis /mɑːts/ *noun*: hands. Possibly from French *main*. See also **sweet and dry**.

mary, mary-ann /meəri/ *noun*: 1 generic term for any gay man; 2 Catholic gay man; 3 exclamation: 'Oh Mary!' Also *muscle mary* – one who spends too long in the gym. Likely origins, Mollie slang and/or US gay slang.

matlock mender /'mætlɒk mendə/ *noun*: dentist.

matlocks /'mætlɒk/ *noun*: teeth.

mauve /məʊv/ *adjective*: someone who appears to be homosexual, e.g. 'she's mauve!'

mazarine /mæzəriːn/ *noun*: platform below stage. Theatrical slang.

measures, medzers, metzers, metzes /meʒəz/ *noun*: money.

meat and two veg /miːt ən tuː vedʒ/ *noun*: a man's penis and testicles. Euphemism.

meat rack /miːt ræk/ *noun*: 1 male brothel; 2 any place where large numbers of men are sexually available.

medzer, madzer /medzə/ *noun*: half. From Italian *mezzo*.

medzer caroon /medzə kə'ruːn/ *money*: half-crown.

mental /mentəl/ *superlative*: 'That's mental!' – that's the best (or the worst). 1960s slang.

meshigener /meʃɪgnə/ *adjective*: crazy. From Yiddish.

metties, metzies /metiːz/ *noun*: money. From the word 'metal'.

mezsh /meʒ/ *noun*: money. Contraction of *measures*.

mince /mɪns/ *verb*: to walk with short steps in an affected manner. 'Mince' dates back to the sixteenth century, and was originally used to describe the movement of females. By the middle of the eighteenth century, the verb was also used with reference to males ('The men are all puppies, mincing and dancing and chattering' – Foote, 1753):

> *Julian*: Through these portals have minced England's top male models.
>
> (Bona Male Models)

minces /mɪnsəz/ *noun*: eyes. Derived from Cockney rhyming slang: 'mince pies'.

minge /mɪndʒ/ *noun*: vagina. Derogatory. Early-twentieth-century slang, most probably from the Army or Navy, and used to refer to female company. Linked with *binge* (alcohol), e.g. 'His problem is minge, mine is binge.'

minnie /mɪni/ 1 *noun*: homosexual man; 2 *verb*: walk.

moey, mooe /'muːi/ *noun*: 1 mouth; 2 face. From Romany *mooi*.

mogue /məʊg/ *verb*: to mislead or lie.

molly /mɒli/ *noun*: homosexual man. Also *margery*.

montrel /mɒntrel/ *noun*: clock or watch. From French *montre*.

mother /mʌðə/ *pronoun*: me, myself. Often used by older gay men to friends when they're talking about themselves, especially in the phrase *your mother*: 'pull up a chair and tell your mother all about it'.

muck /mʌk/ *noun*: stage makeup. From theatrical slang.

mudge /mʌdʒ/ *noun*: hat.

multy, multi /mʌlti/ *quantifier*: very, much, many, a lot. From Italian *molto*.

mungaree, mangare, munjarry, manjarie, manjaree, monjaree, munja, numgare /mən'dʒɑːri/ 1 *noun*: food; 2 *verb*: to eat. *Mungaree* probably comes via Parlyaree, from the Italian *mangiare* (to eat). See also **jarry**.

munge /mʌndʒ/ *noun*: darkness.

N

nada /nɑːdə/ *quantifier*: none. The phrase 'nada to vada in the larder' means that someone is not particularly well endowed.

naff, naph /'næf/ *adjective*: 1 tasteless; 2 heterosexual. *Naff* is a word that has found its way into late-twentieth-century English slang and is used among heterosexuals and homosexuals alike. However, it has an intriguing history as a Polari word. The *Oxford English Dictionary* (1994) cites the word 'niffy-naffy' as meaning inconsequential or stupid. One story claims that it began as an acronym slang-word used by the American Army in the Second World War, meaning 'not available for fucking', but somehow passed over into the gay male lexicon at this time. This is credible – in *The Naked Civil Servant*, Quentin Crisp describes how, once the Americans entered the war, London became full of sexually available uniformed men.

Partridge (1970), however, claims that *naff* is prostitutes' slang, and gives two possibilities as to its origins: one from the French *rien a faire*, the other from 'not a fuck'. As well as the original acronym, Hugo Young (via e-mail) suggests that *naff* could stand for 'normal as fuck', or as a truncation of the slang phrase 'nawfuckingood'. Another slang forces' acronym in Partridge's slang dictionary is 'Naffy' (NAAFI), which means 'No aim, ambition or fucking initiative', also 'no ambition and fuck-all interest' (from e-mail correspondence with Paul Larkhall), so perhaps *naff* is a truncation derived from *Naffy*. James Gardiner (1997) cites *naf* in his Polari lexicon as being backslang from 'fanny'.

Another source claims the word originated in the late 1970s after the arrival of the National Association for Freedom (NAF). 'Naff off!' was a term hurled by CPBM–L (Communist Party of Great Britain Marxist–Leninist) students at their extreme right-wing fellow students (from e-mail correspondence with Isabel H, Vancouver). However, as Julian and Sandy were already using *naff* as a Polari word in the late 1960s, we can probably discount this.

Given that nine possible origins of the word *naff* are listed here, it is unlikely that any one source can be held responsible for its creation. Nor is it possible to determine which source (if any) came first. However, whether from the Army, prostitutes or French, it found its way into the Polari lexicon. Once taken up by gay men, it was used as a Polari word to refer to objects, people, items of clothing etc. that were of bad taste, ugly or not worth bothering about sexually because they were heterosexual:

Sandy: Oh, those horrible little naff gnomes. Oh no!

(Bona Homes)

Sandy: You've got to sell yourself. Go on.
Julian: No. In a close-up my knees is dead naff. I mean they're all wrinkled.

(Bona Promotions)

By the 1980s, *naff* had crossed over into mainstream English slang, meaning something worthless or tasteless: 'It is naff to call your house The Gables, Mon Repos or Dunroamin', *Sunday Telegraph*, 21 August 1983. Although it came to be used by heterosexuals, the original meaning of *naff* – as a pejorative word levelled at them by gay men – was not widely known. The new users would have understood the semantics of the word, but not the initial target. By this time, however, the 'ownership' and the target of the word had changed sufficiently for the original meaning not to matter.

namyarie, nanyarie /'næmjɑːri/ 1 *verb*: eat; 2 *noun*: food. A possible variant of *mungaree*.

nanna /nɑːnə/ *adjective*: awful.

nanti, nantee, nanty, nunty, nuntee /nænti/ *negator*: can be used to mean no, none, don't or nothing. From Italian *niente*:

Mr Horne: I'm suffering from insomnia.
Julian: Nanti kip, eh?

(Bona Nature Clinic)

Sandy: When he's in the theatre he's in another world.
Julian: Another world.
Sandy: Offer him a chocolate? Nanti!

(Bona Song Publisherettes)

nanti dinarly /nænti dɪnɑːli/ *noun phrase*: no money.

nanti polari, nanty panarly /nænti pæ'lɑːri/ *imperative*: don't say anything.

nanti pots in the cupboard /nænti pɒtz ɪn ðə kʌpbəd/ *noun phrase*: no teeth.

nanti that /nænti ðæt/ *imperative*: leave it alone, forget about it.

nantoise, nantoisale /næntwɑz:/ 1 *negator*: no. 2 *adjective*: inadequate.

nanty worster /nænti wɜːstə/ *vocative*: no worse.

nawks /'nɔːks/ *noun*: bosom.

nelly /'neli/ *noun*: effeminate gay man.

nellyarda /neliːɑːdə/ *verb*: to listen.

nishta, nish, nishtoise, nishtoisale /nɪʃtə/ *negator*: nothing, no. Similar to *nix*:

Sandy: Pull yourselves together, nish the chat!

(Bona Seances)

nix /nɪks/ *negator*: don't, no, not. Possibly from German *nichts*. 'Nix my dolly' meant 'never mind'. To 'keep nix' was to keep watch in nineteenth-century slang.

nix mungarlee /nɪks mʊndʒɑːli/ *noun phrase*: nothing to eat.

nobber /nɒbə/ 1 *numeral*: nine; 2 *noun*: one who collects money for a street performer. From Italian *nove*.

nochy /nɒtʃi/ *noun*: night. From Italian *notte*; Spanish *noche*.

nosh /nɒʃ/ *noun, verb*: to perform oral sex. From Yiddish.

NTBH /en ti: bi: eɪtʃ/ *adjective*: not available, or ugly. Acronym of 'not to be had'.

number /'nʌmbə/ *noun*: person, usually sexually attractive: 'check out the butch number over there!'

O

ogle, ogale /ɒgəl/ /əʊgəl/ 1 *verb*: look longingly at a man; 2 *noun*: eyes. From eighteenth-century Cant. Also from Italian *occhio*: eye.

ogle fakes /əʊgəl feɪks/ *noun*: spectacles. This compound noun is sometimes used with the order of its component parts reversed: *fake ogles*.

ogle filters /ɒgəl fɪltəz/ *noun*: sunglasses (see also **ogle shades**).

ogle riah fakes /ɒgəl raɪə feɪks/ *noun*: false eyelashes.

ogle riahs /ɒgəl raɪəz/ *noun*: eyelashes.

ogle riders /ɒgəl raɪdəz/ *noun*: eyebrows or eyelashes. Most probably derived because they 'ride' above the eyes, or as a possible mishearing of *ogle riahs*.

ogle shades /ɒgəl ʃeɪdz/ *noun*: sunglasses/glasses.

omee, omi, omy, omme, omer, homee, homi /'əʊmi/ *noun*: man. *Omee* has a long history, coming to Polari as a Parlyaree word used by actors to refer to each other. It is most probably a corruption of the Italian word for man: *uomo*. *Omee* is first recorded in Hotton's (1864) dictionary of slang, as meaning 'master' or 'landlord'. By the end of the nineteenth century it had come to have a more general meaning as 'man'. The additional /h/ sound at the beginning of the word was probably added as a result of contact with East London communities, which co-incidentally takes it close to the word *homo*. However, for most Polari speakers the /h/ is usually silent.

omee-palone, homee-palone /'əʊmi pəˈləʊn/ *noun*: homosexual man. The word is a combination of *omee* (man) and *palone* (woman), meaning man-woman:

> *Sandy*: We can get you the great omee-palone. He's one of ours, isn't he Jules.

> (Bona Performers)

on the team /ɒn ðə tiːm/ *adjective*: gay.

on your tod /ɒn jɔː tɒd/ *adjective*: alone. Rhyming slang. Short for 'Tod Sloan' (occasionally used in full) the name of a US jockey (1874–1933).

oney /wɒni/ *numeral*: one.

onk /ɒnk/ *noun*: nose.

opals, ocals /ˈəʊpəlz/ *noun*: eyes.

orbs /ɔːbz/ *noun*: eyes.

order, orderly /ˈɔːdəli/ *verb*: 1 leave, go; 2 to experience orgasm (to come). From Parlyaree.

orderly daughters /ɔːdəli dɔːtəz/ *noun*: police.

otter /ɒtə/ *numeral*: eight. From Italian *octo*.

outrageous /aʊtˈreɪdʒəs/ *adjective*: extrovert, loud, camp.

oyster /ˈɔɪstə/ *noun*: mouth.

P

packet /pækɪt/ *noun*: man's crotch. Also *lunch*, *bulge*.

palaver /pəlɑːvə/ 1 *verb*: to talk; 2 *noun*: an argument. From Italian *parlare*: to talk.

palliass /pæliːæs/ *noun*: back.

palone, polone, polony, pollone, paloney, polonee, palogne /pəˈləʊn/ *noun*: woman, girl. *Palone* possibly comes from the seventeenth-century slang word *blowen*, meaning wench or prostitute. It can also be used to mean an effeminate man.

palone-omee /pəˈləʊn ˈəʊmi/ *noun*: lesbian. Just as *omee-palone* means homosexual man, the reverse ordering means lesbian.

pannam, pannum /pænəm/ *noun*: bread.

parker /ˈpɑːkə/ *verb*: 1 pay out; 2 give. From Italian *pagare*: to pay.

parker the measures /ˈpɑːkə ðə meʒʌz/ *verb*: pay the money.

parkering ninty /pɑːkərɪŋ nɪnti/ *noun*: wages.

parnie, parnee, parney /ˈpɑːni/ *noun*: 1 rain water; 2 tears.

passive /pæsɪv/ *adjective*: a homosexual man who takes the insertee role in anal intercourse, and may also be quiet and effeminate.

pastry cutter /'peɪstri kʌtə/ *noun*: a man whose oral sex technique involves digging into the skin of the penis with his teeth.

pearls /pɜːlz/ *noun*: teeth.

phantom /fæntəm/ *noun*: from 'phantom gobbler'. A *phantom* would usually be a closeted gay man in the Merchant Navy who would go round the cabins at night, lifting the sheets of the other sailors to administer oral sex while they slept (or pretended to sleep). See also **BMQ**.

pig /pɪg/ *noun*: elephant.

pig's lattie /pɪgz læti/ *noun*: sty on the eye. One of the more creative uses of Polari: *pig's lattie* literally translates to 'pig's house', commonly known as a pigsty.

plate /pleɪt/ *verb*: oral sex. Rhyming slang (and prostitutes' slang) from 'plate of ham' = *gam*, which is a truncation of *gamahuche*. Also, *plate* is rhyming slang for 'fellate' or 'plates of meat' = 'eat'. To 'plate someone's dish' is to *rim* them.

plates /pleɪts/ *noun*: feet. Rhyming slang from 'plates of meat'.

pogy, pogey /pəʊgiː/ *adverb*: a little. From Italian *poco*.

polari, polare, palare, parlaree /pæ'lɑːri/ 1 *noun*: gay language; 2 *verb*: to talk. Most likely from Italian *parlare*.

polari lobes /pæ'lɑːri ləʊbz/ *noun*: ears.

polari pipe /pæ'lɑːri paɪp/ *noun*: telephone.

poll /pɒl/ *noun*: wig. Molly slang.

pont, ponce /pɒnt/ *noun*: pimp. From French *pont*.

ponte, poona /pɒnt/ *noun*: pound. From Italian *pondo*: weight.

pots /'pɒtz/ *noun*: teeth.

pouf /puːf/ *noun*: homosexual man.

pretty face /prɪti feɪs/ *noun*: attractive man.

punk /pʌnk/ *noun*: male homosexual.

purple hearts /pɜːpəl 'hɑːts/ *noun*: the drug Drynamil.

putting on the dish /pʌtɪŋ ɒn ðə dɪʃ/ *verb*: to apply lubricant to the anus, in preparation for anal sex. Also 'putting on the brandy'.

Q

quarter, quater /kwɔːtə/ *numeral*: four. From Italian *quattro*.

quartereen /kwɔːtəriːn/ *noun*: a farthing.

quean's dolly /kwiːnz dɒli/ *noun*: female friend of a gay man.

queen, quean /kwiːn/ *noun*: *queen* is a slang word used by many Polari speakers to refer to themselves, although, like *trade*, it is a word that holds several meanings, which are dependent on the user, the target and the context of the situation. *Queen* was a word the Mollies used about one another, although, as a slang word, it has a history of being used about women as much as, or more than, about men. A female who was known as a queen was either one whose rank or pre-eminence (often in a specified sphere) was comparable to that of a queen (beauty queen, queen of hearts, May queen), or an attractive girl or a girl-friend; in parts of the country (e.g. Lancashire), *queen* was a slang term of address similar to that of 'dear'. The gay use of *queen* is probably taken from an older word, *quean*, which from the Middle Ages meant a woman, especially one who was ill-behaved, a jade, a hussy, a harlot or strumpet. Both *queen* and *quean* resulted from the rejoining of two related old English words, *cwen* and *cwene*, rooted in the common Indo-European based *gwen* (meaning woman). One form became used to denote those at the top of the social scale (royalty, those who were best at something etc.), while the other experienced downward mobility, and was eventually connected to homosexuality.

Queen can be used to refer to any homosexual man, but it can also refer to various types of homosexuals: those who are effeminate, those who take the *passive* role in intercourse, or older men. Used in conjunction with other nouns, *queen* can simply denote someone who is 'into' a particular sexual scene; for example, *drag queen* (a man who wears feminine clothing, not a transsexual), *seafood queen* (one who pursues sailors), *bean queen* (one who prefers Mexican partners) etc. In the excerpt below, Sandy introduces a note of ambiguity in his use of *queen*:

Sandy: Don't denigrate yourself. He's of the blood royal. A queen's blood flows in his veins. Yes!

(Bona Abbey)

This is an example of a triple innuendo. As well as the surface meaning: 'Julian is related to royalty', there is the secondary meaning, that Julian is a *queen* himself. A third meaning that the queen's blood does not actually belong to Julian, but was put into him by another *queen* (via sexual activity), would probably only be noticed by a minority of the audience. Although *queen* may be aimed at gay men by outsiders with pejorative intent, used by gay men to each other it is neutral or affectionate.

queeny /kwiːni/ *adjective*: effeminate.

queer ken /kwi:ə ken/ *noun*: prison. From Cant.

quongs /kwɒŋz/ *noun*: testicles.

R

randy comedown /rændi kʌmdaʊn/ *noun*: desire to have sex after the effect of taking drugs starts to wear off. From 1960s drug-users' slang.

rattling cove /rætəlɪŋ kəʊv/ *noun*: taxi. Derived via Cant.

real /ri:əl/ *adjective*: really, i.e. not drag. *Real girl* is used to refer to someone who's not a *girl* (i.e. homosexual man) or a *drag queen* in the Polari sense.

reef /ri:f/ *verb*: feel, especially to feel the genitals of a person. Initially *reef* was a criminal word meaning to pull up the lining of a pocket so as to steal the contents. Possibly derived from backslang.

remould /ri:məʊld/ *noun*: sex-change.

rent /rent/ *noun*: male prostitute. Used as early as 1828 to refer to money or cash exchanged for 'criminal activity', *rent* had entered the slang lexicon used by the armed forces by the twentieth century. By the 1960s, its slang meaning had narrowed to mean gay prostitution, and could now be used to refer to the prostitute rather than the fee.

renter /rentə/ *noun*: male prostitute.

riah /'raɪə/ *noun*: hair. Originates from backslang – the word is simply 'hair' spelt backwards.

riah shusher /'raɪə ʃʌʃə/ *noun*: hairdresser. Literally, one who *shushes* or *zhooshes* the riah.

rim /rɪm/ *verb*: oral–anal sex. Early-twentieth-century US slang. Perhaps a variant of 'ream'.

rogering cheat /rɒdʒərɪŋ tʃi:t/ *noun*: penis. Literally 'thing that fucks'. From Cant.

rosie /rəʊzi/ *noun*: rubbish bin. From nautical slang.

rough /rʌf/ *noun*: masculine aggressive man. As famously described by Quentin Crisp in *The Naked Civil Servant* (1968).

royal /rɔɪəl/ *adjective*: queenly.

S

sa, say /seɪ/ *numeral*: six. From Italian *sei*.

salter, saltee, salty, saulty /'sɒltə/ *noun*: a penny. From Italian *soldi*.

savvy /'sævi/ 1 *verb*: to know or understand. 'Savvy?' means 'Do you understand?'; 2 *noun*: knowledge, practical sense, intelligence. Possibly from Jamaican-English via French or Spanish.

say dooey /seɪ duːi/ *numeral*: eight. Literally 'six and two'. Most probably from Parlyaree.

say oney /seɪ wɒni/ *numeral*: seven.

say tray /seɪ treɪ/ *numeral*: nine.

scarper, scaper, scarpy, scapali /'skɑːpə/ *verb*: run, escape. Either from Italian *scappare*, or via rhyming slang: 'Scapa Flow' – to go.

scat /skæt/ *noun*: faeces, especially when used for sexual gratification. Earlier meanings of scat have included: a shower of rain, whisky, a style of music, heroin and treasure. Its Polari meaning may be connected to a further meaning of *scat* which meant 'animal dung'.

schinwhars, chinois /ʃinwɑːz/ *noun*: Chinese man or woman. From French.

schlumph /ʃʌmf/ *verb*: to drink. Possibly from Yiddish.

schonk /ʃɒŋk/ *verb*: to hit. Possibly from Yiddish.

schvartza /'ʃvɑːtzə/ *noun*: black man. From Yiddish. Derogatory. Also *schvartza homie*: black man; *schvartza palone*: black woman.

scotches /'skɒtʃəz/ *noun*: legs. Rhyming slang from 'scotch peg'.

screaming /skriːmɪŋ/ *adjective*: loud, effeminate mannerisms. Also *screaming queen*: outrageous homosexual man.

screech /skriːtʃ/ *noun*: 1 mouth: 'Oh, shut your screech'; 2 face.

screeve /skriːv/ 1 *verb*: to write; 2 *noun*: written material. Parlyaree.

sea food /si: fuːd/ *noun*: (homo)sexually available sailor.

sea queen /si: kwiːn/ *noun*: 1 a gay sailor, particularly a steward or waiter in the Merchant Navy; 2 a gay man with a particular penchant for having sex with sailors.

send up /send ʌp/ *verb*: to make fun of.

setter /setə/ *numeral*: seven.

shamshes /ʃæmʃəz/ *noun*: possible backslang for 'smashers'. From Kenneth Williams' diary (Davies 1994), Friday 24 October 1947, 'Met 2 marines – very charming. Bonar Shamshes.'

sharda /'ʃɑːdə/ *vocative*: what a pity. From German, introduced into a version of Polari used in Ipswich in the 1970s.

sharper, sharp /ʃɑːpə/ 1 *verb*: to steal; 2 *noun*: a policeman. Parlyaree, most likely a variant spelling of *charper*.

sharping-omee /ʃɑːpɪŋ ˈəʊmi/ *noun*: a policeman.

she /ʃiː/ *pronoun*: third person, used 1 to refer to women; 2 to refer to gay men: 'She's a wicked queen!'; 3 to refer to heterosexual men, sometimes deliberately in order to deliberately undermine a case of self-assured masculinity. Also *her*.

sheesh /ʃiːʃ/ *adjective*: showy, fussy, elaborately ornamented or unnecessarily affected. Probably a truncation of the French *chichi* (pronounced /ʃiːʃiː/). Like *bijou*, it is another way of marking an object or thing as being connected in some way to homosexuality:

Julian: Let's look through the wardrobe and see if we can find you some bona drag.
Sandy: Here, here what about this? What about this? Very sheesh.
(BBC Studios)

shush /ʃʌʃ/ *verb*: to steal. Possibly a variant of *zhoosh*.

shush bag /ʃʌʃ bæg/ *noun*: swag bag.

shyckle, shyker, shietel /ˈʃaɪkəl/ *noun*: wig. From Yiddish *sheytl* – a wig worn by married women.

sister /sɪstə/ *noun*: a close friend; also likely to have once been an occasional sexual partner.

size queen /ˈsaɪz kwiːn/ *noun*: one who likes well-endowed men.

slang /slæŋ/ *verb*: to perform on stage. Parlyaree.

slap /slæp/ *noun*: makeup.

sling-backs /slɪŋ bæks/ *noun*: high heels.

smellies /ˈsmeliːz/ *noun*: perfume.

so /səʊ/ *adjective*: homosexual. 'Is he *so*?'

soldi /sɒldi/ *noun*: a penny. From Italian *soldi*: money.

solicit /sɒlɪsət/ *verb*: to *troll* while wearing *drag*. Borrowed legalese.

stamper /ˈstæmpə/ *noun*: shoe. From Cant.

starters /stɑːtəz/ *noun*: any lubricant used for anal sex, e.g. KY Jelly or Vaseline.

steamer /stiːmə/ *noun*: 1 client of prostitute; 2 gay man who seeks passive partners. From rhyming slang: *steam tug* = mug.

stiff /stɪf/ *noun*: paper. *Stiff* used to be slang for a forged note or cheque.

stimp covers /stɪmp kʌvəz/ *noun*: nylon stockings.

stimps /stɪmpz/ *noun*: legs.

stretcher-case /stretʃə keɪs/ *adjective*: exhausted: 'Your mother's a stretcher case.'

strides /straɪdz/ *noun*: trousers.

strillers /strɪləz/, **strills** /strɪlz/ *noun*: 1 musical instrument; 2 musician. Taken from Parlyaree and possibly the Italian word *strillare*.

strillers omee /strɪləz 'əʊmi/ *noun*: pianist.

sweat chovey /swet tʃəʊvi/ *noun*: gym or weights room.

sweet /swiːt/ *adjective*: good.

sweet and dry /swiːt ən draɪ/ *noun*: left and right. Used in conjunction with *martini*. A *sweet martini* was the right hand, while a *dry martini* was the left hand.

swishing /swɪʃɪŋ/ *adjective*: 1 acting flamboyantly grand; 2 acting effeminately camp.

T

tat /tæt/ *adjective*: rubbish. Tat has an early (seventeenth-century) definition as loaded dice. In the nineteenth century it began to be associated with rags, poorly made or tasteless clothes, and thus shabby people. Tat gatherers dealt in old rags. By the mid-twentieth century, *tat* had come to mean rubbish, junk or worthless goods. In twentieth-century Australia the term is applied to false teeth.

> *Sandy*:   Mm, we may have a home for it. For instance, that bundle of rags, it may seem a useless load of old tat, but we'll take it off you.
>
> *Mr Horne*: But that's the suit I'm wearing.
>
> (Bona Rags)

TBH /tiː biː eɪtʃ/ *adjective*: 1 sexually available; 2 gay. Acronym for 'to be had'. See also **NTBH**. Popular from at least the 1920s, as described by Davidson (1977: 149):

> The word 'queer', then hadn't been invented; the cryptic designation was 'so', corresponding *comme ça* in Montparnasse. 'Oh, is he *so*?' one would ask, giving a slight italic tone to the syllable. Another verbal cipher in use was the initials *t.b.h.* 'My dear,' someone might say standing outside Wellington Barracks, 'the one third from the right in the front rank – I know he's t.b.h.!' – meaning 'to be had'; as the modern queer will say 'he's trade'.

that's your actual French /ðæts jə ækʃəl frentʃ/ idiom frequently used by Sandy in the Julian and Sandy sketches to highlight the use of (usually badly pronounced or pidgin) French, giving them a (mostly imagined) air of sophistication.

thews /θjuːz/ *noun*: muscles, probably thighs but possibly used to refer to forearms. The *Oxford English Dictionary* (1994) gives one definition as being 'the bodily powers or forces of man ... muscle development associated with sinews, and hence materialised as muscles or tendons':

Mr Horne: Could you give me some idea of his act?
Sandy: Well, he comes on wearing this leopard skin you see.
             He's a great butch omee, he's got these thews like an
             oak, and bulging lallies. Ohh!

(Bona Performers)

'Thewes' is used in several of Shakespeare's plays, including *Henry VI* and *Hamlet*.

three drags and a spit /ðriː drægz ənd ə spit/ *noun*: cigarette. The phrase *spit and drag* is rhyming slang for *fag*.

timepiece /'taɪm piːs/ *noun*: watch.

tip /tɪp/ *verb*: to give oral sex.

tip the brandy /tɪp ðə brændi/ *verb*: to *rim*. Also 'tongue the brandy'.

tip the ivy /tɪp ðə aɪvi/ *verb*: to *rim*.

tip the velvet /tɪp ðə velvət/ *verb*: 1 oral sex; 2 to *rim*.

titivate /tɪtiːveɪt/ *verb*: to make oneself look pretty. Perhaps derived from the word *tidy*.

tober omee /təʊbə 'əʊmi/ *noun*: 1 rent collector; 2 landlord. From Parlyaree.

tober showmen /təʊbə 'ʃəʊmən/ *noun*: travelling musicians. From Parlyaree. A *tober* is the site occupied by a circus, fair or market.

todge omee-palone /tɒdʒ 'əʊmi pə'ləʊn/ *noun*: the passive partner in gay sex.

toff omee /tɒf əʊmi/ *noun*: rich older male partner or sugar daddy. *Toff* is perhaps a subversion of *tuft*, slang for a titled undergraduate (particularly at Oxford). A *tuft* was the ornamental gold tassle on a cap.

too much /tuː mʌtʃ/ *adjective*: excessive, over the top.

tootsie trade /'tʌtsi treɪd/ *noun*: the sexual pairing of two effeminate gay men.

tosheroon /tɒʃəruːn/ *noun*: half a crown.

town hall drapes /taʊn hɔːl dreɪps/ *noun*: uncircumcised penis.

trade /treɪd/ *noun*: male sex. Trade, which is broadly a euphemism for a casual sexual partner, dates back to the Molly words of the eighteenth century, and has taken on several shades of meaning. Earlier, in the seventeenth century, 'the trade' was used as slang to refer to prostitution, whereas, by the twentieth century, 'trade' was used by the Navy to refer to the submarine service. Common Polari usages implied a gay pickup, or a gay prostitute. It can also be used collectively, to refer to male prostitutes or gay men as a group:

Sandy: Hello. Thank you, yes, we're Bona Books. We're just filling in as book publishers. Normally, if you'll forgive me the expression, we're actors by trade.

Julian: Trade's been a bit rough lately.

(Bona Books)

The *rough trade*, to which Julian refers, is a particular kind of homosexual – one who perhaps becomes violent or demands money after sex. *Trade* can also refer to a heterosexual man who is available for casual sex, usually only allowing himself to be fellated, or taking the active role in anal intercourse.

trade curtain /treɪd kɜːtən/ *noun*: from Merchant Navy slang. Sailors sometimes were eight to a berth, and in order to maintain a degree of privacy during gay sex, they would hang a curtain round their bunk.

tray /treɪ/ *numeral*: three.

treash /'treʒ/ *noun*: term of endearment from Julian and Sandy. A truncation of 'treasure'.

troll /trəʊl/ *verb*: *troll*, which has several meanings, is probably derived from an earlier definition which is to do with 'to move, walk about to and fro, ramble, saunter, stroll or roll', which dates back at least to the fourteenth century. Other definitions of 'troll' are also to do with movement: it can be a bowling term, or mean 'to spin', 'to wag the tongue', 'to turn over in one's mind', 'to sing something in a round', or 'to draw on a moving bait'. Another meaning is concerned with witchcraft; trolls were mythical creatures – formerly in Scandanavian mythology they were conceived as giants, and more recently as dwarfs or imps. The word *trolla* in Sweden means 'to charm or bewitch'. It is possible that the Polari use of *troll* has taken aspects of both of these other sets of meanings into consideration: to walk around, seeking to charm a man into the act of copulation.

trollies /trəʊliːz/ *noun*: trousers. Derived perhaps from a combination of *lallies* and *troll*. A *trolley-dolly* (contemporary gay slang) is a gay flight attendant.

trummus /trʌməs/ *noun*: bum.

trundling cheat /trundəlɪŋ tʃiːt/ *noun*: car.

turn my oyster up /tɜːn maɪ ɔɪstə ʌp/ *verb*: make me smile.

tush /tʌʃ/ *noun*: bum.

two and eight /tuː ənd eɪt/ *noun*: state. From rhyming slang.

U

una /uːnə/ *numeral*: one. Parlyaree.

uppers and downers /ʌpəz ən daʊnəz/ *noun*: drugs.

V

vacaya /vækɑːjə/ *noun*: originally used to refer to any mechanical or electrical device that emits sound, such as a jukebox or record player (e.g. 'cod sounds in the vacaya'), but has evolved to refer to mobile phones.

vada, varda, vardo, vardy, varder /'vɑːdə/ *verb*: to look. A *vardo* was a gypsy caravan in Romany, while in Lingua Franca the word meant to keep watch, or a warden.

vadavision, vardavision /'vɑːdəvɪʒən/ *noun*: television.

vaf /væf/ *imperative*: acronym standing for 'vada, absolutely fantabulosa!' upon seeing an attractive person.

vaggerie, vagary, vagarie /'veɪgəri/ *verb*: go, travel, leave. Probably from Italian *vagare*.

vera /viːrə/ *noun*: gin. From rhyming slang: Vera Lynn = gin.

versatile /vɜːsətaɪl/ *adjective*: bisexual.

voche /vɒtʃi/ *noun*: 1 voice; 2 singer. From Italian *voce*.

vodkatini /vɒdkətiːni/ *noun*: an alcoholic drink – a mixture of vodka and martini.

vogue /vəʊg/ 1 *noun*: cigarette; 2 *verb*: to light (a cigarette) – e.g. 'vogue us up ducky' (from *A Storm in a Teacup*, Channel 4 1993).

vonka /'vɒnkə/ *noun*: nose. Possibly Yiddish.

W

wallop /'wɒləp/ *verb*: to dance. Earlier meanings of this word included to gallop, noisy bubbling movements made by water, a resounding blow or whack (which is the accepted usage today), an alcoholic drink, a flapping or fluttering rag, and a violent, clumsy, noisy movement of the body – suggesting that at one point to call a dancer a 'walloper' might have implied that he or she wasn't very graceful. Possibly from Italian *gallopare*: to dance on stage.

walloper /'wɒləpə/ *noun*: dancer.

wedding night /'wedɪŋ naɪt/ *noun*: refers to the first time two men have sex together.

willets /wɪləts/ *noun*: breasts.

winkle /wɪŋkəl/ *noun*: small penis. Initially the penis of a young boy.

Y

yews /ju:z/ *noun*: eyes.

your actual /jə ækʃəl/ idiomatic phrase used by Julian and Sandy to emphasise something, e.g. 'that's your actual French', 'we are your actual homeopathic practitioners'.

Z

zelda /zeldə/ *noun*: 1 woman; 2 witch.

zhoosh, jhoosh /ʒu:ʃ/ 1 *noun*: clothing:

> Julian: Oh come on, let's have a vada at his zhoosh.
> Mr Horne: Clothing, that's translator's note.
>
> (Bona Rags)

2 *noun*: trim or ornamentation; 3 *verb*: to zhoosh one's riah: to comb one's hair; 4 *verb*: to zhoosh off: to go away; 5 *verb*: to zhoosh something: to swallow something; 6 *verb*: to zhoosh oneself up: to titivate clothing or makeup.

One set of meanings of the word *zhoosh* is derived from its onomatopoeic quality, and is concerned with a slipping or sliding movement: going away, taking things from a shop, or the action of something going down someone's windpipe. Another set has to do with personal appearance: clothing, doing one's hair, or titivating oneself.

zhooshy /ʒu:ʃi:/ *adjective*: showy.

Notes

Chapter 1: What is Polari?

1 Pullum (1991: 151–71) has demonstrated that this particular case of over-lexicalisation is a myth: Eskimos do not have as many words for snow as some researchers have claimed.

2 Stanley (1970: 47) explicitly founds her study of 'homosexual slang' on the intuitive assumption 'that the homosexual subculture was homogeneous'.

3 The Sexual Offences Act, which partially decriminalised homosexuality, was passed in 1967 as a result of Lord Wolfenden's recommendations from ten years earlier.

4 For example: 'The Problem of Ego Identity' (1956). *Identity and the Life Cycle* (1959).

Chapter 2: Historical origins

1 One exception to this is the police, who in the past have collected lexicons from gay and criminal subcultures.

2 The Mollies have been discussed, most notably by Norton (1992), but see also Trumbach (1977), Spencer (1995) and Bray (1982).

3 Burgess (1980: 17) notes that some of Partridge's etymologies were shaky, but that he preferred a shaky etymology to none at all.

4 See Alan Corré's website on Lingua Franca at http://www.stg.brown.edu/webs/corre/franca/go.html

5 Only the spelling of this word suggests an influence from Yiddish, as the pronunciation and meaning are French.

Chapter 3: Polari as a language system

1 These words were: *bevvy, bitch, blow, bona, camp, cottage, dish, dolly, drag, lally, naff, nanti, omi, Polari, riah, send up, TBH, The Dilly, trade* and *vada*.

2 These percentages are based on an analysis of the words in the Polari dictionary (Appendix).

3 With regard to the terms *sex*, *gender* and *sexuality*, I make a distinction between *sex* as referring to 'biological' males or females, and *gender* as referring to socially constructed categories of behaviour; for example, masculine or feminine. *Sexuality*, on the other hand, refers to degree of preference for opposite- or same-sex partners.

4 Stanley (1970: 48) notes in her study of 'homosexual slang' that divergent meanings are attributed to slang words in different parts of the US.

5 As a piece of anecdotal evidence, I recall that my gym teachers always referred to the all-male class as 'girls' when they wanted to criticise our behaviour.

6 Interestingly, at the time of writing, the word *mate* or its online equivalent *m8* is enjoying a revival among gay Internet chatroom users in the UK, some of whom employ it, perhaps in order to index masculine working-class identity constructions of themselves and each other.

7 'She minceth, she brideleth, she swimmeth to and fro', Jack Juggler, Roxb. Club (1562), cited in *Oxford English Dictionary* CD-ROM (1995).

8 'The men are all puppies, mincing and dancing and chattering', Foote: Eng. in Paris i. Wks I: 36 (1799), cited in *Oxford English Dictionary* CD-ROM (1995).

9 'And thus hath he trolled forth this two and thretty wynter', Langl. P. Pl. B. xviii, 296 (1377), cited in *Oxford English Dictionary* CD-ROM (1995).

10 'Two men-of-war that are cruising here to watch for prizes', G. Etherege *She Would* ii. i. (1668), cited in *Oxford English Dictionary* CD-ROM (1995).

11 Source, Val Brown (*Pink Paper*, 5 December 2000: 40).

12 In a similar way, it would be expected that women could be referred to as 'he', but I was unable to find any definite cases of this.

13 Channel 4 (1993), *Summer's Out. A Storm in a Teacup*.

14 See Chapter 7 for a fuller description of this data.

15 Another argument for Polari having a grammar which makes it distinct from English comes by noting that the ordering of *fake* when paired with another word is a reversal of its translation. A direct translation of spectacles or 'fake eyes' would be *fake ogles*. However, the Polari phrase is *ogle fakes*.

Chapter 4: Uses and abuses

1 There is a growing wealth of literature on this subject, and readers are referred to David (1997) and Jivani (1997) for more detailed accounts.

2 Quentin Crisp (1968: 104–5) describes how neighbours had spied through his windows and reported him to the police.

3 Polari use was not confined only to men. Lesbians had their own slang, some terms apparently borrowed by gay men (such as *butch* and *femme*), and, as part of the gay scene, they would have been familiar with many Polari words. The extent to which lesbians knew or used Polari has yet to be fully explored. Also, heterosexual men and women who worked in the entertainment industry, especially in London, would be familiar with Polari.

4 University of Wisconsin: The Safe Space http://www.uwlax.edu/SAC/Diversit/safe_space.htm

5 *Quean*, a variant spelling of *queen*, traditionally means 'prostitute'.

6 Mrs Shufflewick was a female impersonator who had a regular cabaret act at the New Black Cap in Camden.

7 Interestingly, 'Bona Eke' employs a great deal of linguistic wordplay, especially in its second half which is meant to 'explain' Polari, although in fact it is more confusing at times, deliberately giving incorrect interpretations: e.g. 'my heart starts a racket every time I see your packet' is translated as 'I get so excited when I look at your *wages*' and similarly 'I'd even grease my dish' is 'I'd even *cook* for you'. The terms *tatty* and *cod* are also subverted from their Polari meanings – *tatty* is implied to mean 'potatoes', while *cod* is associated with 'fish'. Therefore, like some of the Julian and Sandy jokes, there are triple meanings associated within the lyrics.

8 Alf Garnett was a racist character in the British sitcom, *Till Death Us Do Part* (1964–74), which ran as *All in the Family* in the US.

Chapter 5:   Julian and Sandy

1 Of the Polari speakers I interviewed, over half of them had listened to *Round the Horne* when they were growing up.
2 *Salad Days* (commissioned in 1954) is a musical about a young couple who discover a piano that has the power to make all who hear it dance. *The Boyfriend* is a musical spoof set in the 1920s.
3 The Julian and Sandy sketches were not the only ones in *Round the Horne* to make use of innuendo. Another popular sketch was Rambling Syd Rumpo (again played by Kenneth Williams), a folk singer who peppered his songs with a great deal of nonsense language which had been invented by the writers. In some ways Rambling Syd Rumpo uses an even more extreme example of innuendo, as the words often had no real English translations, whereas, at least with Julian and Sandy, secondary meanings could be read into the dialogue, and Polari was also used to refer to male body parts. Barry Took told me, 'Of course, moulies didn't really mean testicles, but all the same, the audience thought it did, and they found it funny.'
4 For examples, see Ellis (1965), Wyden and Wyden (1968) and Marmor (1965).
5 Kenneth Williams' diaries, published posthumously, reveal that he was often unhappy about his sexuality (Davies 1994).
6 There is no record of Took or Feldman publicly identifying as anything other than heterosexual.
7 A further example of Polari wordplay – the traditional dish 'jugged hare' is referred to as 'jugged riah' – hair and hare being homonyms of one another. Thanks to chef, Richard Maggs, who helped interpret this line.
8 The notion of 'audience' is multiple here. The typical 'family' audience would have comprised both children and adults, who would have had different levels of comprehension of the jokes. Then there would have been gay men and lesbians who would have perhaps understood the content of the sketches more clearly. Finally, Polari speakers would have derived greater enjoyment from the sketches, being able to decode more of the hidden meanings. Of course, these are not discrete categories – it is the case that the father (or mother) of a family could be leading a secret gay life and thus would have to pretend to understand the jokes less than they actually did.
9 There is a fourth meaning of *dish*, used by gay speakers, which has its origins in America and means to viciously chastise someone verbally: 'to dish someone'.
10 The last time Julian and Sandy ever 'performed' for the public was in December 1987, when Barry Took wrote a special sketch for a television show hosted by Terry Wogan which celebrated many years of BBC Radio. This was the first time that Julian and Sandy had ever performed on television. Kenneth Williams died three months later and Hugh Paddick passed away in 2000. Barry Took died in 2002, shortly before this book was published.

Chapter 6:   Decline

1 It is debatable whether any gay spaces can be viewed strictly as 'public' but here I wish to make a distinction between commercial establishments and social situations which occur 'at home'.
2 More recently, this viewpoint has been reversed: Medhurst (1997: 280) notes that the Queer Theory 'take' on camp is that 'Sontag got it wrong'.
3 Although Raban talks of gay slang, his article is a response to McIntosh's article on Polari. McIntosh used Polari as a term that was interchangeable with 'gay slang'.

Chapter 7:   Revival

1   For example, the repeal of Clause 28; a legal recognition of gay relationships; anti-discrimination and anti-bullying legislation in order to combat homophobia in the workplace and in schools; an equalisation of the laws involving multiple sexual partners; equalisation of laws involving sex in public spaces (at present gay men can be convicted of importuning and gross indecency, but the laws for public heterosexual sex are much less stringent); and an end to the 'homosexual panic' motive which is used by defence lawyers in legal cases where gay men are murdered by straight men, usually resulting in much reduced sentences.

2   Chris Denning's website http://www.cygnet.co.uk/~cdenning/polari.html
Michael Quinion's World Wide Words: http://clever.net/quinion/words/articles/polari.htm
Richard Dunn's website http://members.xoom.com/MrRDunn/games.html
Hugh Young's Polari lexicon http://www.homeusers.prestel.co.uk/cello/Polari.htm
Kevan Mai's Julian and Sandy page http://www.fabulosa.force9.co.uk/page6.htm

3   One of the few films which dealt with British lesbian subculture in any depth in the 1960s was *The Killing of Sister George* (1967). The title character (played by Beryl Reid) is called George (a shortened version of Georgina) by everyone in the film. It is possible that the use of 'George' is a reference to this film.

4   St Muriel's London OPI Home Page: http://www.users.dircon.co.uk/~snag/ (This site appeared to have closed when I tried to access it recently.)

5   If we view the debate in terms of 'turn-taking', it is clear that the media can choose which voices it wishes to represent, exclude or 'interrupt'. To be fair to *Boyz*, the magazine published both 'for' and 'against' Polari arguments, but this in itself might not reflect the actual proportion of calls. For example, there could have been 100 'for' calls and only 3 'against', but in order to create an interesting and controversial 'debate', Boyz published equal numbers of 'for' and 'against' arguments.

6   *Straight-acting* is a term that has grown from gay personal advertisements. However, some gay men prefer *non-camp*, as it doesn't imply an 'act'.

References

Aitchison, J. (1991) *Language Change: Progress or Decay?*, Cambridge: Cambridge University Press.

Akmarjian, A., Demers, R., Farmer, A. K. and Harnish, R. M. (1997) *Linguistics: An Introduction to Language and Communication*, Cambridge, Mass.: MIT Press.

Allingham, P. (1934) *Cheapjack*, London: William Heinemann.

Anonymous (1729) *Hell Upon Earth: Or The Town in an Uproar. Occasion'd by The late horrible Scenes of Forgery, Perjury, Street-Robbery, Murder, Sodomy, and other shocking Impieties*, London.

Austin, J. L. (1962) *How To Do Things with Words: The William James Lectures Delivered at Harvard University in 1955*, Oxford: Clarendon.

Baker, R. (1972) *Quorum. Issue 3*, Harrow: S & H Publications.

Bakhtin, M. (1984) *Problems in Dostoevsky's Poetics*, Minneapolis, Minn.: University of Minnesota Press.

Barnstein, K. (1998) *My Gender Workbook*, New York: Routledge.

Barrett, R. (1997) 'The "Homo-genius" Speech Community', in A. Livia and K. Hall (eds) *Queerly Phrased*, Oxford: Oxford Studies in Sociolinguistics, pp. 181–201.

Barthes, R. (1967) *The Elements of Semiology*, London: Cape.

BBC2 (1997) *It's Not Unusual*, London: BBC (produced by Face to Face Productions; broadcast April 1997).

BBC Online (2000) *The Gay to Z of Queer Street*. http://www.bbc.co.uk/choice/gay/gaytoz.shtml (accessed 12 June 2000).

BBC Radio 4 (1995) *Word of Mouth*, London: BBC (broadcast 19 September 1995).

BBC Radio 4 (1998) *The Bona History of Julian and Sandy*, London: BBC (broadcast 12 December 1998).

BBC Radio Collection (1992) *Julian and Sandy*, London: BBC Worldwide.

BBC Radio Collection (1996) *The Bona World of Julian and Sandy*, London: BBC Worldwide.

Becker, H. (1963) *Outsiders: Studies in the Sociology of Deviance*, New York: Free Press.

Beier, L. (1995) 'Anti-language or Jargon? Canting in the English Underworld in the Sixteenth and Seventeenth Centuries', in P. Burke and R. Porter (eds) *Languages and Jargons*, Cambridge: Polity Press.

Blachford, G. (1981) 'Male Dominance and the Gay World', in K. Plummer (ed.) *The Making of the Modern Homosexual*, London: Hutchinson, pp. 184–210.

Bloomfield, L. (1933) *Language*, New York: Holt, Rinehart & Winston.

Bolinger, D. (1975) *Aspects of Language*, 2nd edn, New York: Harcourt Brace Jovanovich.

Bone, R. (ed.) (1972) *Lunch*, London: London Co-ordinating Committee of the Campaign for Homosexual Equality.

Bopp, F. (1836) *Vocalismus*. Oder Sprachvergleiche Kritiken über J. Grimm's deutsche Grammatik und Graff's althochdeutschen Sprachschatz, mit Begrundung einer neuen Theorie des Albauts. Berlin (cited in O. Jespersen) (1922) *Language, Its Nature, Development and Origin*. London: Allen & Unwin.

Borrow, G. (1982) *Romano Lavo-Lil. A Book of the Gypsy*, Gloucester: Alan Sutton. Originally published 1874, London: John Murray.

Bourdieu, P. (1991) *Language and Symbolic Power*, Cambridge, Mass.: Harvard University Press.

Boyz (1999) June, issues 408–10, London: Chronos Publishing.

Bray, A. (1982) *Homosexuality in Renaissance England*, London: Gay Men's Press.

Britton, A. (1979) 'For Interpretation – Notes Against "Camp"', *Gay Left*, vol. 7, pp. 11–14.

Bronski, M. (1998) *The Pleasure Principle*, New York: St Martin's Press.

Brown, P. and Levinson, S. C. (1978) *Politeness: Some Universals in Language Usage*, Cambridge: Cambridge University Press.

Brown, V. (2000) 'Ever Decreasing Circles' *Pink Paper*, 5 December, pp. 30–41.

Burgess, A. (1980) 'Partridge in a Word Tree', in D. Crystal (ed.) *Eric Partridge in His Own Words*, London: Andre Deutsch, pp. 26–30.

Burton, P. (1979) 'The Gentle Art of Confounding Naffs: Some Notes on Polari', *Gay News*, 120, p. 23.

Butler, J. (1990) *Gender Trouble: Feminism and the Subversion of Identity*, New York: Routledge.

Cage, K. (1999) 'An Investigation into the Form and Function of Language Used by Gay Men in South Africa', Unpublished MA thesis, Rand Afrikaans University.

Calder, A. (1969) *The People's War. Britain 1939–45*, London: Jonathan Cape.

Cameron, D. (1997) 'Performing Gender Identity: Young Men's Talk and the Construction of Heterosexual Masculinity', in S. Johnson and U. L. Meinhof (eds) *Language and Masculinity*, London: Blackwell, pp. 47–64.

Carson, M. (1988) *Sucking Sherbert Lemons*, London: Black Swan.

Channel 4 (1993) *Summer's Out. A Storm in a Teacup*, London: Channel 4 (broadcast 19 August 1993).

Chesney, K. (1972) *The Victorian Underworld*, New York: Schocken Books.

Chomsky, N. (1965) *Aspects of the Theory of Syntax* (special technical report, Massachusetts Institute of Technology, Research Laboratory of Electronics, 11), Cambridge, Mass.: MIT Press, pp. 237–45.

Clarke, J., Hall, S., Jefferson, T. and Roberts, B. (1975) 'Subcultures, Cultures and Class: A Theoretical Overview', in S. Hall and T. Jefferson (eds) *Resistance Through Rituals*, London: Hutchinson, pp. 9–74.

Coelho, F. A. (1880) 'Os Dialectos romanicos ou neolatinos na Africa, Asia e America', *Boletim da Sociedade de Geografia de Lisboa*, vol. 2, pp. 129–96.

Cory, D. W. (1965) 'The Language of the Homosexual', *Sexology*, vol. 32, no. 3, pp. 163–5.

Cox, L. J. and Fay, R. J. (1994) 'Gay-speak, the Linguistic Fringe: Bona Polari, Camp, Queerspeak and Beyond', in S. Whittle (ed.) *The Margins of the City: Gay Men's Urban Lives*, Aldershot: Arena, Ashgate Publishing, pp. 103–27.

Crisp, Q. (1968) *The Naked Civil Servant*, London: Jonathan Cape.

Crowley, M. (1968) *The Boys in the Band*, New York: Dell Publishing Co, Inc.

David, H. (1997) *On Queer Street*, London: HarperCollins.

Davidson, M. (1977) *The World, the Flesh and Myself*, London: Quartet Books.

Davies, R. (ed.) (1993) *The Kenneth Williams Diaries*, London: HarperCollins.

Deignan, A. (1997) 'Metaphors of Desire', in K. Harvey and M. Shalom (eds) *Language and Desire*, London: Routledge, pp. 21–42.

D'Emilio, J. (1993) 'Capitalism and Gay Identity', in H. Abelove, M. A. Barale and D. M. Halperin (eds) *The Lesbian and Gay Studies Reader*, New York: Routledge, pp. 467–79.

Derrida, J. (1972) *Positions*, Chicago: University of Chicago Press.

Dillard, Y. L. (1972) *Black English*, New York: Vintage Books.

Donaldson, S. (1990) 'Seafaring' (encyclopaedia entry), in W. R. Dynes (ed.) *Encyclopaedia of Homosexuality*, Garden City, New York: Garland Publishing, pp. 1172–5.

Dorian, N. C. (1981) *Language Death: The Life Cycle of a Scottish Gaelic Dialect*, Philadelphia, Pa.: University of Pennsylvania Press.

Duncan, P. L. (1996) 'Identity, Power and Difference. Negotiating Conflict in an S/M Dyke Community', in B. Beemyn and M. Eliason (eds) *Queer Studies: A Lesbian, Gay, Bisexual and Transgender Anthology*, New York: New York University Press, pp. 87–114.

Dynes, W. R. (ed.) (1990) *Encyclopaedia of Homosexuality*, Garden City, New York: Garland Publishing.

Ellis, A. (1965) *Homosexuality: Its Causes and Cures*, New York: Lyle Stuart.

England, L. (1950) 'A British Sex Survey', *The International Journal of Sexology*, February, vol. 3, no. 3.

Epstein, S. (1998) 'Gay Politics, Ethnic Identity: The Limits of Social Constructionism', in P. M. Nardi and B. E. Schneider (eds) *Social Perspectives in Lesbian and Gay Studies*, London: Routledge, pp. 134–59. Reprinted from *Socialist Review 93/94* (May–August 1987), pp. 9–54.

Erikson, E. (1956) 'The Problem of Ego Identity', *Journal of the American Psychoanalytic Association*, vol. 4, pp. 56–121.

Erikson, E. (1959) *Identity and the Life Cycle. Psychological Issues Monograph 1*, New York: International Universities Press.

Farrell, R. A. (1972) 'The Argot of the Homosexual Subculture', *Anthropological Linguistics*, vol. 14, no. 3, pp. 97–109.

Ferris, P. (1993) *Sex and the British*, London: Michael Joseph.

Flexner, S. B. and Wentworth, H. (1960) *A Dictionary of American Slang*, New York: Ty Crowell.

Foote, S. (1753) *The Englishman in Paris. A comedy in two acts (and in prose)*, London.

Foucault, M. (1978 [French publication 1976]) *The History of Sexuality. Volume 1: An Introduction*, trans. Robert Hurley, New York: Pantheon.

Franklyn, J. (1960) *A Dictionary of Rhyming Slang*, London: Routledge & Kegan Paul.

Freud, S. (1977) 'Group Psychology and the Analysis of the Ego', in *Pelican Freud Library, Volume 12* (first published 1921), Harmondsworth: Penguin.

Frost, T. (1876) *Circus Life and Circus Celebrities*, London: Tinsley.

Frye, M. (1983) *The Politics of Reality: Essays in Feminist Theory*, Trumansburg, New York: The Crossing Press.

Gardiner, J. (1997) *Who's A Pretty Boy Then? One Hundred and Fifty Years of Gay Life in Pictures*, London: Serpent's Tail.

Gaudio, R. P. (1994) 'Sounding Gay: Pitch Properties in the Speech of Gay and Straight Men', *American Speech*, vol. 69, no. 1, pp. 30–7.

Gay Liberation Front (1979) *Manifesto* (revised from 1971), London: Russell Press.

Gay Times (2000) Uncredited article: 'Watch Out', April, London: Millivres Press.

Gleason, P. (1983) 'Identifying Identity: A Semantic History', *Journal of American History*, vol. 69, no. 4, pp. 910–31.

Goffman, E. (1963) *Stigma: Notes on the Management of Spoiled Identity*, Englewood Cliffs, NJ: Prentice-Hall.

Goldsmith. E. S. (1997) *Modern Yiddish Culture. The Story of the Yiddish Language Movement*, New York: Fordham University Press.

Goodwin, J. P. (1989) *More Man Than You'll Ever Be: Gay Folklore and Acculturation in Middle America*, Bloomington, Ind.: Indiana University Press.

Gordeno, P. (1969) 'The Walloper's Polari', *TV Times*, 18–25 October 1969, p. 44.

Graddol, D., Leith, D. and Swann, J. (1996) *English, History, Diversity and Change*, London: Routledge.

Green, J. (1987) 'Polari', *Critical Quarterly*, vol. 39, no. 1, pp. 127–31.

Green, J. and Williams, J. (1999) *The Big Book of Filth*, London: Cassell.

Grose, F. (1785) *The Classical Dictionary of the Vulgar Tongue*, 3rd edn, 1796, London: S. Hooper.

Gumperz, J. (ed.) (1972) *Directions in Sociolinguistics: The Ethnography of Communication*, New York: Holt, Rinehart & Winston.

Habermas, J. (1979) 'Moral Development and Ego Identity', in *Communication and the Evolution of Society*, Boston, Mass.: Beacon Press, pp. 69–74.

Hall, S. and Jefferson, T. (1975) *Resistance Through Rituals*, London: Hutchinson.

Hall-Carpenter Archives (1989) *Walking After Midnight. Gay Men's Life Stories*, London: Routledge.

Halliday, M. A. K. (1978) *Language as a Social Semiotic: The Social Interpretation of Language and Meaning*, London: Edward Arnold.

Halsey, A. H. (ed.) (1972) *Trends in British Society since 1900*, London: Macmillan.

Hancock, I. (1984) 'Shelta and Polari', in P. Trudgill (ed.) *The Language of the British Isles*, Cambridge: Cambridge University Press, pp. 384–403.

Harman, T. (1567) *A Caveat or Warening for Commen Cursetores vulgarely called Vagabones*, London: William Gryffith (included as 'A caveat for common cursitores' in Gamini Salgado (ed.) *Cony-Catchers and Bawdy Baskets: An Anthology of Elizabethan Low Life*, Harmondsworth: Penguin, 1972).

Harris, D. (1997) *The Rise and Fall of Gay Culture*, New York: Hyperion.

Hayes, J. (1976) 'Gayspeak', *The Quarterly Journal of Speech*, vol. 62, pp. 256–66. Reprinted in J. W. Chesebro (ed.) (1981) *Gayspeak: Gay Male and Lesbian Communication*, New York: Pilgrim Press, pp. 43–57.

Haynes, T. (1998) *Velvet Goldmine*, London: Faber & Faber.

Heywood, J. (1997) '"The Object of Desire is the Object of Contempt." Representations of Masculinity in Straight to Hell Magazine', in S. Johnson and U. L. Meinhof (eds) *Language and Masculinity*, London: Blackwell, pp. 188–207.

Higgins, P. (1993) *A Queer Reader*, London: Fourth Estate.

Hindle, P. (1994) 'Gay Communities and Gay Space in the City', in S. Whittle (ed.) *The Margins of the City: Gay Men's Urban Lives*, Aldershot: Arena, Ashgate Publishing.

Hockett, C. (1958) *A Course in Modern Linguistics*, New York: Macmillan.

Hotton, J. C. (1864) *Slang Dictionary*, London: Charles Camden Hotten.

Hudson, R. A. (1980) *Sociolinguistics*, Cambridge: Cambridge Textbooks in Linguistics.

Humphreys, L. (1970) *Tearoom Trade*, London: Duckworth.

Humphries, S. (1988) *A Secret World of Sex: Forbidden Fruit: The British Experience 1900–1950*, London: Sidgwick & Jackson.

Innes, S. A. and Lloyd, M. E. (1996) 'G. I. Joes in Barbie Land: Recontextualizing Butch in Twentieth-Century Lesbian Culture', in B. Beemyn and M. Eliason (eds) *Queer Studies: A Lesbian, Gay, Bisexual and Transgender Anthology*, New York: New York University Press, pp. 9–34.

Jespersen, O. (1922) *Language, Its Nature, Development and Origin*, London: Allen & Unwin.

Jivani, A. (1997) *It's Not Unusual: A History of Lesbian and Gay Britain in the Twentieth Century*, London: Michael O'Mara.

Johnson, T. (1998) *Cleo, Camping, Emmanuelle and Dick*, play performed by Royal National Theatre, London.

Jowell, R., Brook, L., Prior, G. and Taylor, B. (1992) *British Social Attitudes, the 9th Report*, Aldershot: Ashgate.

Jowell, R., Curtice, J., Park, A., Brook, L. and Thompson, K. (1996) *British Social Attitudes, the 13th Report*, Aldershot: Ashgate.

Jowell, R., Curtice, J., Park, A. and Thomson, S. (1999) *British Social Attitudes, the 16th Report: Who Shares New Labour Values?*, Aldershot: Ashgate.

Jowell, R., Park, A., Thomson, K., Jarvis, L., Bromley, C. and Stratford, N. (2000) *British Social Attitudes, the 17th Report: Focusing on Diversity*, London: Sage.

Kahane, H., Kahane, R. and Tietze, A. (1958) *The Lingua Franca in the Levant. Turkish Nautical Terms of Italian and Greek Origin*, Urbana, Ill.: University of Illinois Press.

Katzner, K. (1986) *The Languages of the World*, London: Routledge.

Kenrick, D. (1979) 'Romani English', in I. Hancock (ed.) *International Journal of the Sociology of Language: Romani Sociolinguistics*, The Hague: Mouton de Gruyter, pp. 111–20.

Labov, W. (1972) *Sociolinguistic Patterns*, Philadelphia, Pa.: University of Pennsylvania Press.

Lakoff, R. (1973) 'Language and Women's Place', *Language in Society*, vol. 2, pp. 45–80.

Lave, J. and Wenger, E. (1991) *Situated Learning: Legitimate Peripheral Participation*, Cambridge: Cambridge University Press.

Leap, W. (1996) *Word's Out: Gay Men's English*, Minneapolis, Minn.: University of Minnesota Press.

Legman, G. (1941) 'The Language of Homosexuality: An American Glossary', in G. Henry (ed.) *Sex Variants: A Study of Homosexual Patterns*, New York: P. B. Hoeber, pp. 1147–78.

Le Page, R. B. (1968) 'Problems of Description in Multilingual Communities', *Transactions of the Philological Society*, pp. 189–212.

Le Page, R. B. and Taboret-Keller, A. (1985) *Acts of Identity: Creole-Based Approaches to Language and Ethnicity*, Cambridge: Cambridge University Press.

Lester, S. (1937) *Vardi the Palary* (out of print); cited in Partridge, E. (1974) *A Dictionary of Slang and Unconventional English, Volume 2*, 8th edn, London: Routledge, p. 1318.

Levine, M. P. (ed.) (1979) *Gay Men: The Sociology of Male Homosexuality*, New York: Harper & Row.

Long, S. (1993) 'The Loneliness of Camp', in D. Bergman (ed.) *Camp Grounds*, Massachusetts: University of Massachusetts Press, pp. 78–91.

Longman (1984) *Longman Dictionary of the English Language*, London: Longman.

Lovric, M. (1997) *The Scoundrel's Dictionary. A Copious and Complete Compendium of 18th-Century Slang*, Oxford: Past Times.

Lucas, I. (1997) 'The Color of His Eyes: Polari and the Sisters of Perpetual Indulgence', in A. Livia and K. Hall (eds) *Queerly Phrased*, Oxford: Oxford Studies in Sociolinguistics, pp. 85–94.

Lucas, I. (1994) *Impertinent Decorum*, London: Cassell.

Lumby, M. (1976) 'Code Switching and Sexual Orientation: A Test of Bernstein's Sociolinguistic Theory', *Journal of Homosexuality*, vol. 1, no. 4 (Summer), pp. 383–99.

Lyons, J. (ed.) (1970) *New Horizons in Linguistics*, London: Penguin.

Magee, B. (1973) *Popper*, London: Fontana.

Mallik, B. (1972) *Language of the Underworld of West Bengal*, Research Series 76, Calcutta: Sanskrit College.

Marmor, J. (1965) *Sexual Inversion: The Multiple Roots of Homosexuality*, New York: Basic Books.

Mason, A. and Palmer, A. (1996) *Queer Bashing: A National Survey of Hate Crime Against Lesbians and Gays*, London: Stonewall.

Mazower, D. (1987) *Yiddish Theatre in London*, London: Museum of the Jewish East End.

McIntosh, M. (1972) 'Gayspeak', *Lunch*, vol. 16, pp. 7–9.

McIntosh, M. (1997) 'Class', in A. Medhurst and S. R. Munt (eds) *Lesbian and Gay Studies: A Critical Introduction*, London: Cassell, pp. 233–49.

McMahon, M. S. (1994) *Understanding Language Change*, Cambridge: Cambridge University Press.

Medhurst, A. (1997) 'Camp', in A. Medhurst and S. R. Munt (eds) *Lesbian and Gay Studies: A Critical Introduction*, London: Cassell, pp. 274–93.

Meinhof, U. L. and Johnson, S. (1997) 'Introduction to Language and Masculinity', in S. Johnson and U. L. Meinhof (eds) *Language and Masculinity*, London: Blackwell.

Merriam-Webster (1993) *Merriam-Webster's Collegiate Dictionary*, 10th edn, Springfield, Mass.: Merriam-Webster.

Meyer, M. (ed.) (1994) *The Politics and Poetics of Camp*, London: Routledge.

Moonwomon, B. (1985) 'Toward the Study of Lesbian Speech', in S. Bremner, N. Caskey and B. Moonwomon (eds) *Proceedings of the First Berkeley Women and*

Language Conference, Berkeley, Calif.: Berkeley Women and Language Group, pp. 96–107.

Moran, J. (1991) 'Language Use and Social Function in the Gay Community', paper presented at NWAVE (New Ways of Analyzing Variation) 20, Georgetown University, October.

Nettle, D. and Romaine, S. (2000) *Vanishing Voices. The Extinction of the World's Languages*, Oxford: Oxford University Press.

Newton, E. (1993) 'Role Models', in D. Bergman (ed) *Camp Grounds*, Massachusetts: University of Massachusetts Press, pp. 39–53.

Norton, R. (1992) *Mother Clap's Molly House. The Gay Subculture in England 1700–1830*, London: Gay Men's Press.

O'Grady, W., Dobrovolsky, M. and Katamba, F. (1996) *Contemporary Linguistics: An Introduction*, 3rd edn, London: Longman.

Orwell, G. (1933) *Down and Out in Paris and London*, London: Penguin.

OUP (1994) *Oxford English Dictionary*, on CD-ROM, 2nd edn, Oxford: Oxford University Press.

Partridge, E. (1950) *Here, There, and Everywhere: Essays Upon Language*, London: Hamish Hamilton.

Partridge, E. (1961) *A Dictionary of Slang and Unconventional English, Volume 1*, 5th edn, London: Routledge.

Partridge, E. (1964) *A Dictionary of the Underworld*, London: Routledge & Kegan Paul.

Partridge, E. (1970) *Slang, Today and Yesterday*, London: Routledge.

Partridge, E. (1974) *A Dictionary of Slang and Unconventional English, Volume 2. The Supplement*, 8th edn, London: Routledge.

Plummer, K. (1975) *Sexual Stigma: An Interactionist Account*, London: Routledge & Kegan Paul.

Podgorecki, A. (1973) *'Second Life' and its Implications*, mimeo (Halliday, 1978), London.

Porter, K. and Weeks, J. (eds) (1991) *Between the Acts: Lives of Homosexual Men 1885–1967*, London: Routledge.

Pratt, M. L. (1987) 'Linguistic Utopias', in N. Fabb, D. Attridge, A. Durant and C. MacCabe (eds) *The Linguistics of Writing: Arguments between Language and Literature*, Manchester: Manchester University Press, pp. 48–66.

Pullum, G. (1991) *The Great Eskimo Vocabulary Hoax and Other Irreverent Essays on the Study of Language*, Chicago: University of Chicago Press.

Queen, R. M. (1997) '"I Don't Speak Spritch"; Locating Lesbian Language', in A. Livia and K. Hall (eds) *Queerly Phrased*, Oxford: Oxford Studies in Sociolinguistics, pp. 233–56.

Raban, J. (1973) 'Giggling in Code', *Lunch*, vol. 20, pp. 16–17.

Ramat, P. (ed.) (1983) *Linguistic Reconstruction and Indo-European Syntax*, Amsterdam: Benjamin.

Rampton, B. (1998) 'Language Crossing and the Redefinition of Reality', in P. Auer (ed.) *Code-Switching in Conversation*, London: Routledge.

Ribton-Turner, C. J. (1887) *History of Vagrants and Vagrancy, and Beggars and Begging*, London: Patterson Smith.

Rigelsford, A., Brown, A. and Tibballs, G. (1995) *Are You Being Served?*, San Francisco: KQED.

Rodgers, B. (1972) *The Queen's Vernacular*, San Francisco: Straight Arrow Books.

Ross, A. (1989) *No Respect, Intellectuals and Popular Culture*, New York: Routledge.

Ross, A. (1993) 'Uses of Camp', in D. Bergman (ed) *Camp Grounds*, Massachusetts: University of Massachusetts Press, pp. 54–77.

Rust, P. C. (1996) 'Sexual Identity and Bisexual Identities: The Struggle for Self-Description in a Changing Sexual Landscape', in B. Beemyn and M. Eliason (eds) *Queer Studies: A Lesbian, Gay, Bisexual and Transgender Anthology*, New York: New York University Press, pp. 64–86.

Sagarin, E. (1970) 'Languages of the Homosexual Sub-culture', *Medical Aspects of Human Sexuality*, April, pp. 34–48.

Salgado, G. (1977) *The Elizabethan Underworld*, London: J. M. Dent & Sons.

Saussure, F. de (1966) *Course in General Linguistics*, C. Bally and A. Sechehaye (eds), trans. R. Harris, London: Duckworth.

Savage, L. (1998) *Lily Savage: A Sort of A–Z Thing*, London: Headline.

Scroggie, W. (1999) 'Producing Identity. From the Boys in the Band to Gay Liberation', in P. J. Smith (ed.) *The Queer Sixties*, Routledge: New York, pp. 237–54.

Seidman, S. (1993) 'Identity and Politics in a "Postmodern" Gay Culture: Some Historical and Conceptual Notes', in Warner, M. (ed.) *Fear of a Queer Planet: Queer Politics and Social Theory*, Minneapolis, Minn.: University of Minnesota Press, pp. 105–42.

Seligman, D. (1973) 'Coming Out', *Lunch*, vol. 45, pp. 10–12.

Sontag, S. (1966) 'Notes on "Camp"', in S. Sontag, *Susan Sontag Against Interpretation and Other Essays*, New York: Farrar, Straus & Giroux, pp. 275–92.

Spencer, C. (1995) *Homosexuality: A History*, London: Fourth Estate.

Stanley, J. P. (1970) 'Homosexual Slang', *American Speech*, vol. 45, pp. 45–59.

Stanley, J. P. (1974) 'When We Say "Out of the Closets!"', *College English*, vol. 36, pp. 385–91.

Sunday Mirror (1963) 'How to Spot a Possible Homo', April.

Took, B. and Feldman, M. (1974) *Round the Horne*, London: Woburn Press.

Took, B. and Feldman, M. (1976) *The Bona Book of Julian and Sandy*, London: Robson Books.

Trumbach, R. (1977) 'London's Sodomites: Homosexual Behaviour and Western Culture in the 18th Century', *Journal of Social History*, vol. 11, no. 1, pp. 1–33.

Trumbach, R. (1991) 'The Birth of the Queen: Sodomy and the Emergence of Gender Equality in Modern Culture, 1660–1750', in M. B. Duberman, M. Vicinus and G. Chauncey (eds) *Hidden From History*, London: Penguin, pp. 129–40.

Tyler, C.-A. (1991) 'Boys Will Be Girls: The Politics of Gay Drag', in D. Fuss (ed.) *Inside/Out: Lesbian Theories, Gay Theories*, New York: Routledge, pp. 32–70.

Wardhaugh, R. (1986) *An Introduction to Sociolinguistics*, 2nd edn, Oxford: Blackwell Textbooks in Linguistics.

Wardhaugh, R. (1993) *Investigating Language: Central Problems in Linguistics*, Oxford: Blackwell.

Warner, N. (1982) 'Parliament and Law', in B. Galloway (ed.) *Prejudice and Pride: Discrimination Against Gay People in Modern Britain*, London: Routledge & Kegan Paul.

Waugh, T. (1996) 'Cockteaser', in J. Doyle, J. Flatley and J. Muñoz (eds) *Pop Out: Queer Warhol*, Durham, NC: Duke University Press, pp. 51–77.

Webbink, P. (1981) 'Nonverbal Behavior and Lesbian/Gay Orientation', in C. Mayo and N. Henley (eds) *Gender and Non-Verbal Behavior*, New York: Springer, pp. 253–9.

Weeks, J. (1977) *Coming Out*, London: Quartet.

Weeks, J. (1981) *Sex, Politics and Society*, London: Longman.

Weeks, J. (1985) *The Meaning of Diversity: Sexuality and its Discontents*, London: Routledge.

Weightman, B. A. (1981) 'Towards a Geography of the Gay Community', *Journal of Cultural Geography*, vol. 1, pp. 106–12.

White, E. (1980) 'The Political Vocabulary of Homosexuality', in L. Michaels and P. Ricks (eds) *The State of the Language*, Berkeley, Calif.: University of California Press, pp. 235–46.

Wigg, D. (1977) 'Are You Being Unfair?', *Daily Express*, 12 October 1977, p. 5.

Wilde, W. C. (1889) 'Some Words of Thief Talk', *Journal of American Folklore*, vol. 11, no. 7, pp. 301–6.

Wyden, P. and Wyden, B. (1968) *Growing Up Straight: What Every Thoughtful Parent Should Know About Homosexuality*, New York: Stein & Day.

Young, A. (1972) 'Out of the Closets, into the Streets', in K. Jay and A. Young (eds) *Out of the Closets*, New York: Douglas.

Index

Some terms (Polari and non-Polari) are discussed at length in the book and are presented here in *italics*. For further information on Polari terms, see the Appendix on page 161.

An environmentally friendly book printed and bound in England by www.printondemand-worldwide.com